D0215866

LIB051005 R3/78

SIMON FRASER UNIVERSITY LIBRARY

Unless recalled, all materials
due on last date stamped

RES 24HR   RES 3DAY

Challenging Ways of Knowing

Challenging Ways of Knowing:
In English, Mathematics and Science

Edited by

Dave Baker, John Clay and Carol Fox

 **Falmer Press**

(A member of the Taylor & Francis Group)
London • Washington, D.C.

UK   The Falmer Press, 1 Gunpowder Square, London, EC4A 3DE
USA   The Falmer Press, Taylor & Francis Inc., 1900 Frost Road, Suite 101,
        Bristol, PA 19007

© D. Baker, J. Clay and C. Fox, 1996

*All rights reserved. No part of this publication may be reproduced, stored
in a retrieval system, or transmitted in any form or by any means, electronic,
mechanical, photocopying, recording or otherwise, without permission in
writing from the Publisher.*

First published in 1996

**A catalogue record for this book is available from the British
Library**

**Library of Congress Cataloging-in-Publication Data are available on
request**

ISBN 0 7507 0524 8 cased
ISBN 0 7507 0525 6 paper

Jacket design by Caroline Archer

Typeset in 10/12pt Times by
Graphicraft Typesetters Ltd., Hong Kong.

*Printed in Great Britain by Biddles Ltd., Guildford and King's Lynn on
paper which has a specified pH value on final paper manufacture of not
less than 7.5 and is therefore 'acid free'.*

Contents

Acknowledgments   vii

Introduction   1

Part I: Changing the Subject Boundaries   11

     Introduction   11

1   Good Science or Good Art? or Both?   13
     Shirley Brice Heath

2   Evolving Shared Discourse with Teachers to Promote Literacies for
     Learners in South Africa   19
     Alan and Viv Kenyon

3   Mathematics, and its Learning, as Narrative — A Literacy for the
     Twenty-first Century   29
     Leone Burton

**Part II: Literacy Practices Inside Schools, Outside Schools and
     in Higher Education**   41

     Introduction   41

4   Scientific Literacy: A Functional Construct   43
     Edgar W. Jenkins

5   Family Literacy Programmes and Home Literacy Practices   52
     David Barton

6   Enlarging the 'Ways of Taking' from Literary Texts:
     Mode-switching in the Primary Classroom   62
     Henrietta Dombey

7   Frames of Knowledge   71
     Terezinha Nunes

8   Children's Formal and Informal School Numeracy Practices   80
     Dave Baker

9   'How Can You "Discuss" Alone?': Academic Literacy in a
     South African Context   89
     Lynn Hewlett

Contents

10 Academic Literacies   101
    Brian V. Street

Part III: The Role of Texts in Literacies for Learning   135
        Introduction   135

11 An Agenda for Research on Text Materials in Primary Science
    for Second Language Learners in Developing Countries   137
    Alan Peacock

12 'Focusing on the Frames': Using Comic Books to Challenge
    Dominant Literacies in South Africa   146
    Peter Esterhuysen

13 Book Learning: Literacy and Information   159
    Margaret Meek

Part IV: Questioning Dominant Canons and Practices   171
        Introduction   171

14 Dominant and Subversive Literacy Practices: The Case for
    Literature   173
    Carol Fox

15 Scientific Literacy: Whose Science? Whose Literacy?   184
    John Clay

16 Calculating People — Origins of Numeracy in India and the West 194
    George Gheverghese Joseph

Notes on Contributors   204

Author Index   209

Subject Index   212

Acknowledgments

The editors are indebted first to their colleagues in the Faculty of Education, Sport and Leisure in the University of Brighton, particularly those who participated so fully in our symposium *Alternative Ways of Knowing*; Katrina Fry, Roy Hawkey, Avril Loveless, Carole King, Heather Mines, and Muriel Robinson. Their interest and encouragement have been invaluable to us. Without the day-by-day support of Jinny Briant and Joanna Cheetham, completion of the typescript on time would have been impossible. We are grateful to Jeremy Mulford for employing all his patience and editorial skills in helping us with the final draft. Many thanks to Sue Bowles for typing up some of the manuscript at short notice. Thanks also to the contributors of original documents in the chapter by Brian Street. Finally our thanks to Les Cross for the photograph on page 53.

Dave Baker, John Clay and Carol Fox

Introduction

The papers collected together in this volume first appeared in draft form at the symposium *Alternative Ways of Knowing*, sponsored in February 1995 by the University of Brighton's Faculty of Education. Long before the symposium took place, the editors of this book — Dave Baker, John Clay and Carol Fox — had been working together on the issues raised by the literacies and numeracies of their disciplines in teacher education: Mathematics, Science, and English respectively.

Dave Baker, for example, had been questioning the commonly held model of numeracy as culture- and value-free, and proposing instead that numeracies be viewed as social practices. The implications of this second model for the classroom had been of particular interest to him as it could be used to investigate the ways in which the diverse numeracy practices that children employed in the course of their everyday lives, and brought with them to school, tended to be marginalized by their teachers in the classroom.

John Clay, working with groups of future science teachers who were mainly female, was interested in the ways in which many of his students had problems in making the discourses of science their own so that they could feel confident and comfortable with them. Were those discourses too rigid in their denial of a range of non-expository genres — poetry, narrative, and the more personal and affective modes? What were the scientific discourses of non-British cultures like, and what might they teach science educators and their students?

Carol Fox had spent some months in South Africa in 1994, and had become aware of the ways in which academic literacies in the English language were not easily accessible to black students, many of whom had beaten their way through formidable obstacles to obtain a place at a prestigious university. Her colleague on the same visit, Shirley Brice Heath, also helped her to see that many kinds of literacy flourished in children's street shelters, community theatre groups, and other non-educational settings, although the practitioners of these literacies were often assumed by the educated to be non- or semi-literate.

The disciplines of mathematics, science, and English have very different traditions, histories and values, yet all three editors found that similar questions and problems emerged when they began to consider the literacies and numeracies that people used on a daily basis without thinking much about them, and to compare these to the ways in which literacy and numeracy practices were made strange, and often 'difficult' or inaccessible, in many educational contexts. A focus on the value that education bestows on some literacy/numeracy practices compared to others provided the cross-disciplinary themes of this book.

Shirley Brice Heath and Brian Street, ethnographers of literacy whose work had inspired our earliest collaboration on the educational issues surrounding plural notions of literacy and numeracy, were able to attend our symposium. The Universities of the Witwatersrand and of Cape Town, together with Cape Town College of Education, sponsored South African colleagues to join us, while the British Council supported Peter Esterhuyzen, of the Storyteller Group (a South African non-government organization which publishes an extraordinary range of educational comics), to come too. In addition to our international participants, colleagues from mathematics, science, and English departments of many British universities swelled our numbers to seventeen writers of draft papers.

The idea was to circulate papers among all the participants before the symposium, so that the time at the event itself could be profitably spent discussing the implications of what we had written. Over three days, the group of seventeen, augmented by colleagues from the University of Brighton, discussed all the papers in a group of thirty, facing one another around a rectangular table. The revised form of those papers is the content of this book.

In introducing the major themes and ideas of this book, we need to define some of the terms that reappear across its four sections. The writers here, for example, tend to refer to litera*cies* (as plural), *literacy practices*, and numera*cies* (as plural). Let us begin with our plural notion of literacies and literacy practices.

Literacy practices refers to literacies in action, that is, reading and writing events that happen in different social contexts, with different functions, in a diverse array of social groups and domains. To construe literacy in this way is to resist the more familiar tendency to regard literacy as a single psychological entity, something acquired, or learned, or taught, once and for all — or not, as the case may be. This definition also resists assumptions about people or groups who are often described as *illiterate*, as if illiteracy, too, were a clearly definable state of being. The research of some of the contributors to this book, in particular Shirley Brice Heath, Brian Street and David Barton, has shown us that communities and individuals in their home settings move very fluidly between oral and literate practices, and that the gulf between orality and literacy, hitherto believed to be clear and unproblematic, cannot now be assumed to exist for most people at all.

By regarding literacy practices as a multiplicity of activities and events around literacy in different communities, we find that clear-cut definitions elude us. Of course, once literacies are seen as located in social practices, they become ideological, containing within them, often in ways that are concealed or taken for granted, embedded relationships between readers and writers, relationships that usually have much to do with the relative power and status positions of those participating in literacy events. Nowhere are the ideological implications of literacy practices more apparent than in educational contexts, whether we are referring to the ways in which whole subject disciplines are constructed, written down, and enshrined in law (as in the National Curriculum for England and Wales), or to the written materials used in educational settings for learning, or to the implicit rules that seem to dominate academic writing in higher education, or to the kinds of knowledge, written and spoken, that educators regard as appropriate in the classroom or lecture hall.

In our consideration of the terms associated with mathematics in this book, some important issues are similar to those surrounding the terminology of literacy, and others are rather different. In the literature on *numeracy*, there is an ongoing debate about the meaning of several terms. These debates are concerned with the meaning of *numeracy*, its relationship to *mathematics* and the value or dangers of the term *innumeracy*. These concerns are best seen in relation to two different perceptions of numeracy. The first has to do with the breadth of the content of numeracy, and the second questions whether numeracy is value-free or is firmly positioned in cultural contexts and therefore value laden.

On the one hand, there is a broad understanding of the term *numeracy*. This defines individuals as *numerate* when they have acquired the mathematical skills and concepts required to function effectively in their group or community. This in turn means being comfortable with numbers, the ability to make use of mathematical skills and concepts in handling problems in everyday life, the ability to process information and data in a mathematical form. On the other hand, the narrower view is that individuals are *numerate* when they can do basic arithmetic calculations, involving the four rules of addition, subtraction, multiplication and division on whole numbers. Both these views entail corresponding negative notions that people who cannot carry out the specified activities are *innumerate*.

These views of numeracy are both usually grounded in the commonly held view that numeracy is an autonomous skill, independent of social context and universally true across space and time. In this respect, they parallel similar constructions of literacy referred to above. An alternative view is that numeracies are social practices, learned and used in social and cultural contexts and imbued with political, ideological, and cultural influences. Regarding numeracies as social practices carries with it implications of power relationships and contests over meanings and resources. Whilst the contributors to this book in general hold the broader rather than the narrower view of numeracies, they also regard numeracies as social practices and are aware of ideological and political implications of this position.

Our contributors were concerned that the use of the word *numeracy* did not imply an acceptance of, or support for the narrower view of *numeracy* described above. The use of the word *numeracy* rather than the word *mathematics* in their papers is intended to draw attention to the parallels that exist between the work being done on numeracy practices and that on literacy practices. In consequence, they use the term *numeracy* to mean the collection of *numeracy practices* that people engage in — that is the contexts, power relations, and activities — when they are doing mathematics. The words *numeracy* and *mathematics* are therefore seen as equivalent. The choice of the term *numeracy practices* is intended to make the links between numeracy and literacy visible, and does not imply a restricted view of the activities involved. A numeracy event, in parallel to a literacy event, is any occasion where mathematics is integral to the nature of the participants' interactions and their interpretative processes. It needs to be made clear here, too, that an activity may be a literacy event, or a numeracy event, or even both. The nature of the activity will determine the label.

Our readers will expect this book to treat the terminology of science in the same way, regarding scientific practices, too, as socially and culturally embedded. However, there is a difficulty here in that science does not yet have a term equivalent to *literacy* and *numeracy*. Where our contributors refer to science practices or events, they often use the term *scientific literacies* as a substitute for what, logically, ought to be the term scien*cies*. Since this term would be a new coinage, we have resisted it, but we ask our readers to think of scientific practices in the same way as we have asked them to think of literacies and numeracies. In this definition, *scientific literacies* is interpreted as meaning activities that involve people in using scientific skills and concepts, whether or not reading and writing are involved.

Our reflections on literacies and numeracies as social practices inevitably face us with the dominance of some literacy/numeracy practices over others, particularly in educational contexts where there are implications to do with access, with the different worlds of school and non-school, with qualifications and examinations, and eventually with employment, status, and life opportunities. Nowhere can these implications be seen more clearly and dramatically than in post-apartheid South Africa, where the majority who were formerly excluded from most of the literacy and numeracy practices of education are now attempting to gain access to them in large numbers. This is made doubly problematic by the fact that the language of instruction is English. Not only must English be acquired as a second or third, or fourth or even fifth language for many students, but it must be acquired in the specialized forms and discourses associated with the literacy and numeracy practices of university departments. What is often called *academic literacy* is a good example of a *dominant literacy*; a set of literacy practices as often found in mathematics and science departments as in those of subjects apparently more linguistically based.

Several writers here discuss the dominant academic literacies required by their own universities. Lynn Hewlett, for example, writing from a South African perspective, looks at the problems encountered by her students, studying in a language other than their mother tongue, in acquiring writing conventions that seem to them not only alien and intimidating, but also at times incomprehensible. Brian Street, in a British context, uses a collection of responses to his own writing from academic colleagues, reproduced in this book in their original form, to *show* in the very reproduction of those forms, how academic texts conceal the assumptions they make about their relationships to readers. He and his correspondents, and Lynn Hewlett too, raise the issue of whether initiates to academic disciplines can be helped to gain control over the dominant academic literacies by having the power relationships implicit in academic texts made explicit and transparent. In fact a major question of this book concerns the usefulness or otherwise of laying bare the rules of the dominant literacy and numeracy clubs, with all their attendant ideological and political implications. Another way of coming at this question is to ask whether it is the literacy and numeracy practices of education themselves that need to become more flexible, more broadly based, and more strongly related to the out-of-school/college experiences of learners (particularly groups of learners who do not come from powerful or dominant social backgrounds), or whether there are proper rationales for the prevailing literacy and numeracy practices of different domains.

Several contributors to this book look critically at the issues raised by these questions in terms of their examination of the literacy and numeracy practices of school subjects, in and out of — that is in the world beyond — classrooms. Leone Burton claims not only that mathematics is a 'socio-cultural artefact', but that 'success at mathematics is socially construed, just as the mathematics itself is'. She suggests that a narrative approach be adopted to the learning of mathematics, that we can 'tell the socio-cultural story' of mathematics, and that pupils' narratives of their own numeracy practices would place mathematics in a context, personalize it, and make it come alive. Alan and Viv Kenyon show how scientific thinking and literacies can be developed in under-resourced classrooms in South African townships through the poetry, song, and folk-tales of the children's vernacular languages and cultures. Their paper has important implications, both for the development of scientific literacies through genres not usually regarded as 'scientific', and for the ways in which education might value and develop the oral, as opposed to literate, cultures that children bring with them to school. In the UK context, Henrietta Dombey argues too that, in learning to read, children whose communities are not the dominant and powerful ones in society should not be denied access to high-quality literacy practices (i.e., well-written stories): rather, the dominant literacies should be opened up to them by the inclusion of their own voices and experiences in their encounters with literary texts.

We have deliberately not organized this book into subject categories, because the cross-disciplinary implications of many of our papers would then have been obscured. Indeed, the opening section is called *Challenging the Subject Boundaries*. The three contributors to this section do not argue that the disciplines of mathematics, science and English are no longer useful, or that the subjects should merge into one another, or that they should disappear and be replaced by something else. Instead, each suggest that our *ways of knowing* — in poetry and literature, in mathematics, and in science — may be more compatible with one another, and perform a greater service to one another, than is usually thought to be the case. Opening the book with a poem by Wallace Stevens, Shirley Brice Heath discusses the ways in which education has traditionally forced apart our aesthetic and scientific ways of knowing. Heath argues that we do not really apprehend the world in this artificially divided way, but that our natural response to requests for exposition on this or that topic takes a narrative form. A recognition of narrative as a major mental structuring device and as a humanizing force in education is a theme that is revisited in other sections of this book. So fundamental a force is narrative seen to be in many of the papers presented here that we must ask ourselves, as Alan and Viv Kenyon and Leone Burton do in the other two papers of this section, whether mathematics and science can afford to ignore its ubiquity and universality as a way of knowing. The Kenyon and Burton papers provide excellent demonstrations, in the face of traditionally competing and divided ways of seeing and understanding, of the essential wholeness argued in Heath's introductory essay.

The papers in Part Two, the largest section of this book, are again drawn from mathematics, science, and English. They show us literacies and numeracies in action, in classrooms, in colleges, and in the community beyond educational institutions, and each author contrasts the mathematical, scientific, and reading and writing practices that adults and children use for their own real purposes in every-day life with the rather different demands made on literacies and numeracies by educators. What becomes clear through all the papers here is that educators, albeit with the best intentions that schooled literacies and numeracies should effect a transformation in the lives of their students, tend to work with deficit models of the knowledge that learners have acquired and used in their lives outside school or college.

Edgar Jenkins, in urging qualitative studies of scientific literacies among the public at large, speaks of 'an emphasis . . . on the dignity of respondents' know-ledge and the importance of context in understanding'. Surveying some fascinating studies of groups of elderly people whose ways of managing their fuel and heating needs do not match 'scientific' conceptions of their problems and the solutions to them, Jenkins exposes the gap between different levels of understanding of *energy* and *heat*. If we look at science in action in this way, Jenkins claims, 'science as coherent, objective and well-bounded gives way to science which is problematic and fluid'.

Similar notions of literacy practices emerge from David Barton's paper on family literacy. At home people engage in an enormous range of functional literacies — literacies that are 'used to get things done'. Barton moves our perceptions of literacy practices away from book reading, learning to read in the early years, and attendant notions of literacy/illiteracy, and shows that adults who identify them-selves as having difficulties with literacy nevertheless participate in a large number of reading and writing events. Family literacy programmes, he concludes, need to move beyond deficit models that aim to make literacy practices at home more like those at school: 'rather than regarding homes as needing to replicate what schools do, family literacy could support the things people do in their everyday lives'.

In contrast to the studies of vernacular literacies presented by Jenkins and Barton, Henrietta Dombey moves us back into the classroom of the Infant and Junior school. She discusses the potentially alienating experience for some working-class children of learning to read from well-written and pleasurable stories. On the one hand, such texts teach more powerful reading lessons than most educational reading materials, on the other, teachers can by no means take it for granted that children will automatically find such texts meaningful and rewarding: 'Texts rich in mean-ing for some readers may seem remote, arid and even empty to others who come to them with a different set of understandings.' Dombey argues that all children need to have access at least to parts of the dominant culture, and locates the nature of the interaction in school between reader and text as the site where culture is either extended or opened, or silenced. In classrooms where children are encour-aged to interact orally with the print, moving 'between the children's oral vernacu-lar and the language of the printed text', children are empowered to take control of what might otherwise be alienating and dominating. While Barton shows how home literacies can become positive models for school literacy, Dombey urges that home vernaculars be brought into school literacy rather than left at the classroom door.

In her paper *Frames of Knowledge*, Terezinha Nunes regards mathematics as a 'social product whose boundaries are culturally defined'. Like Barton, she shows that mathematical knowledge has many functions and forms outside school, though education tends to be blind to most of them. She explains that mathematics has developed multiple systems of signs, which become 'frames of knowledge' for those who use them. These frames make possible certain kinds of reasoning and constrain others: the tools we use to think with have a direct relationship to the kinds of thinking we are enabled to do. Nunes proposes that a plurality of frames, appropriate for different functions, social situations, and kinds of thinking, would liberate learners from the constraints of single or dominant systems.

Baker, in a study of the numeracy practices of two year six girls in a primary school classroom, contrasts the children's use of numeracy practices in formal and informal settings. The informal practices referred to are like Barton's family literacies and Jenkins' elderly groups' scientific literacies: they are mathematics used to solve the children's own problems, numeracies in action for the children. The children's formal numeracy practices, however, illustrate the constraining effects of singular frames of knowledge referred to in Nunes' paper.

We conclude Part Two with papers by Lynn Hewlett and Brian Street. Their papers have been briefly described earlier in this 'Introduction'. Suffice it to add here that they extend the arguments of Jenkins, Barton, Dombey, Nunes and Baker to the problems of acquiring academic literacies in the context of undergraduate degree courses. Again, they show how joining a particular literacy club can be very problematic for those who are trying to learn its rules of entry from non-dominant, even disadvantaged, positions in the power structures of both the university and the society in which the university is embedded. In both papers, there are important implications for democracy, equal opportunities, and social justice.

Although the papers in Part Two take a critical stance to the ways in which educational frames of knowledge fail to recognize the 'dignity' of learners' under-standings, and fail to use them in school and college settings, the writers here should not be read as 'teacher bashers'. On the contrary, they imply that looking at vernacular and functional kinds of knowledge outside educational contexts can enrich the institutions of education — curricula, subjects, teachers themselves — by making them socially more real.

One major aspect of education highly pertinent to literacies and numeracies is its use of printed materials, which are the main focus in Part Three. The first paper, by Alan Peacock, is concerned with the complex problems of producing meaning-ful and educative science materials in African countries. Accepting that, for the present, science textbooks are going to be the dominant printed form (an assump-tion that Peter Esterhuyzen's paper, following him, challenges by implication), Peacock describes six major problematic areas in getting the books matched to the learners' needs. The six areas have already been anticipated in Part Two; the *cultural appropriateness* of resources has surfaced in the papers of Hewlett, Alan and Viv Kenyon, and Dombey. Peacock also discusses the expository genres of science texts and their non-narrative structures, another theme that runs throughout this book. His analysis of the enormous difficulties of producing good science textbooks for schools in the Third World serves to show up problems which, though less dramatic and more concealed, are nevertheless present in Britain.

Peter Esterhuyzen, a comic book publisher who has produced and distributed five million comics free in South Africa, shows us how creative the enterprise of employing a popular medium to promote literacy can be. Indeed, Esterhuyzen's publications have moved well beyond a consumer notion of reading, to one in which readers themselves produce their own texts, as in the case of the comic *Heart To Heart*. By working with young people, schools and teachers, Esterhuyzen demonstrates how the authority of the textbook can be challenged and replaced by literacy practices that are both subversive and empowering.

Part Three closes with Margaret Meek's paper on the literacy practices of reading for information. Distinguishing the genre from textbooks, Meek asks us to examine what *learning, knowledge*, and *information* mean as they are constructed in the pages of the thousands of expensive publications currently targeted at the education market. She warns that a new authority is emerging which 'will divide the text-makers, who put on disk what is authorised as knowledge, from the teachers who let the machine do the teaching.'

The final section of this book comprises papers by writers from each of our three core subjects. By using the examples of four different groups involved in literacy practices, from pre-school children to university students, Carol Fox argues that, in our consideration of powerful and authoritative canonical texts, literature is a special case. Not only does literature resist authority in its own content and its ways of telling that content, but the acts of reading we engage in when we encounter these texts make us think about our own literacy practices. She proposes that international/multicultural literature, a new canon, shows readers how dominant literacies can be subverted and their authorities challenged.

John Clay, in turn, discusses the dominant literacy that informs current science curricula in the West. He revisits the themes of earlier papers, in particular the marginalization in education of the scientific knowledge possessed by groups outside education. He argues that current positivist models of scientific knowledge are increasingly undemocratic and incompatible with new notions of *environmental citizenship*.

The book closes with a paper that extends the multicultural concerns of the papers by Clay and Fox. George Gheverghese Joseph looks at the history of Indian mathematics, showing us that canons of knowledge and authority are neither inevitable nor permanent, but are — to use Leone Burton's phrase — 'socio-cultural arte-facts'. Gheverghese Joseph's paper gives a fascinating account of the basis of Indian and Arabic mathematics in language, showing how mathematics, poetry, story and myth were integrated in other forms of knowing. His themes are a powerful reminder of Heath's opening paper, where she argues that the division of art and science is irrelevant and inappropriate in an age when 'education is currently looking more than ever for multiplying possibilities of knowing'.

This book raises many more questions than it can find answers for, but one of its fundamental propositions is that literacies and numeracies provide an excellent focus for cross-disciplinary research and enquiry, research that also vitally needs intercultural collaboration. While it has concentrated on the core subjects of the English National Curriculum, there are many more literacy and numeracy domains to be studied in the future. Some are suggested by the papers here. Heath, Meek, and Esterhuyzen, for example, signal that the visual and computer literacies of the age of information need to be explored. And we need to know much more about the kinds of knowing involved in people's self-directed activities outside educational institutions. In the contexts where literacies and numeracies are used for purposes other than learning how to do them, we also need to consider, as Nunes' paper suggests, the difference made to frames of knowledge by writing things down, whether in mathematics, science or English.

Part I: Changing the Subject Boundaries

Introduction

This book is a cross-disciplinary and intercultural enterprise. Inevitably its collaborators raise questions about the traditional divisions of subject fields, and suggest that a focus on literacy and numeracy practices is a productive way to look at the problem of the divided curriculum. The most original and creative writers resist the authorities of subjects, genres, conventions, and rules, replacing them with new forms, new ways of knowing. And these writers are not only poets like Wallace Stevens, whose poem opens Shirley Brice Heath's paper. In the science/technology field we recall David Macaulay's book *The Way Things Work* (Dorling Kindersley, 1988) across whose pages ambles a woolly mammoth. The mammoth's story, with its hilarious sepia illustrations, is not merely a huge entertainment but a way of reminding the reader that technical knowledge can be represented in many forms, for all the principles of levers, pulleys, magnets or whatever that are presented in the technical drawings and texts can also be learned from the fictional mammoth. Heath's plea for more integrated and personally directed ways of knowing in a new age of information, where the old divisions of Arts and Sciences seem arbitrary and irrelevant, is richly illustrated by the papers from Alan and Viv Kenyon, and Leone Burton. The Kenyons show us vividly how stories and songs from traditional cultures in vernacular languages can be ways of presenting science to young children — woolly mammoths for the classroom. Leone Burton uses the idea of narrative, a structuring device that reappears throughout this book, in mathematics activities in a new way, suggesting that what teachers need to admit to their pedagogies are the different and competing stories of children's numeracy practices.

1   Good Science or Good Art? Or Both?

Shirley Brice Heath

Many readers will be familiar with Shirley Brice Heath's Ways With Words, *her ethnographic study of three literate communities in the Piedmont Carolinas, a ground-breaking work which informs, directly or indirectly, many of the papers in this book. Here Heath turns her attention to the division between the Arts and Sciences, each with their competing discourses and literacies. Illustrating her argument with a poem by Wallace Stevens she proposes that our knowing is not naturally so divided and reminds us that the barriers between subjects and disciplines are artificial. She shows us that in the evolution of scientific ideas the process is one of 'narrating possibilities and merging types of knowledge to achieve a project'. Arguing that the processes of how science is done are not accessible to inspection she points out that what scientists and artists say about their thinking is remarkably similar. In spite of these 'mergers' in the two kinds of enterprise, education splits the wholeness of our coming to know into narrower and more limiting discourses. In the age of information, she suggests, 'just learning the facts' will not do — 'The claim must increasingly be for the creative rather than the uniform, the search for possible worlds rather than simply acquiring actual worlds as previously defined or delineated by others.' Heath's paper sets the cross-disciplinary tone of this book, and links in different ways with all the papers that follow it.*

Opusculum paedagogum.
The pears are not viols,
Nudes or bottles.
They resemble nothing else.

. . .

They are not flat surfaces
Having curved outlines.
They are round
Tapering toward the top.

. . .

The pears are not seen
As the observer wills.

Stevens, 1955

The American poet, Wallace Stevens (1955), by daylight an insurance adjuster and by evening a poet, merged science and art in his poetry. In 'Study of Two Pears', quoted above, he forces the reader to look again and again at two pears and to see, perhaps for 'the first time, the contrapuntal of the stretch between the familiar and the strange. Most of us have seen two pears; many of us have seen them in their 'real' form, as well as in animated shapes in children's alphabet books, and in artistic reproduction in still life, film, or computer image.

At this moment, we recall two pears in our visual and mental image again, as we read Stevens' poem to open this chapter. We know as teachers and teacher educators that these two pears are within the next few pages of print about to become something else for us again: two objects symbolic of concepts well removed from the usual way in which we engage with pears. Our experience with reading chapters such as this let us know also that, as we read further, we must keep all our *experience* about and of pears juggled within our heads. At this point, we suspect also that the point of this chapter will be that nothing with which we have had experience escapes both our artistic and scientific ways of knowing. We appreciate, feel, remember, and sense, while we at the same time know that the pear has components, a scientific name, and that diagrams in information books on seeds, fruit, and botanical reproduction will show the inside of pears and give explanations of how they grow from seeds into trees, need grafting, have varieties, and grow only in regions where combinations of soil and climate meet their needs. Such juggling encompasses the science and art of Stevens' poem.

Yet most of us had to put together these ways of knowing pears on our own, for our ordinary formal education kept these ways separated in classrooms — often both spatially and temporally. We learned about the aesthetic qualities of fruit during art period or on visits to art galleries, or even in the cafeteria, while in classrooms, we learned to dissect, categorize, and analyze pears and their life cycle. Later as we grew older and had biology classes, we further took apart pears to look at them in numerical and categorical terms, and we may well have changed their state in order to be able to talk about calories and nutrients, as well as water content. We read about them in information books on fruits, as well as in sections of textbooks devoted to processes.

For 'factual' evidence, we label, enumerate, distinguish, and collect phenomena in order to separate them from other objects and features of the environment about them. With labels, weights, and facts, we think we *know* pears. Later, as adults, we return to an orchard we visited as a child, and we venture into an orchard flavored with memories of an old friend. Once again, we taste the pears we had eaten there years ago; we take two back to the cottage and they catch us unawares on the dark wood table as they glow in the fading sunlight of the late day. We have now another mediated form of engaging with the pears. Whereas in our classification and description of pears, we mediated our knowledge through a series of steps of labelling and measuring given by the methods of science, now we filter our expression through emotion as well as aesthetic and practical perceptions. Now as adults we are at last free to put together our science and art of knowing pears.

For too long, as we have taught science to young children, we have looked for the correct combination of ways of segmenting as well as combining phenomena. We have asked children to count the number of pears, to calculate how to divide two pears among five children. As Stevens tells us, we search for combinations of ways of knowing and then still must agree that 'the pears are not seen as the observer wills.' They are interpretable and hence open always to expanding ways of seeing.

Too often the material objects of teaching as well as the process of 'training' teachers still set forth the myth that science offers one way of seeing, mathematics another, and the arts of pictorial and literary representation yet others. Textbooks, constraints of school schedules, and the process of 'training' teachers set apart art and science. Moral and material incentives, as well as personal likes and dislikes (some do not like pears as well as apples) rarely enter academic discussions of seeing and knowing, except by young children as yet sufficiently unregimented not to know they must not shout out in the classroom, 'But these pears are too hard to eat!' Young children uninitiated into formal education's way of seeing things only one way at a time strangely resemble us as adults, who resist directives that try to transmit only certain bits and pieces of knowledge and one or another particular way of seeing pears — or anything else that matters to us.

Narrating Life in Knowing

True scientific knowledge . . . demands abandonment to the very life of the object. (Hegel, Preface to *The Phenomenology of Mind*)

Leaving aside the matter of 'true,' we recognize that Hegel (along with Stevens, imaginative hungry children, and adults full of memories) abandons transmission from others as the only way to know something. We are urged into the 'very life of the object,' and that means into placing objects into projects and plans, or into scenarios that we imagine and create based on our prior experience. This chapter and others of this volume suggest that we devote considerable effort to creating lives of knowing with and for learners and that we not simply cook the pears to determine their calorie count or their mineral content but think instead of placing pears within narratives of life — our own and that of the objects.

Observers or readers have known for years that when asked what a chapter of a textbook is about, most learners narrate their responses. They are less likely to respond 'the process of decomposition that makes soil' than they are to say 'what the author talks about is how soil is made.' This response initiates a narrative in which the author is telling a story, and the suggestion is of an active author, agents playing roles in the making of the soil, and readers as active knowers. English speakers often give written texts animacy and report them as 'trying to say' or as 'telling us.' We may even go further in our explanation by saying 'you know when you leave a pile of leaves and garbage in your garden long enough, it becomes soil . . .' In ordinary conversation, we initiate answers to questions often by engaging the listener in an animate experience of *project* within a particular scenario —

making compost in the garden — before we proceed to talk about nitrogen, aeration, and other actors in the story of making soil. Inevitably, if engaged, our conversational partner asks, 'But what if . . . or how do . . . ?'

Narration carries knowledge for us because it animates, giving us actors with agentry who go about doing things and also wondering what will happen to change the scenario if they take certain other actions. Jerome Bruner tells us

> . . . the humanities have as their implicit agenda the cultivation of hypotheses, the art of hypothesis generating. It is in hypothesis generating (rather than hypothesis falsification) that one cultivates multiple perspectives and possible worlds to match the requirements of those perspectives. (1986, p. 52)

Some call this 'the believing game' or the act of 'embracing contraries' (Elbow, 1986). The learning taking place in narrating ourselves or others into a scenario of learning is acting out what often becomes reduced to 'the scientific method' in classrooms or in reductionist versions of school learning. This believing game method is that of narration, of putting an animate being within a scenario and pondering consequences of certain actions and processes. This method lies at the heart of art, creativity, and the humanities.

Enjoying the Disagreeable Idea

In numerous studies of how scientific ideas emerge and evolve, the process of both individuals and groups is that of narrating possibilities and of merging types of knowledge to achieve a project — an outcome projected into a future. Such projects are often directed by what scientists refer to as a 'disagreeable idea,' a set of hypotheses that seek to alter what has just been said or done and to believe in the emergence of new results. Chains of change follow from alertness to the unexplained in the outlying phenomena. Imagining and following such chains is what both science and art are all about.

Ironically, few who call themselves scientists believe the problem of how science is done is amenable to scientific research. Artists whether literary or otherwise, believe the same of their work. The particular language of thought is embedded in not only the history of an individual, but in unique and socialized ways of representing to the self and others a sense of inquiry (John-Steiner, 1985). Thus, this process as it actually occurs and in terms of the possible worlds it opens is rarely discussed. Terms such as 'insight,' 'intuition,' or 'happenstance' dominate. Major scientists, such as Albert Einstein or C.P. Snow, have acknowledged the texture and the subjectivity of the process of the making of science (Gardner, 1993). Writers again and again talk of 'just keeping your eyes and ears open' and 'going on insight' as their initial process.

What sets science apart *in the end* from art and the humanities is the fact that the results of science are subject to uniform control; art and the humanities escape this end most of the time. Hence the context of discovery is the same; that of justification differs. The laboratories of famous scientists, such as that of the Copenhagen school of physics, which included Niels Bohr and Werner Heisenberg, have been noted as having a certain 'joy in the contemplation of nature that could lead at times to flippancy' (Thomsen, 1986). Many enjoyed music as well as pictorial art, seeing in these ways of searching out patterns, sensing dissonances, and looking behind and beyond (Root-Bernstein, 1989).

Writers and artists, talking of their art in numerous collections with titles such as 'writers on writing' certainly do not claim 'uniform control' in the end. But they do talk of the hard work that follows inspiration and of the need to 'whip ideas into shape' or 'crack the whip over the sentences.' Almost all artists speak of their art as 'a way out' of an uneasiness with the way things are. They talk also of their preparation for art, through reading, observing, and 'finding the right moment' (Sternburg, 1980; Halpern, 1995).

It is instructive to hear the strategies for pioneering scientific research that some of the most prominent scientists of the late twentieth century offer. They ring in parallel to prescriptions given by artists, especially literary figures:

1. Learn well and deeply, experience life itself; remember that 'chance favors the prepared mind . . .'.
2. Direct action is always preferred over indirect.
3. Be different in your experiences, hobbies, philosophy, and goals.
4. Learn the experiences of the masters; read biographies and stories (of science and of literature); learn different styles of knowing from them.
5. Try many things; never be afraid to cast your line in various parts of the river.
6. 'Do what makes your heart leap!' and remember that joy and play, along with commitment, go together with discovery.
7. Think in unexpected ways, and don't be afraid to think big.
8. Look for novelty, and remember that truth comes often out of error.
(Root-Bernstein, 1989, pp. 410–20)

Formal education stands, more often than not, in opposition to these recommended mergers of art, aesthetics, emotion, reason, and experience. We have somehow enfranchized the view that rules and procedures must come before discovery and will be the primary science learning of most of us.

There are those who tell us that facts now double every five years and, for those with access to technology, their access to facts doubles each year. Clearly, 'just learning the facts' is no longer possible (if it ever was!) for any learner. We must now question seriously old academic habits based on different domains of facts and determine some way to enable students to learn to be discriminating, eager, and lifelong learners. We now know that we can no longer segment our choices of experiences and areas of knowledge into arbitrary domains or different arenas of facts. Instead, *areas of study* or *projects of learning* must replace these, and to the extent possible in schools, be grounded in ways to catch curiosity and talents, as well as to take advantage of local resources, for such projects and areas will not come easily in textbooks or pre-designed materials. Education is currently looking more than ever for multiplying possibilities of knowing. Projects and portfolios — terms and entities borrowed from the adult worlds of science and art — now abound in classrooms. Many teachers enable students to work in groups on projects and to document their strategies for others to question and debate. The sense of efficacy, practice, and experience — emotional, cognitive, and social — feeds the motivation for further learning. Teachers and students are gradually granting themselves equal rights and privileges in trying out mixed modes of learning and displaying knowledge (Ben-Peretz, 1995).

The study of science and of scientists, as well as of art and artists, offers many parallels. Both build upon wonder, curiosity, and imagination; both depend ultimately, though not initially, on rigor, practice, patience, and numerous areas of uniformity. These realities of the fields at large need to guide teaching and learning more and more. The claim must increasingly be for the creative rather than the uniform, the search for possible worlds rather than simply acquiring actual worlds as previously defined or delineated by others. Widening the limits of what is perceived to be possible generates scientists and artists, science and art. Neither their languages nor ways of knowing can stand far apart. The continuing goal should be to embrace a project of knowing, of creating a sense of wonder in which teachers and students think and work as animate agents in creating a scenario with projected outcomes, in being observers that will.

References

BEN-PERETZ, M. (1995) *Learning from Experience: Memory and the Teacher's Account of Teaching*, Albany, NY: State University of New York Press.

BRUNER, J. (1986) *Actual Minds, Possible Worlds*, Cambridge, MA: Harvard University Press.

ELBOW, P. (1986) *Embracing Contraries: Explorations in Learning and Teaching*, New York: Oxford University Press.

GARDNER, H. (1993) *Creating Minds*, New York: Basic Books.

HALPERN, D. (ed.) (1995) *Who's Writing This? Notations on the Authorial I with Self-portraits*, Hopewell, NJ: Ecco Press.

JOHN-STEINER, V. (1985) *Notebooks of the Mind: Explorations of Thinking*, Albuquerque: University of New Mexico Press.

ROOT-BERNSTEIN, R.S. (1989) *Discovering: Inventing and Solving Problems at the Frontiers of Scientific Knowledge*, Cambridge, MA: Harvard University Press.

STERNBURGH, J. (1980) *The Writer on her Work*, New York: Norton.

STEVENS, W. (1955) *Collected Poems of Wallace Stevens*, London: Faber and Faber.

THOMSEN, D.E. (1986) 'Going Bohr's way in physics', *Science News*, 129, pp. 26–7.

2 Evolving Shared Discourse with Teachers to Promote Literacies for Learners in South Africa

Alan and Viv Kenyon

In this paper Alan and Viv Kenyon draw on their collective experience as teacher educators and, more importantly, as story tellers in promoting literacies in intending teachers and school students. They have achieved considerable success in advancing the acquisition of complex literacies in two ways. Firstly, by valuing and recognizing the rich and varied culture that learners possess and bring to education, and by developing ways of thinking and doing through the poetry, song, and myths/legends of the learners' vernacular languages and cultures. Secondly, in their teacher education programmes, they have developed bold and exciting ways of planning, delivering, and evaluating teaching material where student teachers are engaged as partners rather than as recipients of privileged knowledge delivered from 'experts'. Like Heath, Alan and Viv Kenyon argue that science and the arts can be integrated in learning, and they demonstrate this for us in their account of primary science teaching in township classrooms in South Africa. Their analyses of the poetry and song texts that children know as part of their culture show that these literary forms are capable of carrying detailed and accurate knowledge of the environment. This knowledge becomes the beginning of scientific enquiry by starting from where the children are rather than from where the teacher or the 'science' is. Their emphasis on the uses of narrative in science education links this paper to the ensuing one by Leone Burton.

A Story

In January 1994 9-year-old Nonkokheli, a Xhosa speaker, found herself in an English medium 'Model C' school[1] in Cape Town, barely able to communicate with her peers and teacher. She had come from a rural area to stay with an aunt who 'in the child's best interests' sent her to what had previously been a whites only school. Nonkokheli, already reading and writing in Xhosa, now struggled to speak, read and write in English.

In August we went to her school to tell and work with stories, changing and adapting them and making books. For Nonkokheli the story of Demane and Demazana unlocked the door to English print literacy. A traditional story from her culture was given status in English. Suddenly there was reason to engage in print literate behaviour in a language other than her own. Her culture was valued and she had something to say. She could bring what she knew to her learning experiences and she wrote! Previously it had been a struggle to write two or three sentences in English but now it was hard to stop. With the continued support of her teachers, Nonkokheli is now participating enthusiastically and thoughtfully in literacy events in English.

Nonkokheli is one of the small group of pioneers known by township teachers as the 'five-per-centers'. These are children to whom real opportunities to gain literacy are denied because what they bring to the learning situation is rarely acknowledged and counts for nothing. But what about the 95 per cent who remain in what were Department of Education and Training (DET) schools, where the curriculum and methods which prevail in classrooms bear little relation to their culture and life experiences? Doors to various literacies are closed to these children as well.

The 95 Per Cent

The average school learner in a primary school in South Africa struggles to become literate on a number of fronts:

- On the home front, against *the disadvantages of severe poverty*.
- At school, to make sense of and succeed in *a repressive and inefficient education system*, which will inevitably outlive the eras that spawned it.
- In broader social and cultural terms, to participate in the creation of a better, more equitable society with *diminishing resources*.

To transcend the past and climb out of poverty, school learning is given priority in the minds of most stakeholders. To move towards success in education children must confront, make sense of, and then take possession of significant aspects of a whole range of literacies — ways of articulating and interpreting meaning — from basic print-literacy and numeracy, to other more subtle and complex literacies from fields like science and technology, art, music, history, health sciences, and geography. There are also other emerging and competing fields such as environmental education (eco-literacy) and computer literacy. Not only do learners have to do this from the perspective of disadvantage and impoverishment, but *they are expected to do it mostly in a language that is not their own*.

For the vast majority of children in disadvantaged DET schools the big question then becomes: How well equipped are teachers to support these disadvantaged learners given the inadequacy of teacher preparation programmes, inappropriate teacher support systems and unrewarding opportunities for further professional development?

Teacher Development

Teachers are the key players in effecting educational improvement. In South Africa there have been many attempts in the past to remedy the ills of apartheid education. Over the years, university research projects and non-governmental organizations (NGOs) have proliferated programmes which make attempts to understand and ameliorate a complex and problematic education system that is wasteful in its execution, and less than 50 per cent effective at its terminal stage.

In our work in teacher education and development we attempt to be eclectic and to evolve patterns of interaction that incorporate student teachers or teachers as partners alongside lecturers or INSET workers. We try to be culturally sensitive and contingently responsive to the contextual and social realities of teachers and learners as well as to their current needs. An ongoing process of collective inter-action provides a way forward which develops and shapes a shared discourse based on the immediate and emergent problems teachers face in their work. This draws on a range of different literacies that participants bring with them. Learning be-comes two-way.

Shared Discourse

The roots of the notion of evolving a shared discourse came from our work at a rural teachers' college in the Eastern Cape during the 1980s. Here we learned that some of the endemic problems of South African teacher education could resolve themselves if student teachers and college lecturers collaborated officially in tack-ling real teaching tasks as a team.

Abandoning the traditional approach and blocking time for teams of lecturers to work in partnership with whole groups of students was an alternative we invest-igated (Kenyon and Kenyon, 1991). Real teaching tasks were collaboratively tack-led with pupils. Through a negotiation process, up to 120 students and from 6 to 10 lecturers shared the ownership and responsibility for the careful planning and preparation of weekly sets of lessons that were then taught to pupils. These co-planned, co-owned lesson attempts were carefully observed and reflected on, and a loose form of action research was regularized into the college programme.

We established a risky process at the college that involved student teachers as partners in the direct discussion of the business of teaching rather than talking about teaching from a safe distance. This produced interesting results. There was a remarkable increase in personal and professional confidence on the part of the students. The lecturers gained a more sensitive awareness of the complex demands of teacher preparation in a developing education setting. It was clear that time spent in serious task-related talking was time well spent. If both lecturers and students were regularly learning from each other, there was the chance for a shared dis-course to emerge and for a shared set of understandings to develop as a base for future action. Lecturers could no longer work at the level of 'nice ideas'. Students could no longer be blamed for 'not getting it right'. Student teachers and lecturers began to operate more powerfully from the grounding of a shared set of multi-level literate behaviours.

The Primary Science Programme — Western Cape

Subsequent consultancy work for the Primary Science Programme (PSP) has provided an opportunity to extend the notion of the development of a *shared discourse* as a basis for educational development work in the specific field of primary science. The alternative is to impose or adopt an established discourse, which inevitably exacerbates the weaker position of the teacher as novice. Many teachers in less privileged circumstances are isolated from the world of academic and theoretical discourse. They do not believe that they have a place in such a debate and they lack the means and the confidence to join in and participate. Too often the day-to-day grind of school routine and classroom work leaves teachers isolated from chances to participate in carefully considered talk about their work. Their deep concerns, current needs and professional aspirations are rarely expressed overtly.

Part of the purpose of PSP has been to model in our practice and interaction with teachers the promotion and development of a shared discourse. We concentrate on the quality of talk and discussion in an open way and nurture the development and refinement of an inclusive common language. This leads to an emerging shared understanding of the real task demands of science teaching in the context of township and rural Western Cape schools. This emergent shared discourse encompasses an increasing range of fields. We need to:

1. talk about science content, science concepts, the conventions of science discourse, and the way science is written;
2. take account of talk about teaching science and learners learning science; talk which encompasses pedagogy and curriculum;
3. think carefully about the relationship between languages and science learning:
   - about reading, writing and talking science (science literacy) in more than one language;
   - about the fact that in using science process skills, learners are also using different language functions;
4. talk about how all these things come together as children try to make sense of science and teachers attempt to make science sensible to children.
5. consider how we can communicate our shared understandings to a wider audience and engage in broader debate.

Modelling the development of shared discourse has two potential outcomes. Firstly, if teachers come to value the possibility of building the links between cultural and classroom experiences on the one hand and talk and discussion on the other then the opportunity might emerge for the development of children's literate thinking. We would argue that learners can never be actively science literate without first developing broad literate thinking in relation to the science activities and concepts they are exposed to. Secondly, teachers themselves become better equipped to participate in mainstream debate from a position of strength.

Over the past two years we have found that DET classroom teachers have begun to volunteer with confidence to present papers, posters or workshops at mainstream national conferences and are involving themselves in local and national curriculum and policy debate. What processes have led to this developing confidence?

Enabling Conditions and PSP Work

An important PSP consideration is the extent to which teachers themselves are in the driving seat (Raubenheimer, 1992). In the Western Cape, teachers have had increasing autonomy in influencing the direction and thrust of the programme. We believe it is crucial to *trust* that teachers will assume more and more confidence and authority over time. It is important that the tasks and problems are 'real', and that outcomes are concrete and practical. Only then will deeper needs emerge and more critical underlying problems reveal themselves so that subsequent action can be both *responsive* and *progressive*.

Teachers identify topics of concern at a mass planning meeting at the beginning of any year. Rotating panels of teachers participate in the specific planning of each cycle of workshops on a topic. Some teachers with special interests or abilities are invited to join in the presentation of the workshops.

At workshops we review science content and consolidate related background knowledge, usually in a mind-mapping process. Collectively, we consider a range of different potential methodologies and approaches that emphasize teaching science in a practical and relevant way. We test the ideas co-developed in the workshops in a classroom setting with up to seventy pupils. Then we spend time collectively reflecting on the apparent outcomes that we observe. At the end of a cycle of workshops we produce a booklet that accurately documents the workshop process. We then distribute these support materials to the workshop participants.

The content and ideas in a workshop report are not regarded as final. Rather they are a record of a developing process and can always be improved upon, and often are, in that teachers tend to request a repetition of topics over a period of years. Revisiting and refining topics is now seen to be a critical element of ongoing support.

Language, Literacy, Science and the PSP

In the Western Cape, taking account of theories about the relationship between language and learning as well as second language learning, we have been selectively drawing on theory and infusing relevant ideas into our practice. In this way we have adopted and adapted aspects of theory in order to make them authentically and implicitly our own. An example would be the relationship between talking and writing. For most African children the culture of the home is predominantly oral. Henderson Mafu, a primary school teacher in the township of Khayelitsha, is concerned that learners in his classes who reveal powerful oral skills and dominate lessons, are the very same pupils who are incapacitated and fail badly when formally assessed in written examinations. So, in lessons we co-prepare and present, we try to signal clearly the means by which learners can make links between the spoken and the written. We model ways in which pupils can transfer their understanding from direct hands-on experience, through talk in the primary language, to pictures and labels in English with some spoken English, and finally, to more formal written scientific English.

In our work with children who live and learn in more than one language we have developed a practice which we call productive bilingualism. Watching a young teacher, Selby Ngcelwane, taking a science lesson on measurement of area caused a rethink and a radical shift from the view that one should use either one language or another. Selby used the primary language judiciously to draw on and consolidate the learners' contextual experiences of spreading margarine on bread, of painting or covering surfaces, and clearing a plot for planting. Then he moved on to use simple everyday English to re-establish what had been learned using a commercially produced poster. Finally he used the chalkboard, textbooks and more formal science language conventions to formulate the notes in English with pupils.

Learning science involves a whole range of symbolic systems, each with different possibilities and limitations. The important thing may be to allow for a greater flexibility so that learners practise and develop a facility in translating across symbolic systems, moving between different literacy forms, and different language conventions.

What Makes Science Teaching Problematic?

In our scientific and technocratic age, science discourse is probably one of the most powerful discourses. In contrast with a competitive world economy based on highly sophisticated scientific and technical development, one finds that science and technology education is relatively under-developed and unproblematized. There is a lack of deep concern for the way in which the majority of learners are systematically 'cooled out' and switched off the sciences.

In South Africa, science education tends to remain focused on the fixed and rather sterile products of science, mediated through written texts which stress the facts, correct terminology and technical explanations of science content. Science discourse has evolved specific ways of encoding its own invented world in the written form (Halliday and Martin, 1993), and this effectively excludes the less advantaged, the less confident and the less powerful. Do the powerful in science rely solely on conventional scientific, written language when they think scientifically? Einstein claimed that such language played little part in his mental operations: signs, images and even muscular sensations played a far more important role.[2]

Nobel Prize winner, Richard Feynman, identified playing around experimentally, switching representations, being alerted to noticing things, having interesting discussions, translating ways of seeing and imagining as important aspects of his developing interest in science (Sykes, 1994).

Another problem in science teaching is that what our common sense tells us about reality often is not the case when looked at more closely, carefully, or more systematically in order to find out. Do teachers ever realize this and/or try to make this fact explicit? Do they unpack with learners the fact that scientific understanding can often seem counter-intuitive? How can they take account of the apparent contradictions between the way things are seen through a common-sense frame and the way science discourse sets things out? If we want learners to operate more powerfully in science, what changes are needed to help teachers effect a more inclusive, learner-friendly science education for young children?

Young Learners and Science

We found in workshops that teachers of young children are quick to draw parallels between the natural curiosity of their pupils and the science process skills conventionally associated with scientists. Going through an excerpt from Paley's research (1981), describing very young children's science discourse, many science process skills were evident: problem solving, experimentation, prediction, hypothesis and comparing.

If very young children exhibit these scientific process skills naturally, what happens in primary schools to the incipient science they bring with them? How does it get deformed, stunted and shut off? How can teachers find ways to take account of and give status to children's capabilities? What aspect of the culture of the home, of the riches of African languages and of the oral tradition lend themselves to being incorporated into the day-to-day life of school?

Another Story

Introducing lessons on frogs, a local teacher and accomplished storyteller, Maureen Figlan, appropriates the Frog Prince story but makes it completely her own and imbues it with many elements that are culturally part of African oral literature. She tells in Xhosa and incorporates traditional sayings and parts of rhymes. The onomatopoeic last line of a well known Xhosa rhyme 'tsi-gxada; tsi-gxada; tsi-gxada' enriches the visual image of the way the frog jumps. The storyteller's ample body transforms itself dramatically as she mimes the frog propelling itself through the water with smooth, powerful thrusts. The crowded class of fifty-plus children sit spellbound. Riveted, they hang onto and relish every nuance of the telling.

Before we look at live frogs the next week, the class discusses how frogs move. Did the storyteller get it right? Does a frog really tuck its forelegs close to its chest when it swims? How accurate is 'tsi-gxada' in describing the arching jump of the frog? Suddenly the room is full of science and other talk, in Xhosa and in English, in gesture and in mime. Hands and arms move and swing in attempts to recapture or represent what is in the mind's eye. Cheeks bulge, eyes roll and frog sounds pervade the room. There is discussion, disagreement and more debate.

Observing frogs and looking at photographs, we find the storyteller was right. Perhaps the implicit knowledge came from her rural experience of listening to traditional tales (intsomi) as a child and an apprenticeship into storytelling conventions where you 'memorise nothing, but remember many things' (Scheub, 1975). When it comes to jumping we observe that the frog kicks off with powerful hind legs and flies spreadeagled in an arc through the air (tsi), lands on its fore-parts first (gxa-) and the hind-parts follow (-da). So there is found, culturally imbedded in the poetry of the language and the conventions of storytelling gesture, scientifically accurate knowledge.

Models, Praise Poems and Plants

In recent years the PSP teachers have been exploring ways to carefully assess the science knowledge children bring with them. We have tried drawing and mind-mapping and have moved on to model making. Modelling, both mentally and physically, is seldom given any conscious attention in the current curriculum. Yet it has always been a powerful African symbolic, expressive form. And in science it is a dominant means by which scientific findings are rendered and made explicit. Young African children improvise ingenious model toy cars from scraps of wire and bottle tops. The notion of modelling is not alien. The idea that a model can also be a tool to help conceptualize something scientific is under-exploited in our primary schools.

The heritage of oral literature for many South African people incorporates praise poets. At the 1994 inauguration of President Mandela, praise poets were part of the ceremony. Spontaneous oral poetry (umbongo) lends itself to formative assessment by revealing what children know in an expressive and lively form rich in metaphor and poetic associations. At a workshop on the 'Value of Plants', teachers tried composing praise poems of their own to plants like aloes, grasses, reeds and umhlonyana (a variety of wormwood). The teachers were quite struck by the way the unconventional exercise tapped and revealed a hidden resource of cultural and factual knowledge not usually given status in school-associated learning. We tried it with children and the results have been quite stunning. Considerable factual and accurate knowledge is revealed, knowledge that makes a particularly appropriate and empowering starting point for subsequent work, knowledge that celebrates what learners bring to school and, in particular, their oral literacy skills and the potency of their primary language.

The following poem comes from a pupil at Sosebenza Primary School in a particularly impoverished shack area on the outskirts of Cape Town. Teachers at this school have been promoting literacy by encouraging children to make their own books.[3]

Inyibiba ngu Ayanda Silumko	**Arum Lily**
Nzwakazi ndini ebuqhaqhawuli	*Queenly, of silky bright appearance*
Nzwanekazi ndini engenasiphako	*Queenlier, blemish free*
Mbelukazi ndini emanzandonga	*Beautiful woman, creamy*
Buqaqawuli besizwe sakowethu	*complexioned, like donga[4] floodwater*
Sihombo sesizwe siphela	*Beauty for all our nations*
Isizwe siyazingca ngawe	*Beauty to appease all our nation*
Awunamdintsi uyathandeka eluntwini	*People, never tiring of your beauty,*
Udumo lwakho lungumangaliso	*love you*
Singayini na isizwe nqaphandle	*Your glory is immeasurable*
kwakho	*Plucked you don't wither or wilt and*
Akubuni ebusika nayiqabaka	*the nation is privileged by your*
Lishushu ilanga uyadlisela	*presence*
	Even winter cannot dry you out
	You thrive on morning dew and in the
	heat of summer look even more proud.
Akulali ebusuku uyaphuthelwa	*You don't sleep at night. No you are*
Nasemini akozeli uyayokozela	*never drowsy*
Imbalela akuzazelento	*By day you don't even doze and your*
Imimoya evuthuzayo ayiluthu kuwe	*beauty is resplendent*
Indudumo zifika ziphinde zigqithe	*You transcend droughts*
Nyibiba ndini engeva zimanga	*Blowing winds are nothing to you*
	Storms come and go without affecting
	you
	Arum Lily! You remain untouched
	regardless. (Not even an unknown
	thing to come can harm you.)

(Inyibiba was translated by Ncebakasi Saliwe and Ndileka Mavumengwana.) This pupil is aware of soil erosion, knows the drying effect of sun and wind, knows that cool air carries less water vapour, knows that some flowers close at night, and that the arum is not a seasonal flower. Most interesting of all, is the way he alludes to new pending ecological dangers.

More About Story

Stories are an untapped resource from the strong cultural tradition of oral literature throughout Africa. There is evidence that many traditional stories provide explanations of natural phenomena which parallel scientific theories (Lévi-Strauss, 1978). Children like Nonkokheli find themselves in the texts of these stories, and, in situations which could otherwise be alienating, they are more likely to feel included when a story from their culture is used. Through using stories we believe teachers are likely to open the doors of the science literacy club to more children.

We believe that stories lend themselves to teaching implicit and incidental lessons. They can also be used to subtly open up cognitive space for subsequent work and talk. People come to learn things by revisiting them in different contexts, at different times, in different modes for different purposes and with differing degrees of interest and attention.

Perhaps a major problem with the development of science literacy for children has been a narrow focus and reductionist approach. You end up with a lowest common denominator type of science education. If the matrix from which children must make sense of science is narrowly framed and the register arbitrary and inflexible, is it any wonder that children vote with their minds and opt out?

Notes

1 'Model C' schools are schools which during the apartheid years were for white pupils only. After the unbanning of the ANC, the Nationalist government declared these schools could open their doors to pupils of all races.
2 Einstein, A., quoted by Koestler, A., in an interview with *Réalité*, Jan. 1966, 182, p. 78.
3 The work of Mrs N. Sishuba described in *Stories into books* (1993) a documentation by Dyer, D. of courses presented by Alan and Viv Kenyon.
4 Donga — a South African term for an eroded gulley.

References

DYER, D. (1993) 'Stories into books', unpublished documentation of courses presented by Alan and Viv Kenyon.

HALLIDAY, M.A.K. and MARTIN, J.R. (1993) *Writing Science*, London: Falmer Press.

KENYON A. and KENYON, V. (1991) 'Doing things differently in DET: A retrospective case-study of an innovation in teacher education' (unpublished) Kenton-on-Katberg Conference, University of Fort Hare, October 1991.

KOESTLER, A. (1966) *Réalités*, January, 182, p. 78.

LÉVI-STRAUSS, C. (1978) *Myth and Meaning*, London: Routledge and Kegan Paul.

PALEY, V.G. (1981) *Wally's Stories*, Cambridge MA: Harvard University Press.

RAUBENHEIMER, D. (1992) 'An emerging approach to teacher development: Who drives the bus?', *Perspectives in Education*, 14(1), pp. 67–80.

SCHEUB, H. (1975) *The Xhosa Ntsomi*, Oxford: Oxford University Press.

SYKES, C. (ed.) (1994) *No Ordinary Genius*, New York: W.W. Norton and Co, pp. 18–25.

3 Mathematics, and its Learning, as Narrative — A Literacy for the Twenty-first Century

Leone Burton

In common with other disciplines, mathematics, like science, attempts to answer the needs of society at any given time. Its solutions to these social imperatives can be told as socio-cultural stories that are reified to provide the dominant and immutable corpus that is school mathematics. Yet learners of anything, and in Leone Burton's view this includes mathematics, explore the meaning of their experiences through narrative — through juxtaposing voices, sharing narratives and frames, discussed further by Terezinha Nunes and Peter Esterhuysen in this volume. The narratives of the learners tell of their experiences in coming to know mathematics. In any classroom there are at least three different narratives: the learner's, the teacher's, and that of mathematics itself. As such, these narratives, differently positioned in space and time, reflect alternative ways of knowing that challenge the reified content of school mathematics and the dominant transmission pedagogy found in schools. If encouraged in mathematics classrooms such narratives would entail different interpretations and perspectives on meanings and knowing, and dialogic negotiation of the development of knowledge. Such an approach would transform current mathematical education practices including the roles and interrelationships of teachers and learners. In Leone Burton's view, a transformation of this kind is vital to enable us to cope with the society of the future; then flexibility, adaptability and the adoption of multiple roles will be essential to manage not only complex technological changes but also complex personal and socio-political patterns.

I think today I began to understand that maths is a way of describing things in reality. A great example is that a ball flying through the air travels the path of a parabola. Because there is an infinite number of ways for the ball to travel there is an infinite number of possible parabolas. Because parabolas can be written mathematically there would be a mathematical function to describe every arc in the world. (Secondary school student reported in Waywood, 1990, p. 53)

The Nature of Narrative

Narrative, I want to claim, is an attempt to impose coherent meaning on experience. Connectedness, and consequently coherence, is a necessary part of narrative. Without it, narrative does not gain, or hold, attention. Indeed, narrative always communicates within a community involving story teller(s), sometimes listeners, or readers, and sometimes participants. It engages others in the attempt not only to tell but also to explain and, ultimately, to understand the experience which has provoked it.

Narratives are personal, told by and often about the experience of the narrator vested with the meaning that the narrator chooses to garner and, consequently belonging to the narrator through the very processes of meaning-making. The 'facts' or story spine, are never the same when recounted by different individuals, using different emphases, highlighting or attending to different features, invoking different metaphors or explanatory examples.

Narratives are used to pose, explore, respond to *What if?* type questions. Narratives are a means to examine implications through a process of raising conjectures, and, pursuing and testing them against the substance of the story. As a result, surprise is often an important feature of narrative, sometimes used by effective narrators to confront the listeners with the implications of their own, often unquestioned, presuppositions.

> While it is true that the world of a story (to achieve verisimilitude) must conform to canons of logical consistency, it can use violations of such consistency as a basis of drama. (Bruner, 1986, p. 12)

Narratives may be communicated in many different forms, in speech, in writing and/or pictorially. They may be long or short. However, their 'telling' is not unproblematic and the story teller needs to consider the substance, structure and other characteristics which distinguish stories that arouse our interest. Clearly constructing narrative is a legitimate concern of the classroom. We all recognize and respond to 'good' narrative. However, our education in many cases fails to validate and build upon our childhood abilities to transform our own stories into narratives which our community finds meaningful. Nor is the narrative of 'objectivity' treated as problematic, especially in the mathematics classroom.

Narrative is *a*, possibly *the*, way to explore the meaning of experience. Narrating is participatory, involving a community in telling and responding to a story. Narrative starts from the personal and the particular, often encountering the general in its journey, and returns to the personal again. Narrative is a strategy for seeking possible answers to questions about our world.

Narrative, Mathematics and its Learning

Mathematics is a socio-cultural artefact.

> Mathematical knowledge is not simply a 'parade of syntactic variations', a set of 'structural transformations' . . . Mathematical forms or objects

increasingly come to be seen as sensibilities, collective formations, and worldviews . . . It is . . . math worlds, not individual mathematicians, that manufacture mathematics. (Restivo, 1993, p. 250)

Despite a century of reinforcement for the notion of the Queen of Sciences as objective, universal, certain and infallible, apparently 'a suitable language for stating value neutral descriptive facts' (Skovsmose, 1993, p. 173), recent work by sociologists, philosophers and historians makes the relationship of mathematics to its social and cultural (including political) roots more and more evident. Much of what is taught as immutable mathematics, especially at school level, is a social distillation of the results of refining strategies which have been particular to space and time. However, at present the social nature of mathematics remains a well-kept secret especially amongst the wider lay public who firmly believe that mathematics consists of a body of 'objects', or facts and skills, universally recognizable, and transmissible within a classroom setting (if only teachers were more effective). This is despite accumulating international evidence that learning is rarely about transmission, that current teaching of mathematics is associated with wide-scale learner failure and that mathematics itself is understood differently even from one state to another within the same country (e.g., Australia).

Unfortunately, the widespread acceptance of 'objective' mathematics has, in my view, reinforced a transmission pedagogy. Such a pedagogy is already regarded as necessary to teach a syllabus perceived as heavily loaded with difficult content. The most efficient means of assessing transmission in mathematics is, apparently, to rely on learner recall and reproduction, hence the dominance of tests. This is subject to challenge (see Gipps and Murphy, 1993). However, the very sociocultural nature of mathematics, together with its curriculum experience (syllabus, pedagogy and assessment) has led to a socially differentiated distribution of those who learn it successfully, and those who do not. Achievement at mathematics has become closely linked to power so, for example, mathematics departments in the universities of the developed world are predominantly staffed by white men. In many developed countries identifiable shifts in female performance have led to women comprising almost 50 per cent of university entrants. However, such shifts break down when entry to particular disciplines is examined. Mathematics is a case in point but by no means the worst. Computer science and physics provide examples of two further gendered disciplines, as do the languages, for example, English. Information on 'race' is harder to come by but, at the anecdotal level, colleagues in universities across the developed world confirm the 'white' status of their institutional communities at both student and staff levels. So, it would appear that we have a correlation between mathematics viewed as an objective science, transmission pedagogy, test-based assessment and widespread mathematical failure.

Is this connection causal? Does the mathematics narrative of objective science, with its related components in the educational setting, lead to the success of members of one community, and the failure of many others? In other words, is white, middle-class, male success at mathematics predicated by the mathematics that we reify and teach and the style which we use? I would claim that success at mathematics *is* socially construed, just as the mathematics itself is. The basis of that construction is access to membership of a community. Of what does failure consist? To fail at mathematics is to be excluded from the mathematical community and consequently from its culture, its language, its artefacts, its styles of thinking. Despite evidence that certain communities are more likely to fail than others such failure tends to be imputed to the student as an individual. It is linked with the 'mystery' of mathematics as well as with its 'power', to which, by definition, the failing students do not have access. However, despite failure at school mathematics, many adults successfully participate in mathematical practices as part of their lives (see Cockcroft, 1982). At the same time, it is possible to wonder, with Ole Skovsmose, if 'the teaching of the powerful mathematical language prevent(s) a critical interpretation of a highly technological society?' (1994, p. 5).

How large a part does our current definition of the school mathematics curriculum play in maintaining a low-level of challenge and enquiry in the population? I would offer the example of calculator use to justify a response that the school mathematics curriculum plays a very large part in promoting dependency on experts and knowledge:

> Evidence suggests that the limited use of both calculators and computers in the mathematics classroom cannot simply be attributed to difficulties of access to technology . . . In effect, there seems to be only limited recognition of the potential of both devices to fulfil the different functions of: *working implement* to carry out already standard mathematical processes; *teaching aid* to promote mathematical development; and *thinking support* to underpin novel mathematical strategies. (Ruthven, 1995, original emphasis)

But an approach in the classroom which makes effective use of calculators has been shown to respond to a pedagogy which supports learner independence. Such independence includes questioning, taking responsibility and making decisions and in consequence changes to the curriculum (see Ruthven, 1992; Shuard *et al.*, 1991). It is the pedagogy which is powerful in either mystifying or making clear the mathematics, disempowering or empowering the learners.

What Would a Narrative Approach to the Learning of Mathematics Look Like?

I claim that a narrative approach to mathematics and its pedagogy is consistent with a view of mathematics as being socially derived and with the understanding of mathematics as being socially negotiable. The former is the content, the latter is its pedagogy. With respect to the content of mathematics, instead of presenting it as 'objective', independent and fixed, we can tell its socio-cultural story, seeing it as a solution to a social imperative of a particular culture. Most interestingly we can compare different solutions to the same imperative thereby gaining insight into both the respective cultures *and* the mathematics (see, for example, Joseph, 1991; 1994). By engaging with the narrative, we place the mathematics in its context and personalize it, making it come alive to the conditions of the time. Context provides meaning and consequently learner motivation since it is exceedingly difficult to engage with context-less abstractions, as every teacher of mathematics knows! Contextualizing the mathematics also means that the story is enriched in terms of the interconnections of disciplines since mathematizing is often about geographical, physical, economic, social or historical information. Many sources of information are brought to bear on the problem which is set in a context. By narrating, we make use of our power to employ language to speculate about, enquire into, or interrogate that information.

Narrative in the mathematics classroom is dependent upon pupils assuming responsibility for themselves and their learning and exercising that responsibility judiciously with respect to one another, and their teacher. They must have stories to tell which means that the work that they are doing cannot be replicative. Work must be responsive to questions, have enquiry strategies which drive it and those undertaking it must be convincing in presenting their summative stories. The response of the community to such presentations is to query, to challenge, to request evidence, to pose alternatives, to seek counter-examples, in a word, to engage with mathematical *critique*. To extrapolate from Barbara Tizard's (Tizard *et al.*, 1981) work showing that children's 'interesting' questions are dependent upon adults' 'good' responses, I am proposing that pupils are more likely to generate depth and breadth of mathematical understanding and, indeed, interest in so doing in a classroom which provokes them to engage with 'interesting questions' because of an environment which values, and evaluates, 'good responses'.

Even with the same initial challenge, some narratives might be expected to conflict with others, some might build upon others, some might explore ground that no-one else has attempted to cross. Such practices are unlike those of a conventional classroom where: 'knowledge conflicts cannot emerge. A disagreement will always indicate that somebody has misunderstood something' (Skovsmose, 1993, p. 175). Narrative, on the other hand, presupposes different perspectives, different strategies, different conclusions, allowing knowledge conflicts to emerge naturally and themselves to become the focus of reflection in the classroom.

> The introduction of reflective knowledge . . . means the introduction of knowledge conflicts into the classroom. Therefore monologism has to be replaced by a dialogical interpretation of knowledge development; this will break down the ideology of the neutrality of the mathematical curriculum. (*ibid*, p. 177)

Some narratives might be told, others written or drawn, some might be acted. In 1993, at the Technology in Mathematics Teaching Conference, a party of 18-year-old Polish school pupils performed a version of one section of Lakatos' *Proof and Refutations*. After the performance, they were able to talk very convincingly (in English!) of the mathematical proof which had been the focus of their drama. In

Burton (1984), I showed pupils' narratives (although I was not, then, calling them such) in response to the challenge *Crossing the River*, which stated: 'Two men and two boys want to cross a river. None of them can swim and they only have one canoe. They can all paddle but the canoe will only hold one man or two boys. How do they all get across?'

Two children in a class of 9- to 10-year-olds, described their resolution in language:

CROSSING THE RIVER

First we got cuisenaire cubes
and got out two cubes for the boys
and two cubes for the men.
and made a modle of it all.
We started moving the cubes.
about. It looked easy at first
but we soon found it wasen't
so easy. We were moving the cubes about
for some time and then we had got
it into a posestion that we saw
we were all most there. We
saw the answer and moved the
cubes and they were all on the
other side.

(ibid, p. 53)

Meanwhile, three other children represented their resolution of the same problem visually:

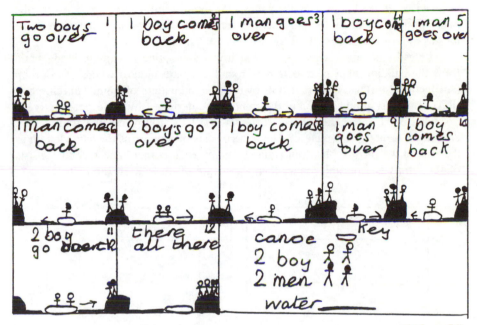

(*ibid*, p. 54)

The Narratives of the Mathematics Classroom

Pupil Narratives — Mathematics

Narrative assumes a shared discourse, but it also assumes dialogic negotiation of meaning:

> The establishing of 'dialogue' as an epistemic concept is implied by giving up the thesis of the homogeneity of knowledge, and accepting that contradictory knowledge claims can rightly be made with the consequence that knowledge conflict becomes a reality. (Skovsmose, 1994, p. 205)

Bruner (1986) lists three necessary features of discourse which are also relevant to mathematical narrative. These are *presupposition*, *subjectification* and *multiple perspective* (pp. 25–6). *Presupposition* allows the creation of implicit meanings. Any mathematics teacher who has presented an investigative challenge to a class can testify to the existence of presupposition as long as the language within which the challenge is couched allows for it. Consequently, as I have pointed out elsewhere, the best investigative situations are those that *encourage* interpretation. *Subjectification* places those who are undertaking the enquiry at its centre, their questions are the important ones, their strategies for investigation are the ones which will be justified or abandoned as the story unfolds. Their outcomes will relate back to their questions. **Multiple perspectives** allow many views on the same piece of world. In a mathematics classroom, multiple perspectives are the many positions held by the students the variety of which permits the exercise of those powerful questions: *What is different? What is the same?*

I recall videoing a Year 8 class which was attempting to capture in algebraic form the building of a picture frame around a square picture where each group (**subjectification**) had constructed its own, different, pattern of frame (**presupposition**). The class produced many different frame designs (**multiple perspectives**). So, what is the same and what is different about the following two frames built around the same square picture? The first consists of four strips the same length as the side of the picture plus four squares, one in each corner. The second consists of four strips all one unit longer than the length of the side of the picture.

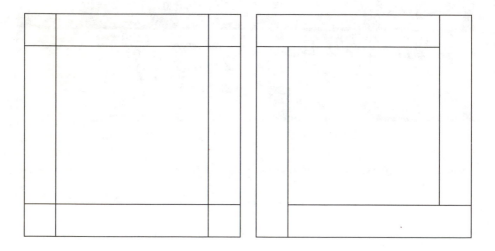

Figure 3.1   Picture frames

Is $(4x + 4)$ equal to $4(x + 1)$? Put like that, and exemplified through their own constructions, the pupils were not in any doubt. They used their discourse to negotiate a meaning both satisfactory to them, and to their teacher, i.e., socially acceptable.

Teacher/Researcher Narratives about Pupils' Learning

There is another form of narrative which is easily found both in classrooms and in the published research literature. It is the narrative told by teachers and researchers about the learning that they observe. An example is provided in Valerie Walkerdine's book *The Mastery of Reason* (1988) where she presents some dialogue between a teacher and a group of 7-year-olds. She writes:

> The teacher had chosen to take a group of children whom she considered
> ready for work on place-value . . . consonant with the current discursive
> practices in which she is inserted, children are taken to 'discover the
> place-value concept'. (p. 159)

The transcript provided demonstrates that three children, Sue, Michael and Anne,
successfully obtain the sum of two double digit numbers, 42 and 38. Sue also
successfully adds 28 and 26 getting 54. The purpose of the activity, to the children,
appears to be to obtain the answers and yet their offerings are ignored. My reading
of this transcript is that these children cannot be said to have no understanding of
place-value. So, what are these children learning during the tedious ninety-nine
lines of transcript? I suggest that they are learning certain socio-cultural lessons
about school mathematics, in particular that it is not important what you *know*,
what is important is that you have learnt what the teacher requires you to know, or
more pertinently, do. In the case of this particular teacher, it is that you count in
bundles of ten and single ones. Valerie Walkerdine interprets 'the relevant event in
the context of the lesson on place-value' as being 'that enough ones have now been
produced potentially to make another bundle' (p. 168). She says 'In all these
examples of the children beginning place value, the teacher, in a sense, *tells* the
children what they are supposed to be experiencing and discovering' (p. 169). In
my view, the teacher does not tell the children 'in a sense', she tells them directly
and without equivocation. The telling might be helpful if you had correctly interpreted the rules of the game which the teacher is playing. These rules have not been
made explicit, hence the need for interpretation, for the teacher, and the researcher,
to impute meaning for their own narratives which provide an 'explanation' for the
pupils' behaviour. My narrative is not about place-value, or the value of place, but
about boredom, mystification and disaffection.

However, independently of the teacher's choice of activity, Michael goes on
to have an exciting time inventing a rule for combining double digit numbers.
'Michael's elation is quite apparent. It seems to be the fact that the algorithm
works, rather than simply getting the right answer, which gives Michael pleasure'
(*ibid*, p. 175). Indeed, the persistence of children in pursuing their own questions
is remarkable when you consider the obstacles which are often placed in their way.
For me, the power of Michael's narrative, is demonstrated when he says: 'Miss.
May I tell you the easy way I found how to do it?' (*ibid*, p. 174). Michael then tells
his story — despite Valerie Walkerdine's assertion that 'mathematical discourse is
written' (p. 171).

Why is Mathematical Narrative a Literacy for the Twenty-first Century?

What do we require of a literacy? It seems to me that a literacy is a facility to
communicate and to receive communications about matters of personal, social,
cultural and political importance. Freire (1972) has drawn our attention to the

political power of literacy, not simply an ability to read and write but to have a reason to read and write because of the need to question, challenge, debate and critique society. As Giroux put it, literacy is 'a precondition for social and cultural emancipation' (1989, p. 148). But a literacy presupposes a language, and consequently a culture which both defines and is defined by that language. To accept the political intent and power of a literacy is to acknowledge that education has political purposes. Above, I indicated that the political purposes of mathematics education have, in effect if not in intent, been elitist distributing power and influence to a small, non-representative group and disseminating mystery and personal disaffection through 'objective' practices. But:

> mathemacy . . . has to be rooted in the spirit of critique and the project of possibility that enables people to participate in the understanding and transformation of their society and, therefore, mathemacy becomes a precondition for social and cultural emancipation. (Skovsmose, 1994, p. 27)

What is this mathemacy of which Ole Skovsmose writes? Of what might it consist? Whose interests would it serve? Is it a literacy for the twenty-first century? I do not believe that we can afford much more of the mathematics education that has been provided in schools. Not just the complex technological base of our society, of which much is frequently made, but the complex personal and socio-political patterns which make up our life styles define educational needs for the coming century which are a long way from being met. Amongst those needs, I believe, are an ability confidently to handle all kinds of information, including mathematical information, and to bring powerful mathematical thinking strategies to bear on the issues and opportunities which we face.

> Mathematics classrooms should be politicized; that is, students should be involved in planning, challenging, negotiating, and evaluating the work that they do in learning mathematics. (Noddings, 1993, p. 150)

Asked to work at a mathematics curriculum for the twenty-first century, high on my agenda would be making use of communicative skills, gaining experience of problem posing as well as problem solving, recognizing complexities including multiple positionings and that most decisions are made in the absence of clear definition and indications and rely upon maximization rather than 'rightness'. Far from wanting to encourage young people to keep discipline areas discrete, I would prefer a curriculum which grew out of a problem-perspective using all appropriate knowledge bases. Of central importance would be self and peer evaluation of responses by the pupils, to match their own objectives. Celebrating and valuing diversity, investigating similarities and differences, would seem to me a far more educative agenda than imposing a spurious mathematical neutrality through which one attempts to homogenize learners.

Certainly we have construed a messy world which is unlikely to be sorted out by the invention, or discovery, of more mathematics. Valerie Walkerdine points to the idea that mathematical proof . . . provides us with a way of dominating and controlling life itself. Such a fantasy is omnipotent because it is unfulfillable. It is . . . an enormous and dangerous fantasy. (1994, p. 74)

Before long, we must resolve human issues with respect to the ways in which members of societies relate to each other, the ways in which societies value their members and involve them in social organization, and the ways in which groups within and across societies interrelate. Such issues require mathematics but, more than that, they demand application of the processes of mathematical enquiry, the results of working at which I have been calling narrative.

References

BRUNER, J. (1986) *Actual Minds, Possible Worlds*, London: Harvard University Press.

BURTON, L. (1984) *Thinking Things Through*, Oxford: Basil Blackwell.

COCKCROFT, W. (1982) *Mathematics Counts*, London: HMSO.

FREIRE, P. (1972) *Pedagogy of the Oppressed*, Harmondsworth: Penguin Educational.

GIPPS, C. and MURPHY, P. (1993) *A Fair Test?*, Milton Keynes: Open University Press.

GIROUX, H.A. (1989) *Schooling for Democracy: Critical Pedagogy in the Modern Age*, London: Routledge.

JOSEPH, G. (1991) *The Crest of the Peacock*, London: I.B. Tauris.

JOSEPH, G. (1994) 'Different ways of knowing: Contrasting styles of argument in Indian and Greek mathematical traditions', in ERNEST, P. (ed.) *Mathematics, Education and Philosophy: An International Perspective*, London: Falmer Press.

LAKATOS, I. (1976) *Proofs and Refutations*, CUP: Cambridge.

NODDINGS, N. (1993) 'Politicizing the mathematics classroom', in RESTIVO, S., VAN BENDEGEM, J.P. and FISCHER, R. (eds) *Math Worlds*, Albany, NY: State University of New York Press.

RESTIVO, S. (1993) 'The social life of mathematics', in RESTIVO, S., VAN BENDEGEM, J.P. and FISCHER, R. (eds) *Math Worlds*, Albany, NY: State University of New York Press.

RUTHVEN, K. (1992) 'Personal technology and classroom change: A British perspective', in FEY, J. and HIRSCH, C. (eds) *Calculators in Mathematics Education*, Reston, VA: NCTM.

RUTHVEN, K. (1995) 'Pressing on: Towards considered calculator use', in BURTON, L. and JAWORSKI, B. (eds) *Technology in Mathematics Teaching — A Bridge Between Teaching and Learning Mathematics*, Bromley: Chartwell Bratt.

SHUARD, H., WALSH, A., GOODWIN, J. and WORCESTER, V. (1991) *Calculators, Children and Mathematics*, London: Simon and Schuster.

SKOVSMOSE, O. (1993) 'The dialogical nature of reflective knowledge', in RESTIVO, S., VAN BENDEGEM, J.P. and FISCHER, R. (eds) *Math Worlds*, Albany, NY: State University of New York Press.

SKOVSMOSE, O. (1994) *Towards a Philosophy of Critical Mathematics Education*, Dordrecht: Kluwer.

TIZARD, B., HUGHES, M., CARMICHAEL, H. and PINKERTON, G. (1981) 'Children's questions and adults' answers', paper presented to Section H, British Association for the Advancement of Science, Salford, England.

Leone Burton

WALKERDINE, V. (1988) *The Mastery of Reason*, London: Routledge.
WALKERDINE, V. (1994) 'Reasoning in a post-modern age', in ERNEST, P. (ed.) *Mathematics, Education and Philosophy: An International Perspective*, London: Falmer Press.
WAYWOOD, A. (1990) 'Mathematics and language: Reflections on students using mathematics journals', in DAVIS, G. and HUNTING, R.P. (eds) *Language Issues in Learning and Teaching Mathematics*, Bundoora, Vic: The Institute of Mathematics Education, La Trobe University.

Part II: Literacy Practices Inside Schools, Outside Schools and in Higher Education

Introduction

The papers in Part Two raise questions about the gulf that commonly exists between what people use literacies and numeracies for in their communities and what they are used for in schools and colleges. The gulf extends beyond the difference between learning mathematics, science, and English as the focus of what we are doing, and using them in the furthering of other enterprises and activities. The writers here move us away from deficit notions about frames of knowledge outside the school gates. Jenkins, for example, suggests that the ways that people construct knowledge to deal with their fuel and energy needs are adequate for the purpose, 'not an incorrect' version of 'real' science. Are school subjects irrelevant for the functional purposes of everyday life? The papers here suggest that we need to know much more about those functional literacies and numeracies than we do. Barton's research on family literacies implies, like Jenkins, that the literacies out there are far from inadequate, and that educationalists make many false assumptions about the literacy skills of those thought to have literacy problems. Dombey's paper, like Hewlett's, reminds us that *oral* vernaculars have a fundamental role to play in the acquisition of literacies, even when their forms are non-standard dialects or non-dominant languages. Nunes argues that the sign systems employed by numeracies and literacies themselves constrain the kinds of thinking we are enabled to carry out within their frames. Dave Baker describes the informal and formal numeracy practices in his research and suggests that we ought to be widening the frames of knowledge in school mathematics to include the practices employed in other areas of our lives. Street's paper also has resonances of the frames Nunes refers to, but here it is the conventions of our literacy practices themselves, exemplified in his presentation of a range of written responses in their original format, that not only set the boundaries of what is or is not permissible within an intellectual field but also conceal power and authority relationships. Hewlett's paper dramatically reflects the interaction between dominant and non dominant groups, with the added important dimension of language itself. Can frames of knowledge become readily accessible to learners who have to encounter them in an imposed and alien tongue?

4   Scientific Literacy: A Functional Construct

Edgar W. Jenkins

In this paper, Edgar Jenkins argues for a conceptual framework that would be more appropriate for determining the essentially functional forms of scientific literacy that certain individuals and groups possess. Within the continuing debate around the public understanding of science, he contrasts qualitative methodologies to the more common quantitative studies where researchers seek to determine how much, or usually how little, scientific knowledge the public possess. The research that Jenkins discusses here on elderly people's understandings of energy conservation shows that the subjects of the research have an understanding of phenomena that makes no distinction between 'science' and 'technology'. Their ways of knowing are intimately related to action and use and though not 'scientifically correct' are well adapted to the particular purposes and contexts in which their knowledge of energy was employed. This paper reminds the reader that simplistic notions of literacy/illiteracy as bipolar opposites should be rethought and succinctly argues for plural forms of scientific literacies that are shaped and suited for specific social purposes. How such an approach to science education can be accommodated alongside 'science for future scientists' is a question that emerges from this paper. Jenkin's research on scientific literacies in the community can be compared to Barton's in this volume on family literacies.

The term 'scientific literacy', characterized as scientific knowledge and attitudes, allied with some understanding of scientific methodology, appears in much contemporary writing about science education. In many countries of the world, it is associated with attempts at science curriculum reform and innovation (e.g., AAAS, 1989; Champagne *et al.*, 1989; Science Council of Canada, 1984), directed principally, but not exclusively, towards school science education. Together with the notion of technological literacy, it underpins the world-wide UNESCO initiative *Education 2000+*, now in its third phase and directed towards the development of a 'world community of scientifically and technologically literate citizens' (UNESCO, 1993). Alongside these attempts at reform, efforts to define, explore and measure scientific literacy sustain a minor academic industry, reflected in conferences, seminars and a journal, *The Public Understanding of Science*. In addition, the promotion of scientific literacy through a variety of media constitutes a major business, augmented by a host of public events as diverse as science weeks, science fairs, and education-industry partnerships.

Quantitative measures of scientific literacy are universally disappointing. Despite some conceptual or methodological differences, the broad conclusion is that science is 'not much understood' by the general public which is mostly scientifically illiterate. However, such measures commonly rest upon a cognitive deficit model of scientific literacy which presupposes that the public should understand science essentially on the scientists' terms. Further objections to this model are that it portrays science as an unproblematic body of knowledge, that scientists' own knowledge is often confined to a speciality, and that they often differ about the procedural aspects of science. It is difficult to take issue with Ziman's (1991) conclusion that a simple 'deficit' model of the public understanding of science, which seeks to interpret findings in terms of public ignorance of scientific literacy, provides a poor conceptual framework for exploring the issues involved.

A different perspective, which this paper seeks to illustrate, is evident in the work of researchers such as Wynne (1991), Layton, Jenkins and Davey (1986) and Yearley (1989). Their work relies on qualitative, rather than quantitative, approaches to data collection and analysis, and focuses on individuals or groups of adults engaged in understanding and/or acting upon some issue with a scientific dimension. The emphasis is on the dignity of respondents' knowledge and the importance of context in understanding. Typical studies relate to elderly people seeking to manage a domestic energy budget within fixed, low incomes; parents raising children born with Down's syndrome; self-help or protest groups concerned with issues relating to health, medication, or the environment; and elected representatives making decisions about such matters as the siting of an airport, a nuclear facility, or the storage and disposal of hazardous waste.

Studies like these show that adults engage in complex processes to deconstruct and rework scientific knowledge in order to articulate it with other understandings, personal knowledge and practical purposes. The corollary is that scientific literacy comes to be understood as essentially functional, interactive, interrogative of science and its estate, and intimately and integrally related to such notions as authority, expertise and power both within and beyond science itself. There are, of course, parallels here with debates taking place elsewhere among those with a scholarly interest in other aspects of literacy. Greenwood, for example, has shown how, like scientific literacy, 'workplace literacy' has long been regarded as unproblematic, whereas, particularly from the workers' perspective, it is rich in tensions and contradictions, and underpinned by powerful economic and socio-political assumptions (Greenwood, 1992).

Consider the case of elderly people, living on their own and managing a domestic energy budget within limited financial resources. Such groups are increasing in many western industrial societies. Not surprisingly, therefore, the well-being of the elderly has become a significant political issue and a determinant of social and economic policy. One aspect of that well-being has received particular attention from central and local government in the United Kingdom as well as from several charitable and other organizations whose especial concerns lie with, or include, the elderly. The concerns include the ways in which elderly people use their financial and other resources to keep warm, eat well and maintain good health. Such needs are not, of course, uniform. The elderly do not form a homogeneous group, partly because of individual variation, partly because their financial and other circumstances differ, but mainly because the group includes people of very different ages, potentially involving a possible span of thirty-five years. Nonetheless, growing old raises distinctive issues in relation to income, mobility and health, all of which depend upon the management of a domestic energy policy. The importance of effective management of such a policy is highlighted in the United Kingdom by the estimated 600–700 deaths annually of elderly people from hypothermia. Such deaths help to account for the particular emphasis placed on keeping warm.

A study, in Leeds, of a sample of thirteen elderly people living on their own, explored the understanding that such people had of the scientific knowledge relevant to their energy concerns, how such knowledge was obtained and the use that was made of it. The study was based on detailed interviews in an approach that can, for brevity, be described as essentially ethnographic (Layton, Jenkins, MacGill and Davey, 1993). Not unexpectedly, the study confirmed that the elderly had no understanding of heat, or more generally of energy, in terms that would have made sense to, or been accepted by, a physicist. The interviews revealed no hint of heat understood in scientific terms as molecular motion. Rather it was understood in terms redolent of eighteenth-century caloric theory as a fluid that could flow, leak, escape or rise. These are descriptions that resonate with those used by heating engineers to model heat and heat transfer and which are reflected in the advisory literature made available to the elderly about how to stop 'heat leaking through the roof', etc. As a corollary, 'cold' was perceived not as an absence of heat but rather as possessing distinctive qualities of its own. Lagging pipes served to keep both the 'cold out' and the 'heat in'. Similarly, a draught was 'concentrated cold' and the glass in windows 'attracted cold', as evidenced by the fact that it always 'feels cold to the touch'. This understanding of heat and cold is by no means confined to elderly people (Bagshaw, 1981) and, however disappointing to some science educators, is hardly surprising since it is attested repeatedly by everyday experience for which it proves an adequate level of explanation. As two of the elderly remarked, 'If I leave this door open, the heat from the fire warms the room next door', and 'By heating the hall, it takes the chill off my bedroom upstairs'.

In exploring the scientific literacy of the elderly interviewed in the study, it is helpful to identify what might be involved in a 'scientific approach' to the management of domestic energy in this context. Such an approach is likely to involve the following elements.

1. Exchanging a larger dwelling for accommodation which is smaller and/or makes fewer energy demands.
2. Choosing a cost effective method of providing heat for warmth and for cooking, e.g., the use of a cheaper fuel, taking advantage of off-peak, lower priced energy supplies.
3. Making optimum use of energy-saving devices such as thermostats, taking

showers rather than baths, switching off unnecessary lights, employing strategies for preparing drinks and meals which minimize energy demands.

4. Reducing heat loss by insulation and double glazing.
5. Monitoring energy consumption both *in toto* and in respect of individual appliances, and, where possible, taking corrective action.
6. Using data, e.g., weather forecasts, to anticipate sharply increased or diminished energy demands, and responding as required, e.g., by adjusting the amount of clothing worn or, in extreme circumstances, heating part, or a smaller part, of a house rather than the entire dwelling.

For many of the elderly people interviewed, moving house was not a realistic possibility. Where it had been considered, it was rejected on grounds other than energy considerations, such as proximity to family who might help in the caring or in an emergency, or the desire to remain close to long-standing friends and neighbours. Similarly, energy costs were not necessarily the determinant of choice between gas and electricity as a means of heating or cooking. For one elderly lady who had once owned a gas cooker, electricity had become the only option. She judged it 'cleaner than gas', mainly (and illogically) by reference to her children's houses where, she inferred, the gas central heating meant that the 'walls get dirty at the back of the radiators'. Safety considerations were also important for another interviewee who commented that she 'used to turn the taps on (accidentally) and . . . I haven't a big sense of smell'.

Each of the people interviewed had given careful consideration to the use which they made of the energy devices to which they had access. Two examples will suffice.

I make . . . up . . . three or four casseroles and put them in the freezer and pop one in the oven as required . . . (This is) more economical . . . you've only got to cook once . . . except for just warming up.

I draw three . . . cupfuls of water and I put that over the pilot light for the night so that in the morning that water is slightly warm, so it doesn't take much to get it boiling.

However, the apparently 'efficient' use of energy appliances was frequently overridden by other concerns. One elderly lady provided additional heating in a room she did not normally use because she chose to be interviewed in this 'best' room in connection with the research. Another switched on an electric fire which would not have been on if the interviewer 'hadn't been coming' and because the simulated fire 'provided something to look at'. A third interviewee abandoned the use of an electrically heated towel rail because her grandchildren would come and 'they got burnt on it', while another always left her heating on 'for her cat'. Similarly, lights were sometimes turned off, or not used, for reasons that had little or nothing to do with efficient energy usage. 'I like a lot of light; it's cosy that way', commented one elderly lady. Curtains, although widely acknowledged as important in thermal insulation, were nonetheless drawn open each morning as a means of signalling to their neighbours that 'all was well' or 'because I couldn't stand a dark room upstairs all day'. Windows, which might be kept closed to retain heat, were opened regularly to allow the entry of 'fresh air', commonly regarded as a 'healthy' strategy.

The effective scientific management of a domestic energy policy inevitably has a quantitative dimension requiring, as a minimum, the monitoring of energy consumption both generally and in respect of particular energy devices. Such monitoring is a formidable task and requires calculations beyond the competence of most of the population (Sewell, 1981; Cockroft Report, 1982). Those interviewed in this study showed a keen sense of the relative energy demands of different appliances, e.g., 'anything that heats is expensive and anything like lighting is comparatively cheap', coupling this with a monitoring of their total energy consumption, sometimes on a daily basis, by reading the appropriate meters. Such diligence, however, owed more to financial prudence to 'live within one's means', than to effective energy management *per se*. 'I allow myself about four units (of electricity) per day', commented one lady. Another, acknowledging that she 'didn't understand therms' . . . , reckoned that 'if it's ten therms more . . . say if I used thirty last time then forty this time, it's going to be about a third more expensive'.

Advice, commonly in the form of literature from government and charitable sources, was acknowledged but frequently ignored. A thermometer, designed to indicate when the temperature of a room fell to a point when the occupant might be at risk from hypothermia, was judged 'just for interest' or dismissed with a comment such as 'If I hadn't got one, I wouldn't bother to get one', since 'I know when to warm myself up'.

Superficially, it would be possible to conclude that the behaviour of the elderly people referred to in the preceding paragraphs was 'unscientific' and that their level of 'scientific literacy', at least in respect to heat energy, was very low. The data necessary for the relevant scientific judgments were not available and decisions about energy management often rested on grounds, such as convenience and comfort, which might be regarded as too personal, subjective or qualitative to sustain a scientific approach.

Such a conclusion, however, involves the assumption that a scientific approach is both appropriate to, and adequate for, an understanding and evaluation of the management of domestic energy by the elderly. This assumption is unlikely to be valid. It fails to acknowledge the complexity of human behaviour and, more particularly, to accommodate the notion that elderly people may understand the management of domestic energy in terms that are significantly different from, but not necessarily less valid than, those of a scientist or heating engineer. The elderly bring judgments to bear which reflect their roles as investors (e.g., in loft insulation), as consumers (e.g., as in using an 'unnecessary' simulated electric fire), as members of a social group (e.g., heating an additional room to greet the interviewer), as expressers of personal values (e.g., decision to remain near one's family), and as problem-avoiders) (e.g., rejecting double-glazing because of a lack of confidence in those who might undertake the work). As a corollary, judgments about energy practice are made in ways that are appropriate to each of those roles.

The management of domestic energy, therefore, is much more complex and subtle than might be understood, or even dictated, by a consideration of the nature of energy itself. More particularly, it is clear that individual and social preferences act as powerful influences upon the ways in which fundamental scientific ideas relating to energy and its conservation are integrated into the everyday practice of the elderly, i.e., there is both a psychology and a sociology of domestic energy use.

The fact that people do not act as isolated, scientifically rational individuals means that if their behaviour, and their scientific literacy, is to be understood, it must be understood using a variety of concepts, explanations and perspectives. Moreover, as far as energy is concerned, it can be conceptualized in a number of different ways which relate to different levels of explanation so that it lacks any single, socially shared, understanding. An understanding of one level of explanation, e.g., of heat energy as the motion of particles, does not necessarily ensure access to understanding at another, e.g., heat energy as a commodity to be purchased. In addition, there is a lack of articulation between the scientific notion of energy as presented in conventional science courses and the understandings that elderly people invoke in the management of it.

The relationship to science of the elderly referred to above was, by design, that of 'user'. For these users (and, by extrapolation, most people) science was less an outstanding manifestation of human curiosity about the natural world, a conceptual cathedral of awe-inspiring construction, than a quarry to be raided, a repository of resources which might further their particular endeavours and assist in the solution or amelioration of particular problems and concerns. Such an understanding of the relationship between scientific knowledge and action has a number of important consequences.

Once the public understanding of science is conceptualized in these interactive, rather than deficit terms, many of the commonplace assumptions about the nature of science lose their validity. Science as coherent, objective and well-bounded gives way to science which is problematic and fluid. The frequent cases of 'expert' scientific judgments in conflict — for example in forensic, disaster diagnosis and risk analysis contexts — serve to emphasize the incomplete nature of the knowledge constructed and, even more significantly, the role of value judgments in scientific decision making. Likewise, as adults engage with issues which have a scientific dimension relating to, for example, diet, medication, or hazards in the home or workplace, the seeming certitude of laboratory science crumbles. A similar comment can be made about many environmental issues, such as ozone depletion, global warming or the long-term storage of radioactive material. As Ravetz (1990) has pointedly observed, from a situation in which 'hard' scientific facts were seen in opposition to 'soft' values, we have moved to one in which inescapably 'hard' decisions have to be made on the basis of a scientific input which is irremediably soft.

In addition, the ignorance of science inherent in a deficit model of understanding can be seen in a new perspective. Such ignorance may reflect a positive choice. For example, parents of children who have Down's Syndrome often choose to disregard chromosomal information and understanding about the origin of the syndrome since they can do nothing about it and their concerns lie with the welfare of their children rather than with underlying causality of the genetic abnormality. Likewise, elected councillors making decisions about the storage or disposal of hazardous waste often chose to 'leave the science' to their expert advisers, a conscious division of labour and a selective ignorance which allows their attention to be focused more effectively on other matters. When the process of integrating scientific knowledge with other personal judgments and situation-specific knowledge does not remove science from the scene altogether, therefore, it frequently relocates it as a peripheral player, as in the management of domestic energy by the elderly.

Attention also needs to be given to what happens to scientific knowledge when it is relocated from one context, e.g., that of generation, to another, notably that of use or action. Aitken (1985), writing about the origins of radio, has commented that 'information . . . generated within one system exists in a particular coded form, recognizable by and useful to participants in that system. If it is to be transferred from one system to another . . . it has to be translated into a different code, converted into a form that makes sense in a world of different values' (pp. 18–19). It is not difficult to think of examples of this translation of scientific knowledge and of the difficulties sometimes associated with it. Epidemiological estimates of increased cancer deaths from a radiation leak are commonly cast in probability terms but these measures are of little direct help to someone who wishes to know whether it is 'safe' to eat the vegetables grown in his garden sited close to the source of the leak. The physicists' understanding of heat as molecular motion is less useful to the householder than the scientifically unacceptable notion of heat as a fluid. Pharmacologists are less interested in classifying substances in terms of their chemical constitution and structure than in terms of their functions as stimulants, depressants, painkillers, etc. In developing countries, where water- and excreta-related diseases account for a very high proportion of all illness, the biological classification of causative organisms as viruses, bacteria, protozoa, etc., is of less practical importance than an understanding of modes of transmission and methods of preventive intervention.

More generally, this issue touches upon the distinction between scientific knowledge and knowledge that might be described as technological. The relationships between science and technology are complex, vary over time and depend upon the science and technology involved (Gardner, 1994). Nonetheless, technological concepts, like that of heat 'flow', are grounded in the context of action rather than of understanding, in contrast to heat conceptualized scientifically in terms of the kinetic theory of matter. There are clear parallels here with the notion of 'situated cognition' and the claim that 'interaction with other people and the use of socially provided tools and schemas for solving problems' is central to everyday cognitive activity (Rogoff and Lave, 1984, p. 4).

It is also important to recognize that, since individuals do not encounter scientific knowledge as free-floating and unencumbered by social and institutional connections, issues such as trustworthiness and reliability are important elements in the development of their scientific understanding. In some cases, as with the local councillors referred to above, their lack of scientific knowledge reflected a confidence, born of experience, in the expertise of their professional officers. In other instances, for example at British Nuclear Fuel's Training College, apprentices were content to know relatively little of the physics of radioactivity, an ignorance they were content to justify by claiming that the relevant scientific understanding had already been incorporated by the specialists who had designed the nuclear facility and established its operating procedures (Wynne, 1991). In other cases, the social institutional origins of the scientific knowledge being offered betrayed values and interests which were antithetical to those of the recipients, with the result that such knowledge was rejected. Accounts of the mental and physical manifestations of Down's Syndrome, provided by members of the medical profession to new parents, were frequently discounted and, in many cases, subsequently refuted by experience (Layton *et al.*, 1993). In the United States, many Native Americans, seeking the repatriation of the bones of their ancestors, reject claims by anthropologists and archaeologists about the importance of these human remains for the scientific study of such phenomena as population migration and paleopathology.

The public understanding of science, therefore, is a much more complex phenomenon than is commonly presented. 'Scientific thinking' will not often be the proper yardstick by which it may estimated, not least because scientific 'ignorance' may be a positive construction with considerable practical advantages. For most of the population, scientific understanding is intimately related to action and use, to be accommodated, or not (in accordance with criteria which may be as much socio-institutional as utilitarian), alongside other knowledges deemed relevant to the context of that action or use. Where such accommodation occurs, it commonly entails the restructuring and re-contextualizing of scientific knowledge in ways that relate to the interests, concerns and priorities of particular groups or individuals. The underlying notion, therefore, is that of a variety of functional scientific literacies for specific social purposes, the implications of which for science education are profound but lie beyond the scope of this paper.

References

AAAS (1989) *Project 2061: Science for All Americans*, Washington DC: American Association for the Advancement of Science.

AITKEN, H.G.J. (1985) *Syntony and Spark: The Origins of Radio*, Princeton NJ: Princeton University Press.

BAGSHAW, M. (1981) 'Domestic energy conservation and the consumer', unpublished MPhil thesis, University of Bradford.

CENTRAL STATISTICAL OFFICE (1984) *Social Trands, No. 14*, London: HMSO.

CHAMPAGNE, A.B., LOVITTS, B.E. and CALINGER, B.J. (eds) (1989) *This Year in School Science 1989: Scientific Literacy*, Washington DC: American Association for the Advancement of Science.

COCKROFT REPORT (1982) *Mathematics Counts*, London: HMSO.

DURANT, J., EVANS, G. and THOMAS, G. (1992) 'Public understanding of science in Britain:

The role of medicine in the popular representation of science', *Public Understanding of Science*, 1(2), pp. 161–82.

GARDNER, P. (1994) 'Representations of the relationship between science and technology in the curriculum', *Studies in Science Education*, 24, pp. 1–28.

GREENWOOD, S. (1992) *The Politics of Workplace Literacy: A Case Study*, Gowen, New York: Teachers College Press.

LAYTON, D., JENKINS, E.W. and DAVEY, A. (1986) 'Science for specific social purposes (SSSP): Perspectives on adult scientific literacy', *Studies in Science Education*, 13, pp. 27–52.

LAYTON, D., JENKINS, E.W., MACGILL, S. and DAVEY, A. (1993) *Inarticulate Science? Perspectives on the Public Understanding of Science and Some Implications for Science Education*, Driffield: Studies in Education Ltd.

MILLER, J.D. (1983) 'Scientific literacy: A conceptual and empirical review', *Daedalus*, 112(2), pp. 29–48.

MILLER, J.D. (1987) 'Scientific literacy in the United States', in EVERED, D. and O'CONNOR, M. (eds) *Communicating Science to the Public*, New York: Wiley.

NATIONAL SCIENCE BOARD (1980) *Science Indicators — 1980*, Washington DC: Government Printing Office.

NATIONAL SCIENCE BOARD (1983) *Science Indicators — 1982*, Washington DC: Government Printing Office.

NATIONAL SCIENCE BOARD (1985) *Science Indicators — 1985*, Washington DC: Government Printing Office.

NATIONAL SCIENCE BOARD (1988) *Science Indicators — 1987*, Washington DC: Government Printing Office.

RAVETZ, J. (1990) 'Some new ideas about science, relevant to education', in JENKINS, E.W. (ed.) *Policy Issues and School Science Education*, Leeds: Centre for Studies in Science and Mathematics Education.

ROGOFF, B. and LAVE, J. (eds) (1984) *Everyday Cognition: Its Development in Social Context*, Cambridge MA: Harvard University Press.

SCIENCE COUNCIL OF CANADA (1984) *Science for Every Student: Educating Canadians for Tomorrow's World*, Report No. 36, Ottawa: Science Council of Canada.

SEWELL, B. (1981) *Use of Mathematics by Adults in Daily Life*, Leicester: Advisory Council for Adult and Continuing Education.

TREFIL, J. (1991) *One Thousand and One Things Everybody Should Know About Science*, New York: Doubleday.

UNESCO (1993) *International Forum on Scientific and Technological Literacy for All*, Final Report, Paris: UNESCO.

WYNNE, B. (1991) 'Knowledge in context', *Science, Technology and Human Values*, 16(1), pp. 111–21.

YEARLEY, S. (1989) 'Bog standards: Science and conservation at a public enquiry', *Social Studies of Science*, 19(3), pp. 421–38.

ZIMAN, J. (1991) 'Public understanding of science', *Science, Technology and Human Values*, 16(1), pp. 99–105.

5   Family Literacy Programmes and Home Literacy Practices

David Barton

David Barton takes the discussion of literacies outside schools and into families and neighbourhoods. His paper vividly illustrates the difference made by ethnographic observation to our understanding of the terms literacy *and* illiteracy, *for real research evidence, as opposed to ill-informed assumptions and conjectures, shows us that family literacy practices are numerous, varied and frequent. Barton argues that the functional literacies of the home—literacies that are used to get things done — are important models for literacy practices in educational institutions. While family literacy programmes have traditionally been oriented to the view of literacy held by the teacher and the school, Barton proposes that schools have a great deal to learn from homes. Like Esterhuysen and Hewlett in this volume he shows that assumptions about the illiteracy of the uneducated are mistaken, but that the literacy practices of families and neighbourhoods are potentially an important educational resource. Barton's paper provides an alternative to Dombey's emphasis on well written books and stories as central in learning to read.*

Introduction

The two words *family* and *literacy* have the wholesome glow of something we surely approve of: we are all in favour of families, however we define them, and we all believe in literacy, however we define it. The difficulty is that family and literacy both mean different things to different people. The two words have been put together to make *family literacy*, an idea which has become prominent in the government's discussion of literacy education, linking adult and child literacy. *Family literacy* is on the public agenda.

In this paper I shall contribute to the general discussion of family literacy by examining the reading and writing that people do in their everyday lives. To do this I will draw primarily on data which has been documenting the ways in which people use literacy in their home lives, taken from the 'Literacy in the Community' project in which I have been involved. In order to relate this to current notions of family literacy I will begin and end with an image of family literacy, typical of those from the educational press.

The picture is of a white women in her early 20s with two children, a girl of about 4 and a boy of about 5. They are all sitting close together looking at a large book the woman is holding. Behind them on the wall are the words 'story corner'. It is an intimate picture which I interpret as a mother with her two children sitting in a school. Although this is in many ways a positive image, I want to challenge it if it is to be the predominant representation of family literacy. I want to question each aspect of this image of family literacy, to move it beyond young mums, beyond 4- and 5-year-olds, beyond books and beyond schools. First, I need to describe what we have learned about home practices from our study of literacy.

Literacy in the Community

The 'Literacy in the Community' study was a detailed four year study of the role of reading and writing in people's day-to-day lives in Lancaster, England. The study included intensive interviews with adults attending basic education classes, a door-to-door survey, a detailed study of fourteen households in one neighbourhood, and interviews with managers of bookshops, the library, advice centres and other access points for literacy in the city. There were also studies of local community associations, detailed observations, and the collection of documents and photographs. Here I will concentrate on what we learned about literacy in people's home lives, drawing mainly on data from the detailed study of one neighbourhood.

We contacted the fourteen households in the neighbourhood study mainly through the door-to-door survey. One member of each household who agreed to take part was interviewed extensively about their everyday literacy practices, covering a wide range of activities at home and in the local area. There were regular household visits with further interviews and observations. According to the people's literacy activities, the study of each person developed in different directions. Often we interviewed other household members and accompanied people on trips to the library and to community associations. Some people kept literacy diaries for us, and others collected documents such as letters from school or junk mail. After a space of more than a year we returned to some of the people who had been interviewed and asked them to reflect on interview transcripts and on our analysis of their literacy practices.

We gradually built up a picture of the role of literacy in people's everyday lives. Here I will summarize our findings about how families and households use literacy, grouping them under four headings.[1]

Households or Families?

We refer to several different overlapping domains in our study, including *family, household, neighbourhood* and *community*.[2] Obviously contemporary families and households come in many forms; sometimes the two terms refer to the same entity, often they do not. There are households of one person, several people, related people, unrelated people, and they can be structured in various ways. Families too are diverse; they can be with or without children, or they can be single parent, or they can take many extended and complex forms; there may be links with other generations or there may be none.[3] What was important for our study of literacy practices was whether or not these categories — *household, family, neighbourhood, community* — were useful in describing people's literacy activities. The validity of the terms became an empirical question.

We found that all four of these terms had a useful role in describing some aspects of people's literacy. We knocked on the doors of *households; households* were the groups of people who shared living space and, usually, ate together in a *home*. Some aspects of literacy related to household management and communication. *Families* were important when people talked about their informal learning of literacy and some networks of support; often people referred to relatives who in some cases lived nearby, on the same street or round the corner, and in other cases lived elsewhere in Lancaster or in nearby towns. The physical *neighbourhood* had some salience, where people relied on neighbours for support, and where common local issues, such as traffic problems and street lighting, were addressed. The notion of *community* is more amorphous, but people nevertheless identified with particular communities of interest, such as allotment associations or as parents of children attending particular schools; literacy often had significant roles in these communities.

Both families and households are important in terms of support for literacy. People used a broad notion of family. We asked adults to recall who were the significant people in their childhoods in terms of education; it was not just mothers and parents they referred to. Often people remembered a particular individual who had been important to them, and in many cases it was a more distant relative or family friend. We referred to such people as *guiding lights*, a term used by one of our informants.[4]

The Diversity of Home Practices

We were struck by the wide diversity of literacy which goes on in the home. There are many literacies, tied in with daily activities, beyond book reading. Often they combine many kinds of reading and writing, drawing upon spoken language, numeracy and much more. People deal with shopping lists, TV schedules and junk mail. They write and receive personal letters and cards; some keep diaries, some write poems; they deal with official letters, bills and forms; they have noticeboards, calendars, scrapbooks, recipe books, address books; they read local newspapers, catalogues and advertisements; people keep records of their lives, and read and write to make sense of this complex world; they belong to community organizations and pursue leisure interests bound by a web of newsletters, magazines, notices, minutes and messages; there are instructions which accompany every consumer good and service, from a bicycle helmet to a gas bill; people are even instructed in writing how, when and where to put out the rubbish. Children are exposed to and participate in this range of practices.

At first we imagined we would encounter a distinct *home literacy* which could be contrasted with *work literacy* or *school literacy*. To some extent this is true. There is a distinctiveness about many home literacy practices, but the range of different literacies, including work and school literacies which are brought home, is more striking.[5] Within the home too, as people participate in different relationships with each other and assert different identities, there are many patterns of how literacy is distributed. Many home literacy practices are patterned through gender; in relation to issues of family literacy, for example, women's literacy lives were complex and could not be defined solely in terms of their relationships with their children's education.

When thinking about adults who have difficulty with their reading and writing, it is important to emphasize that everyone participates in literacy activities. Although parents may have problems with reading and writing they nevertheless engage in a wide range of literacy activities. In our data we have many examples of adults with difficulties who keep diaries, maintain household accounts, write poetry, take phone messages, send letters. They are not the empty people living in barren homes waiting to be saved and filled up by literacy that the media sometimes implies. For the most part such adults are ordinary people leading ordinary lives and, if they have children, they are concerned like everyone else about their children's education.

Home is Distinct from School

Home life is very different from the formal life of the school classroom. There are several ways in which such differences have implications for literacy. In school, literacy is an object of study in that it is explicitly talked about and taught, and is central to many classroom activities. Using literacy for formal learning produces a distinct *school literacy*. At home, while literacy is occasioned by many activities, it is often not itself the main objective, which may be shopping, paying the bills, or finding out local news. Literacy is used to get other things done. Linked to these differing purposes at home and at school are different ways of evaluating whether or not literacy is successful. School reading and writing are usually assessed, sometimes formally, and often in terms of correctness and accuracy. Tasks are often carried out in a way which makes them explicit and open to evaluation. In contrast, home literacy is not usually explicitly evaluated but is successful if it serves its purposes. People at home, in keeping with such a diversity of practices, slip in and out of many different roles with respect to literacy, drawing upon and asserting different identities.[6]

Other aspects of home life affect how literacy is practised. Home and school have different notions of public and private, and different rights over personal space. We are only beginning to describe these differences; as researchers we would emphasize that it is important to find out what actually happens in particular homes, rather than make unsupported assumptions which assume one universal way of using literacy common to home and school. Parents are experts on their own experiences. Rather than intervene in families, teachers and others need to investigate together the reality of literacies in homes and communities. Our overriding impression was that whatever their levels of literacy, all the parents we interviewed were concerned about their children's education. However, they often did not know ways of supporting their children, although many existing practices in homes could be identified and built upon.

Lifelong Learning

Participating in and learning about literacy is not only important at the age of 5 years. People had learned many of the literacies we observed as adults, and when they recalled where they had acquired particular aspects of literacy they talked of learning at work or in an informal manner from friends and relatives. From infancy right up through the school years households are significant places for learning. The teen years are of special importance and in our study parents were involved in the homework projects of their teenage children, as well as supporting younger children in learning to read. Teenage literacies are as important as those concerning the infants class.[7]

Adults of different ages participate in quite different literacy practices, so the literacy demands on 20-year-olds, 30-year-olds and 40-year-olds can be very varied. We were also struck by the fact that those with the fewest resources in society often had the greatest literacy demands imposed upon them. Claiming benefit, for example, demands a complex configuration of reading, numeracy, form filling and background knowledge of the social security system. Life changes such as leaving home, starting a family, getting a job, losing a job, retiring, all make different literacy demands, and people encounter new literacies at all points of their lives. Older adults in their sixties and seventies take on new literacies, sometimes embarking on major new projects such as researching their family tree or writing their memoirs. The different literacy demands of different ages needs to be considered in national discussions of the literacy levels of adults.

Support for literacy also takes many forms; people adopt different roles in the home and support is not solely in one direction. Children may help their parents and take on some of the literacy chores of the home: programming the video recorder, making sense of the letters sent from school, map reading on car journeys, and taking charge of the new home computer. It was when trying to help their children with school work that some adults were confronted with their own difficulties in reading or writing, and sought help. More generally, several adults talked of learning from their children's or grandchildren's school activities, including homework.

Family Literacy Programmes

Through ALBSU, the Adult Literacy and Basic Skills Unit, the government has set up a series of what it calls family literacy programmes in England and Wales. This initiative in June 1994 sparked much media interest. The aim of the initiative is to establish projects which teach both parents and children. Projects include speakers of English as a first or second language (although ALBSU defines literacy as being only in English, or Welsh in Wales). They are located in a variety of settings, including libraries, schools, colleges, family centres, and many projects involve partnerships between two or more providers. Initially, four demonstration programmes were funded for two years and more than two hundred small grants have been awarded to individual projects. A wide variety of activities takes place in these projects. One format, adapted from the United States, is a twelve week course for adults and children where parents might have six hours of tuition, children six hours, with an additional two hours a week of joint time. ALBSU encourages fixed length courses with assessment of both children's and adults' progress. It draws extensively, but selectively on family literacy work in the States where there has been a decade of experience. Following a review of ALBSU's role, the government, in its instructions to the agency published in January 1995, has strongly endorsed the family literacy work; it has supported the idea of linking adult and child provision, and of extending ALBSU's role in the area.

There are other family literacy programmes in Britain unconnected with ALBSU, including some in Scotland, some funded by EC money and some funded locally. In the actual practice of these diverse projects, there are various views of family literacy. In many ways these are exciting developments, offering new possibilities to rethink some fundamental aspects of education. These initiatives give the opportunity to reassess home–school links and to rethink the role of community in education. Schools get the opportunity to involve parents; adult literacy programmes get the opportunity to act upon a need, sometimes expressed by students, to help in their children's learning. Bringing together the British tradition of non-formal adult literacy provision and conventional school provision could produce a fruitful confrontation between distinct philosophies of education. Family literacy provides the possibility of educational innovation which need not be constrained by traditions of formal education.

However, for such an exchange to be productive it is essential to examine the underlying concepts of family literacy most critically and not to accept unchallenged narrow versions of what is possible. Home and school literacies are not accorded equal status. School literacy is dominant, supported by powerful institutions and infiltrating other domains. Some versions of family literacy turn out to be an invasion of school and its practices into the home (see Street and Street, 1991). While there is more than a decade of research evidence on the significance of the bed-time story and reading to children, our research and the research of others suggests that it is important to look beyond book reading at home.[8] Children are observing and participating in a wide range of activities. As others have claimed (e.g., Clark, 1976), a general positive attitude to literacy and children's participation in ongoing literacy activities is important. It is probably inadvisable for parents of pre-school children to take on the teacher's role. Attempting to replicate in the home what children do at school is likely to be mistaken; it may not be effective, could lead to an impoverished notion of literacy, and will alienate some people.

The common media image, often represented in government propaganda, of a mother helping her young children learn to read is one such narrow politically charged concept of family literacy. It is important to deconstruct the rhetoric of blame surrounding the term. There is the rhetoric of falling standards which blames teachers. At the same time, there is often a tendency to blame families for children's lack of progress in school rather than blaming the government for the lack of funding to support children who find learning to read difficult in increasingly overcrowded classes. The term family literacy becomes part of a deficit model which concentrates on what children and families lack, rather than examining their strengths. The newspaper headline 'Toolkit to fix family illiteracy' is part of this. In the United States there is concern at the ways in which such a model of family literacy becomes a way of attacking the family, to the extent of providing a thread of links between the purported problems of US industrial competitiveness and the dynamics of family life; mothers' child-rearing practices take the blame for world economic readjustments.

One of the lessons of the US experience is that family literacy programmes ought to pay attention to the languages people speak in the home; the imposition of English on young children has become a cause for concern in the States (Auerbach, 1995). Forcing English on pre-school children in households where other languages are spoken may be seriously detrimental both to children's development and to family stability as a whole (Wong-Fillmore, 1994). There is a danger that family literacy may come to represent an intolerance of difference and diversity in local realities, in cultures, and in languages.

Another concern, in Britain and the United States, is the way in which a medium level correlation between adults with literacy problems and children with literacy problems slips into being interpreted as a causal relationship in which adults' difficulties are seen as generating children's problems (ALBSU, 1993). Using the published figures, Peter Hannon (1994) has demonstrated that the situation is more complex; while some parents with problems have children with problems, there are also many adults with problems whose children experience no difficulties. Conversely, there are many children with problems whose parents have none. This pattern of connections has implications for family recruitment to literacy programmes. Focusing on families where both the parents and the children have literacy problems may reach some people needing support, but there will be a larger group of potential students who do not fit the criteria for such programmes. Identifying children with problems is not a very efficient way of reaching adults with problems; identifying adults with problems is not a very productive way of reaching children with problems. This very practical issue is crucial in the effective allocation of resources: family literacy programmes may not be the best way of reaching many of the people who need and want provision.

These factors may explain concerns expressed by providers of family literacy programmes both in the United States and in Britain; that such programmes are finding it very hard to locate students who fit their precise criteria, while nearby adult literacy programmes have waiting-lists of potential students needing help. At the same time, at a crucial point in their lives for literacy, young children in British schools may wait a year for their problems to be diagnosed and a further year before any help is offered.

Conclusion

The contribution which studies like the 'Literacy in the Community' project can make to the debate is to provide a view of what actually goes on in the home in terms of literacy. As I hope I have shown, the home is a distinct domain of life, separate from school; home is a place where literacy means different things, where the purposes, values, and roles adopted all contrast with formal schooling. Studying the home reveals a richer literacy than that portrayed in the media image with which we started. Family literacy needs to move beyond the stereotypes, and beyond school literacy. If there is real concern at particular families' underachievement, a detailed examination of family life might reveal hidden strengths and resilience in families. It may be found that literacy is not the root of people's social problems, and that families survive despite odds of extreme poverty and deprivation (see Taylor and Dorsey-Gaines, 1988). Family literacy could draw upon existing strengths, upon vernacular forms of learning and, as Moll (1994) terms it, families' *funds of knowledge*.

Returning to the picture we started with, each aspect of the image of a mother with young children reading a book in school can be challenged. Family literacy needs to move beyond the young mum, to include fathers, other siblings, and the range of relations and family friends which people cite as important in their literacy lives. Focusing exclusively on parent-child relations excludes other important social networks and community resources. We need to observe beyond the reception class, and recognize that homes are significant from infancy right up through the teens, acknowledging that parents learn from children too. Notions of family literacy need to move beyond the book and to take account of children's participation in a wide variety of home activities. Finally, images of family literacy need to move beyond the school as a site of activity; rather than regarding homes as needing to replicate what schools do, family literacy could support the things people do in their everyday lives.

Acknowledgment

I am grateful to Mary Hamilton, Roz Ivanic, Fiona Ormerod, Kathy Pitt and Rachel Rimmershaw for useful comments on an earlier draft of this paper.

Notes

1 For details of other aspects of the study see Barton and Padmore, 1991; Barton and Hamilton, 1992a, 1992b.
2 For more details on the notion of domains and on the other framing concepts used here, such as different literacies and networks of support, see Barton, 1994.
3 For more on the distinction between families and households, see Marsh and Arber, 1992; on shifting notions of community, see Heath, 1995.
4 Examples are given in Padmore, 1994.
5 Klassen, in a study of bilingual literacy practices in a Canadian city, refers to the home as 'the centre from which individuals venture out into other domains' (1991, p. 43), and this is how we came to see the home domain.
6 There are also more informal literacies at school beyond the formal classroom ones which are now being documented, for example in Maybin, 1992.
7 In parallel with recent work in the United States, such as Heath and McLaughlin, 1993, we believe attention needs to be paid in Britain to school age children who have dropped out of school, including children who live in households without any adults.
8 For example, some of the articles in Goelmen, Oberg and Smith, 1984.

References

AUERBACH, E. (1995) 'From deficit to strength: Changing perspectives on family literacy', in WEINSTEIN-SHR, G. and QUINTERO, E. (eds) *Immigrant Learners and their Families*, Washington: Center for Applied Linguistics.

ALBSU (1993) *Parents and their Children: The Intergenerational Effect of Poor Basic Skills*, London: Adult Literacy and Basic Skills Unit.

BARTON, D. (1994) *Literacy: An Introduction to the Ecology of Written Language*, Oxford: Blackwell.

BARTON, D. and HAMILTON, M. (1992a) *Literacy in the Community*, Final Report to ESRC.

BARTON, D. and HAMILTON, M. (1992b) *Collaborative Ethnography*, Final Report to ESRC.

BARTON, D. and PADMORE, S. (1991) 'Roles, networks and values in everyday writing', in BARTON, D. and IVANIC, R. (eds) *Writing in the Community*, Newbury Park, CA: Sage, pp. 58–77.

CLARK, M.M. (1976) *Young Fluent Readers*, London, Heinemann Education Books.

GOELMAN, H., OBERG, A. and SMITH, F. (eds) (1984) *Awakening to Literacy*, London, Heinemann.

HANNON, P. (1994) *Literacy, Home and School: Research and Practice in Teaching Literacy with Parents*, London, Falmer Press.

HEATH, S.B. (1995) Ethnography in communities: Learning the everyday life of America's subordinated youth', in BANKS, J.A. (ed.) *Handbook of Research on Multicultural Education*, New York: Macmillan.

HEATH, S.B. and MCLAUGHLIN, M.W. (eds) (1993) *Identity and Inner-city Youth: Beyond Ethnicity and Gender*, New York: Teachers College.

KLASSEN, C. (1991) 'Bilingual written language use by low-education Latin American newcomers', in BARTON, D. and IVANIC, R. (eds) *Writing in the Community*, Newbury Park, CA: Sage.

MARSH, C. and ARBER, S. (eds) (1992) *Families and Households: Divisions and Change*, London: Macmillan.

MAYBIN, J. (1992) 'Children's writing practices', Centre for Language and Communication Working Paper, Open University.

MOLL, L. (1994) 'Family Literacy Programmes', presentation at International Forum on Family Literacy, University of Arizona Tucson: Arizona.

PADMORE, S. (1994) 'Guiding Lights', in HAMILTON, M., BARTON, D. and IVANIC, D. (eds) *Worlds of Literacy*, University of Lancaster: Multilingual.

STREET, J. and STREET, B. (1991) 'The schooling of literacy', in BARTON, D. and IVANIC, R. *Writing in the Community*, Newbury Park, CA: Sage.

TAYLOR, D. and DORSEY-GAINES, C. (1988) *Growing up literate*, London, Heinemann.

WONG-FILLMORE, L. (1994) 'First Language Attrition in a Second Language Context', presentation at Lancaster University.

6 Enlarging the 'Ways of Taking' from Literary Texts: Mode-switching in the Primary Classroom

Henrietta Dombey

In this paper Henrietta Dombey questions whether it can safely be assumed that children who come from non-dominant cultures will find the well-written books and stories, widely acknowledged to teach young readers the most productive reading lessons, as meaningful as they might be to children who come from bookish and literary homes. Here she does not propose an alternative reading agenda for such children, arguing that they deserve access to this dominant literacy since education, and reading, is about broadening experience and the mind's horizons. Instead, she suggests that teachers need to make full use of children's talk during reading, employing their spoken vernaculars to build bridges between the child's culture and the imaginative world of the text. In this argument, learning to read and reading for pleasure are seen as collaborative enterprises, activities that can be done together in small or larger groups. Dombey's paper has echoes of Leone Burton's with its proposal that the different narratives of children's mathematical processes be admitted to the pedagogies of mathematics classrooms. The interrelatedness of the oral and the literate is a theme which appears, too, in the papers by Alan and Viv Kenyon and Lynn Hewlett. Dombey's insistence that well-written literature is too transformative to be jettisoned reappears in Carol Fox's paper in Part Four, where Fox argues that imaginative literature, even as a dominant or canonical literacy, is a 'special case'.

Inside current concern about the effectiveness of different approaches to the teaching of reading in the early years of school lies a problem of long standing: the markedly different rates of success in learning to read experienced by children from different social groups. This problem has been largely hidden in recent years by a government whose 'league table' ideology denies the importance of social difference. The path it has taken has been to retreat into a view of learning to read as the mastery of a neutral technology.

Every autumn thousands of children in reception classes of British infant schools are introduced to the world of the reading scheme, the set of instructional materials chosen for the purpose of introducing them to the business of reading.

With greater or lesser enthusiasm their teachers strive to interest them in the antics of Ben and Lad, Biff and Chip or perhaps even the denizens of the Village with Three Corners, aware that the linear, technical view of learning to read on which these schemes are built finds favour not only with politicians and journalists, but also, increasingly, with the institutions that govern education in this country (OFSTED, 1994; DfE, 1995).

Against this prevailing 'back to basics' tide, in which learning to read is seen as essentially a matter of rule-following to achieve a technical end, that of 'breaking the code', teachers in other schools maintain that learning to read should, from its earliest stages, involve active engagement in predicting the words on the page and the construction of significant meaning with their help. They see learning to read as a wider and deeper enterprise, involving new forms of reflection. They maintain that the process can take place only when the texts on which children learn to read stimulate and reward them, not bore them as happens so often in the reading scheme classrooms. In addition to giving children opportunities to make sense of 'environmental print', of signs and notices dealing in practical everyday matters, such teachers encourage their children to develop a confident familiarity with texts written primarily to give children pleasure.

But for those likely to experience difficulty in learning to read, could it be that such teachers are merely replacing one form of cultural alienation with another? The books taken home in the plastic book-bag at the end of the school day are not received with the same confident familiarity by all families. For those not from the dominant culture, with its well-established practices of story-book sharing with pre-school children, might not such 'meaningful' texts seem as alien and unsatisfying as Ben and Lad appear to those used to more substantial literary reward? Certainly stocking one's classroom with pleasurable texts does not appear to reduce the disparities between success rates of different cultural groups in the business of learning to read.

Yet encounters with such literature are seen to be central to the richly textured learning that is now held to constitute learning to read. Young children, it is now argued, need to encounter texts that are both predictable in their language and structure, thus supporting the novice reader in the arduous business of identifying words, and also of real interest to the child reader. It is not whim and self-indulgence that have led teachers to move away from reading schemes. A recognition has grown that to be accessible to novice readers, more is required of early reading texts than control over the extent and complexity of their vocabulary and spelling patterns. 'Look, Peter, Look' will no longer do.

Recently published reading schemes claim to take account of such considerations. They certainly deal in more inviting topics in language that is less stilted than their predecessors. But there is a further argument for a change in early reading matter, one less easy for the producers of reading schemes to adapt to. If reading in the earliest stages is to be intrinsically rewarding, their texts need to be written in enticing and memorable language, to lure the novice reader in, to deal in compelling themes and to provide her with substantial semantic reward. Such texts are by definition literary and not to be produced to the simplistic formulae of most reading schemes. So learning to read, in some quarters at least, is now seen in large measure as a literary apprenticeship (Meek, 1982). Indeed a recently published 'scheme', Collins' *Pathways*, written exclusively by established writers, claims that 'From the start children are encouraged to re-read, reflect and re-create the meaning of books', and even incorporates texts originally published elsewhere for children's pleasure (Wade, Minns and Lutrario, 1994). So the divide between 'scheme' and 'non-scheme' texts is no longer sharp and clear.

And of course, not being part of a reading scheme is by no means a guarantee of literary quality in a text. Nor is it easy to define all that the term might encompass. One does not, however, need a universally agreed set of criteria to claim that some books are richer than others, offering greater aesthetic reward and a more ambitious set of potential meanings to the reader, enabling her to enlarge, reorganize and re-evaluate her mental model of the world around her and in her head. The Ahlbergs' *Each, Peach, Pear, Plum*, for example, with its rhyming search for the characters of nursery rhyme and fairy tale who have ventured into each other's territory in unexpected ways, provides a novice reader with a fuller reading experience than does *Ben and Lad* from Ginn's *Reading 360*, in which, through unmemorable language and unremarkable pictures, boy and dog are shown to throw balls, grab sticks and fall in the mud, but are neither guided by larger intentions, nor present the reader with any interpretive challenge.

So far, in terms of semantic reward, the case for pleasurable literary texts as against the empty mundanity of the reading scheme seems strong. But, and this is perhaps especially the case for a novice reader, the richness of semantic reward is not a function of the text alone. The experiences and meanings readers bring to texts, and the consequent psychological and cultural reverberations set off in their minds result in profoundly different readings. Literary works of all kinds exist between the poles of the printed text and the individual reader. Indeed imaginative fiction is never totally explicit, but demands a reader who brings to it an understanding of narrative conventions and a willingness to take on the task of imagining a world. As Genette (1980) puts it:

> The real author of the narrative is not only he who tells it, but also, and
> at times even more, he who hears it. (p. 262)

The more active the reader, the more the world comes alive and the greater the significance of the reading. Metaphors of osmosis and saturation are singularly inappropriate. The experience of reading a narrative is never totally assimilative: the reader does not just soak up the text. The reading of narrative fiction is an interactive process, shaped, coloured and given much of its significance by the knowledge, understanding and values that the reader brings to her encounter with the text.

Texts rich in meaning for some readers may seem remote, arid and even empty to others who come to them with a different set of understandings. When I first started teaching, in a primary school in Inner London, I was quite shocked when Linda, a proficient 9-year-old reader, handed me back the copy of *Swallows and*

Amazons with the words 'I just can't understand it Miss,' and a puzzled look on her face. Näively, I had pressed the book on her, remembering my own sense of liberation on reading it at the same age — at seeing the world through the perceptions and actions of four children who led lives of excitement, physical challenge and adventure, largely independent of adults. Linda's polite but anxious puzzlement made me reassess the easy equation I had made between my reading experiences, heavily coloured by wistful memories of my war-time middle-class early childhood on the edge of England's Lake District, and hers, lived in the working-class central London triangle between her home in the Guinness Buildings, the primary school and the public library.

More recently, working with children from homes where books had played little or no part in their pre-school experiences, in a nursery class with a teacher who regarded pleasure in children's literature as an essential element of early childhood, I saw that the cultural gap was not just a matter of the life-style depicted in the text. The 'universals' of story grammar had to be learned by these 3- and 4-year-old children. Simon seemed typical in his interpretation of adjacent pictures in Judith Kerr's *The Tiger Who Came to Tea* as depicting two distinct tigers. The notion of a central character and his or her continued presence through the story, that the tiger in the right-hand picture was the same tiger as in the left-hand picture, shown at a later point in the sequence of events, was, I came rapidly to see, a cultural construct that could not be assumed.

So what texts should we make available to children who bring with them to school experiences and perspectives other than those of the dominant schooled literacy? Should we draw on only those texts whose uses they have some sense of? Should we confine them to environmental print? If we do introduce narrative, should we provide them with texts culturally close to their own experience? Certainly children need to see themselves and their communities in some, at least, of the texts they read. But should such cultural familiarity circumscribe all their reading? Should we restrict our pupils to stories of characters leading lives culturally similar to theirs, to stories of children from one-parent families struggling to keep afloat? And what if the cultures of our pupils' homes accord no significant place to narrative or to reflective reading?

All children come to school to learn, to develop their skills and capacities, to gain new ways of seeing and doing. All children need access to some aspects of the dominant culture. Certainly teachers need to understand the children they teach and to validate their communities' experience, skills and knowledge, in more effective ways than most manage to do today. But teachers have to do more than this. Their job is also to offer children the possibilities of change. Teachers need not only to develop their understanding of where their children come from; they also need to be concerned with the directions in which change might proceed, with knowing how such change can be brought about and with putting it into action.

This is not to put the findings of such anthropological studies on one side. All school learning must be viewed through the prism of culture. As Heath, Street and many others have shown us, literacy and literacy learning are socially constructed (Heath, 1983; Street, 1984). What is offered by the school, with its attendant value systems, is perceived, construed, accepted, rejected or re-formed according to the values, beliefs and knowledge systems of the families and communities from which its pupils come. But does that mean that school learning is culturally determined by its surrounding community?

Cultures are not entirely homogeneous or monolithic. Our personal repertoires of ways of speaking indicate the plurality of our cultural membership. Nor are individuals merely the passive tools of outside forces: our intentions and desires may involve setting ourselves apart from aspects of our surrounding culture, defining ourselves in terms of contrast instead of inclusion. To regard the culture that surrounds young children's out-of-school lives as determining their future is at once to deny those from non-dominant cultures access to powerful ways of participating in the wider culture, to deny the power that individuals, even young children, have to negotiate their own social identities and to deny the larger society the opportunity of change. It also makes impossible the role of schools serving populations of mixed cultures, which is, of course, increasingly the case in urban schools throughout the developed world.

While there is no doubt that cultural circumstances have an important effect on the nature and 'success' of early school literacy learning, the influence is not just one way. The learning of literacy can provide children with the opportunity to extend the cultural possibilities open to them, to enlarge their notions of who they are and who they might become. Judith Solsken's (1993) study of children in kindergarten and first grade leads her to the conclusion that 'literacy learning is . . . a self-defining social act' in which children must be seen as acting not only within but also upon larger social systems (p. 8). If this is so, then we need to consider very carefully what options we provide for children and the extent and the manner in which we make these available to them.

We need to ensure that all children are given the opportunity to take command of aspects of the discourse of the dominant culture — not to replace their own, but to complement it, to give them the wherewithal to make successful forays into places where important information is found and decisions are made, to ensure that they are not left voiceless on the sidelines, not shut out of the discourse of power. Confident familiarity with the discourses of power will not by itself confer power on its users, but unfamiliarity will assuredly exclude. All children should be helped to become active, reflective and critical readers. This involves critical reading of a variety of complex texts, and giving children from the beginning of their school education, a sense of the rich possibilities of written language.

Powerful writers can make appeals across the barriers of place, time and social class, to introduce new ways of thinking and new ways of using language. Asked to talk about what she really likes to read most, 8-year-old Katie, living a precarious life with her single mother on social security in the centre of a south coastal town, rejects all thought of the letters, notes, notices, cards, magazines and comics she and her classmates have brought for us to include in a survey of the range of their reading, and instead clutches to her a copy of *The Secret Garden* (Burnett, 1911). She gives us an impassioned account of the story — of characters and events and places, all in a literal sense quite remote from her own life, but given their significance in part by the theme of growth and health and the power that apparently powerless children can have to bring these about, and in part by the author's masterly skill in making plot and theme compelling to the naïve and culturally remote reader.

The books children encounter in school and those they take home to share with their parents may be more familiar to those from the dominant culture than to others, and may evoke and imply a world better known to them, through language that is closer to their own, and through narrative forms more familiar to them. But if we are to recognize the power of literature to enlarge children's experience of themselves, of others and of the world in which we live, we should not accept such differences as dictating distinct reading diets, but should seek to find ways to 'bridge the discontinuity of cultures' (Camitta, 1993).

Perhaps we need to shift our attention to the transactions through which these texts are read — to the 'ways of taking' that children encounter in their primary classrooms. In *Ways with Words* Heath (1983) shows the collaborative exploration that characterizes the reading of texts in Trackton, where the evening paper is typically read in the public situation of the front porch as together neighbours find out who has died and explore their connections with the events and the people they are reading about. Baynham (1993) suggests this collective 'mode switching' from written to spoken language might be a key feature of the encounters of members of non-dominant cultures with written texts. But to what extent are such practices welcomed or encouraged in school classrooms? Recognizing the power of culture, Walkerdine (1981) implies that an essential starting point for the teaching of young children is the provision of familiar cultural practices within which they can position themselves. But how far do we succeed in doing this with respect to literacy learning?

'Hearing children read' is still the key instructional context for learning to read in this country, the encounter between individual child, text and teacher; still seen as the key classroom literacy event, on which parent-child interactions at home should be modelled. What happens in this encounter then takes on a particular importance. In a penetrating study of children in a culturally mixed classroom, Gregory (1992) examines the puzzling lack of success in learning to read experienced by the children from monolingual English-speaking homes not oriented towards the culture of the school. These children are less successful not only than their classmates from homes culturally closer to the school, but also than children from Bangladeshi families with a seemingly greater cultural separation from the school. For Gregory the explanation lies in their inability to position themselves within the teacher's metaphor of reading. To these children reading is likely to be seen, not as an enjoyable activity, but as hard work:

> . . . not sharing stories but learning the words, not encouraged by a teacher
> as facilitator but consciously and explicitly taught. (1992, p. 45)

There is now widespread agreement that the school should build on home learning in early literacy teaching. But as Gregory asks: '*whose* home learning is it to be?'

(*op. cit.*, p. 47). She argues that teachers should widen their concerns to include heightening children's awareness of how and why they learn to read. I would argue that alongside this must go a greater openness to the vernacular language forms that have framed children's pre-school experience of life and learning.

And where are the benefits in replacing a strange new practice with familiar aridity? The expectations of school learning which Gregory invokes are curiously similar to the literacy practices Heath documents in the 'Roadville' homes of the blue-collar community. Both seem modelled on certain kinds of school practices; both appear sanctioned less by the evidence of their effectiveness, than by a memory of the institutions that effectively excluded the parents from the dominant culture. To be familiar is not necessarily to be productive.

My own research with nursery children (aged 3 to 4 years) in the category found by Gregory to be problematic, shows that the culturally strange experience of shared reading of such texts as Maurice Sendak's *Where the Wild Things Are* can be successfully translated to the classroom and made 'real' to the children, where certain conditions are met. Analysis of transcripts of 'storytime' carried out over a period of one year showed Simon and his classmates learning to make urgent personal sense of a variety of texts. As she read the text and showed them the pictures, their teacher both allowed the children to take a leading role in the activity — volunteering their own interpretations and 'text to life' and 'life to text' moves in their own vernacular — but also determined to ensure that a clear focus was maintained on the construction of narrative, tolerating no serious deviation from this. Children persistently trying to divert the topic were first ignored, and finally silenced with words such as 'We're not talking about cats now, we're talking about wild things.' But not all contributions were treated with this brusqueness. 'I blink!' said Holly, when she heard how Max tamed the wild things 'with his magic trick of staring into all their yellow eyes without blinking once', to which her teacher responded, 'Well you blink, yes, but Max has got a special trick. He stared at them all without blinking and he tamed them.' Like the other children in this lively class, Holly had not been schooled into passivity, but regularly volunteered her observations, without waiting to be invited to do so. Her teacher's response at once validated Holly's interruption, steered her attention onto the construction of the narrative, and, through contrasting Max's behaviour with hers, made evident its significance.

The children were also invited to predict what would happen, and to test their predictions against the unfolding evidence of the text. Their role was active, initiatory and constructive. Through the familiar vehicle of child-initiated conversational exchanges, these children were enabled to encounter and make personal sense of the culturally new experience of construing a (relatively) complex written narrative.

Their own re-tellings of such narratives became, over the course of a school year, markedly different from these conversational interactions, taking on much of the discourse structure and many other linguistic features of the narratives they were modelled on. In a classroom full of kaleidoscopic diversions, books developed powerful attractions for these children, to the point where by June nearly all the children chose to spend as much as fifteen minutes at a time poring intently over a text as they talked their way through it.

Thus, through such 'mode-switching' between the children's oral vernacular and the language of the printed text, the children took possession of important aspects of the dominant literacy, reproducing features of Sendak's language as they chose to re-tell the story. Instead of subordinating themselves to an alien discourse, they were learning to incorporate aspects of that discourse into their repertoires and to use them for their own purposes.

Such 'mode-switching' has applications well beyond the nursery class. Carole King's (1993) work with 9- and 10-year-olds, documented in the video and accompanying booklet entitled *Creating a Community of Readers* shows its power in extending the range and depth of children's reading at an age when most, including many from the dominant culture, are reluctant to move beyond narratives with familiar content, told in familiar ways. The class is divided into groups of six or so, and each group reads a particular book, undertaking the reading of an agreed amount individually at home, but the focus is on sharing what happens in their minds as they read. Privately the children make entries in individual reading diaries or 'reading-thinking books', which they then use during their group time in school as starting points for discussing their own readings. Again there is a tightly structured boundary set by the teacher, in that both entries in the diary and discussion in school must be prompted by the text. But within that, the initiative belongs to the children, whose contributions vary from such text-to-life moves as 'It makes me think of my brother' and 'I feel like that sometimes' to penetrating observations on the narrative 'It seems like a gorilla telling the story really, like it might be a wish from a gorilla' and observations on its telling 'It's sort of like a script really'. The children enthuse about the way of working 'We're sharing thoughts, we are', 'I understand it more' and 'It's made me read more books. I'm half way through three or four.'

Much has been written about creating environments supportive for learning, but all too seldom is this taken to involve children supporting each other, through the use of conversational practices in which they have a confident expertise. And all over the English-speaking world dark clouds loom in the shape of an increased emphasis on the standard forms of spoken English. We will need to do all we can to help teachers see the central importance of encouraging children to use their own vernacular, not just in the playground, but also to give significance to the texts they read and to help them take these into their possession.

References

BAYNHAM, M. (1993) 'Code switching and mode switching: Community interpreters and mediators of literacy', in STREET, B.V. (ed.) *Cross-Cultural Approaches to Literacy*, Cambridge: Cambridge University Press.

BURNETT, F.H. (1911) *The Secret Garden*, London: Heinemann.

CAMITTA, M. (1993) 'Vernacular writing: Varieties of literacy among Philadelphia high school students', in STREET, B.V. (ed.) *Cross-Cultural Approaches to Literacy*, Cambridge: Cambridge University Press.

DEPARTMENT FOR EDUCATION (1995) *English in the National Curriculum*, London: Her Majesty's Stationery Office.

GENETTE, G. (1980) (Trans. J. Lewin) *Narrative Discourse*, Oxford: Basil Blackwell.

GREGORY, E. (1992) 'Learning codes and contexts: A psycho-semiotic approach to beginning reading in school', in KIMBERLEY, K., MEEK, M. and MILLER, J. (eds) *New Readings: Contributions to an Understanding of Literacy*, London: A & C Black.

HEATH, S.B. (1983) *Ways with Words: Language, Life and Work in Communities and Classrooms*, Cambridge: Cambridge University Press.

KING, C. (1993) *Creating a Community of Readers*, Brighton: Media Services, University of Brighton.

MEEK, M. (1982) *Learning to Read*, London: Bodley Head.

OFSTED (1994) *Draft Working Papers for the Inspection of Primary Initial Teacher Training*, London: Office for Standards in Education.

SENDAK, M. (1967) *Where the Wild Things Are*, Oxford: the Bodley Head.

SOLSKEN, J. (1993) *Literacy, Gender and Work in Families and in School*, Norwood NJ: Ablex.

STREET, B.V. (1984) *Literacy in Theory and Practice*, Cambridge: Cambridge University Press.

WADE, B., MINNS, H. and LUTRARIO, C. (1994) *Pathways*, London, Collins Educational.

WALKERDINE, V. (1981) 'From context to text: A psychosemiotic approach to abstract thought', in BEVERIDGE, B. (ed.) *Children Thinking Through Language*, London: Edward Arnold.

7   Frames of Knowledge

Terezinha Nunes

Terezinha Nunes poses the dilemma that if mathematics is 'about what mathematicians do then it is irrelevant to most members of society'. The alternative is that 'it is a social practice and then everyone can have a portion of it. It should be available to all.' The latter position is supported in this book by the papers of Baker, Burton and Gheverghese Joseph. Nunes further claims that the production and use of all knowledge are socio-cognitive phenomena in which individuals are actively engaged. She seeks similarities rather than differences between literacy, numeracy and science and suggests that all three of them employ systems of signs; all three are also social activities and forms of knowledge; the boundaries of knowing anything are socially defined and these boundaries influence people's views of themselves as learners; learning itself, in her view, is also a social practice. But the frames for knowing that are implicit in systems of signs and representations affect how we learn and how we solve problems: they can enable, constrain and structure reasoning. They frame both knowing and knowledge. She suggests that systems of signs provide us with 'things to think with' but different systems throw light onto different aspects of inquiry and therefore change our ways of seeing. Indeed, she sees knowledge as learned by interacting with the environment though talk and the construction of systems of signs. But she wonders whether the ownership of a particular frame of knowledge inhibits or precludes the acquisition of other knowledge, restricting access to dominant numeracy and literacy practices. The former is also discussed by Burton and Baker, the latter by Hewlett, Barton and Fox, among others.

In this paper I wish to discuss an aspect of literacy that stresses the similarities rather than the differences between literacy, language, numeracy, and other systems of signs and cultural practices that constitute frames of reference for knowing. First I would like to explore the meaning of 'mathematics' and 'mathematical knowledge' and the place of mathematics in school education. Then I will discuss how mathematical systems of signs influence the process of knowing. Finally, I will try to consider the broader question of frames of knowledge and their relationship to cognitive development.[1]

Mathematics and Mathematical Knowledge

Are You Good at Maths?

For many people, this would be the beginning of an embarrassing conversation. They regard themselves as weak at maths and think of their ways of solving everyday problems with numbers, as not really proper maths (Cockcroft, 1982) but 'their own' way of solving problems. Recently, members of a darts team told us that they were very bad at mathematics. How true can this be?

Playing darts requires calculation at least in its final stages. A game of darts is played backwards. A player starts a darts game with 501 points and finishes on exactly zero. At each turn they throw three darts and subtract the score for that turn, giving them their new score, but at about 200, they start planning their moves more precisely. A game must finish on a double — that is, the last dart must hit those special areas on the board where the value is doubled. This requires computation from the players.

Suppose it is your turn and you have only one dart left to try to finish the game. If your current score is an odd number, you don't have a way to finish and your turn is up. That means you must leave yourself an even number to be able to finish. How do you maximize your chances of leaving yourself an even number for the last dart? Well, that depends on your score at the time. For example, if your score is 71, you might want to go for a treble 13, which leaves you with a double 16 to finish. Of course, you could miss the treble 13 and get just 13. That means you can go for double 13 and double 16 and still finish in one turn.

It might seem that experienced players do not have to calculate any of this. They may have memorized the many possible finishes, but that seems unlikely. When learning to count, we don't learn all the numbers in the numeration system by rote. We learn basic examples and the way the system is put together and then we generate number names according to the system. Similarly, when we multiply, we don't memorize all possible combinations but learn the so-called basic multiplication facts, which are the products of single digits, and put together other products on the basis of this knowledge. Knowledge and understanding from darts may be transferable. One darts player claimed to apply 'dart numbers' to other calculations. His example involved solving 7×17, which he sees as treble 17 (51) plus treble 17 plus 17. He says he does it this way because 'he doesn't know how to multiply'. Why should people think of themselves as 'bad at mathematics' when they can solve the very problems they think they are 'bad' at? This leads us to the distinction between 'mathematics' and 'mathematical knowledge'.

Mathematics as a Socially Defined Activity

Mathematics, like literature and sports, is a social product whose boundaries are culturally defined. In western society, we have been acculturated to some of the following beliefs about mathematics:

- Mathematics is a special kind of activity and any other activity is, by definition, not mathematics.
- Mathematics is learned in school — unschooled people don't know any mathematics.
- Mathematics is abstract and not about the everyday world — you don't learn about mathematics in everyday life.
- Mathematics is difficult, few people get qualifications in mathematics — that means few people know mathematics.
- Mathematics is used by mathematicians, scientists, and technologists — these are the people who know mathematics.

It is true that mathematics is a special kind of socially defined activity — just as buying and selling, playing darts, and building houses. This is why we think of these latter activities as 'not mathematics'. But do all the other ideas listed above follow from the fact that mathematics is a special kind of activity?

Mathematics has a double status — it is a particular kind of activity but also a form of knowledge. This is why mathematics, like literacy, is something that should be available to all. Yet the social definition of mathematics blinds us to the mathematical knowledge embedded in other activities. We learn *some* forms of mathematical knowledge at school and become blind to others which do not appear in school. If we were to consider as mathematics only the activities of mathematicians, we would end up concluding that mathematics is so specialized that it need not be taught to all pupils. It is because mathematical knowledge is a form of knowledge that permeates so many activities that mathematics is relevant for all pupils (*cf.* Nunes, Schilemann and Carraher, 1993).

Historically, mathematics has developed several systems of signs such as numeration and measurement systems, algebra, systems of coordinates, etc. These systems involve not only a representation of certain aspects of objects, events, time, and space but also model relations between them. Mathematical representations become then a frame for knowing: we reason and speak about the relations as we see them through mathematical representation. For example, we can say that the relationship between the weight of a fish in the market and its price is *linear* — a property of the graphic representation and not of the relationship. This way of framing the types of relations between variables help us better understand relations in a general way.

The Impact of Frames of Knowledge on Reasoning

Systems of signs provided in mathematics play different, even if related, roles in knowing. Three sorts of role can be distinguished: 1) an enabling role; 2) a constraining role; and 3) a structuring role. Each of these will be briefly discussed below.

An Enabling Role

The *enabling role of systems* of signs relates to their systematic and external nature. The use of measurement systems may illustrate the point. Our perception of length is subject to all sorts of illusions. In the Muller-Lyer illusion (Head, 1985) we fail in comparing two line segments. Further our memory of length is inadequate. Merely looking at a window before shopping would be insufficient to ensure that we order the right amount of curtain material. However, these perceptual and mnemonic limitations can be overcome through the use of measurement systems that allow comparisons of length at a distance and over time by applying a standard unit. Larger and smaller units in a measurement system are often systematically related to each other and this relationship becomes a way of thinking, as Gay and Cole (1967) observed in their studies of estimation of length with US adult subjects. Their subjects were able to estimate large distances rather well in terms of small units, even if the units were not the usual ones for them, such as hand-spans. They did so by estimating first in a familiar unit, yards or feet, and then converting this estimate into the units required. The system of signs worked as a frame of knowledge when estimating. In contrast, the same subjects did not have similar frames of knowledge for estimating large quantities of rice in cups, and their performance was worse on that task. This was not simply a matter of the difficulty of the task *per se* because the opposite trend was observed among Kpelle subjects. Gay and Cole's Kpelle subjects had a system of conversion between smaller and large quantities of rice. They estimated volume quite well but did rather badly in estimating length, where no such system of conversions was available to them.

A Constraining Role

The *constraining role of systems of signs* on reasoning seems to derive from the interaction between the subject's reasoning processes and the signs in a system where the signs become objects to be operated on. This constraining role is best illustrated through research that shows within-individual differences across the use of different systems of signs. When people interact with different system of signs, their reasoning processes are different. They may get hopelessly lost when solving a problem using one system of signs and succeed when using another one, as is illustrated in these two examples.

Finger arithmetic

Moreno (1994) observed young children with hearing problems using a finger algorithm for performing addition. In addition, the sign for one of the addends is signed with one hand while the sign for the other addend is signed with the other hand. When adding children move up the numbers signed on one hand, and move down the numbers on the other hand, as if transferring the value from one hand to the other, until there are no more numbers to be added. The algorithm is useful for children with hearing problems because it frees them from remembering verbal addition facts. However, the system is prone to error. The errors are often responses which are off by 5 or 10 units, because the children confuse 3, 8 or 13. The confusion between 3 and 8 is traced to the way these numbers are signed and used during calculation. Both numbers are signed by putting up 3 fingers albeit different ones. When signing 8, 5 is kept in memory. Children learning the algorithm and adding, for example, 8 onto 7, need to count down from 8, retracting the 3 fingers that were put up, and then go on to count down from 5, which was kept in memory. They often stop when the 3 fingers have been retracted, and obtain 10 as the result of 7 + 8. This error does not emerge if the same children carry out the same operation using blocks to represent the addends. Thus the signing algorithm simultaneously enables the children, by freeing them from the need to memorize verbal addition facts, and constrains their practice of calculation in particular ways.

Written numbers and the plus and minus signs

Nunes (1993) analysed the constraints of solving problems with directed numbers when subjects seemed caught between two different practices involving the same systems of signs. In written arithmetic + and − stand for operations to be performed. When dealing with positive and negative numbers, learners have to cope with the fact that −20 and −30 need to be added together although they are preceded by the minus sign, which could indicate subtraction. These two practices may conflict in solving problems. In contrast, in oral arithmetic, where the numbers and operations are not represented in written form, the conflict is absent.

To analyse how oral and written practices constrain reasoning about directed numbers I tested children and adolescents from three grade levels either orally or in written form (Nunes, 1993). All the problems related to gains and losses of a hypothetical farmer with different harvests, a situation familiar to all subjects. The written test required subjects to write the numbers before solving the problem whereas pencil and paper were not available in the oral test.

Subjects in the oral situation performed significantly better than those in the written test. An analysis of the errors displayed in the written test indicated that errors resulted from the conflict of two written arithmetic practices, pointed out above. These difficulties could not be simply attributed to subjects' lack of understanding. First, subjects were randomly assigned either to the oral or to the written situation and subjects in the oral test performed almost at ceiling level. Second, subjects in the written condition often realized that they had made a mistake when asked to explain how they arrived at the result. They often self-corrected during this oral explanation and concluded by saying 'I can't do it on paper, I can only do it in my head.' For example, the following problem was given to JC: 'Seu Severino (the farmer's name) started the season with a debt of 10 *cruzados* (Brazilian currency). He planted manioc and beans. He had a profit of 20 on the manioc and a profit of 10 on the beans. What was his situation at the end of the year?' JC wrote down 10 without a sign, plus 20 underneath (a profit), and then 10 in a third row below the 20 without a new sign. He added all the numbers and wrote 40 for the answer. However, when asked whether that was a profit or a loss, a question routinely asked when subjects did not indicate the direction of the value, JC answered: 'No, it's not that. I can't do it on paper. He took his profit from the beans, paid the 10 he owed, and he still has the 20 from the manioc.'

These two examples illustrate how systems of signs and cultural practices constrain subjects' reasoning. The systems of signs used during calculation seem to become the objects on which we operate. While we interact with these objects, our reasoning process is a product of this interaction; the systems of signs both enable and constrain what we can achieve with them.

A Structuring Role

The *structuring role of signs* in concept formation is rather more difficult to illustrate. When subjects use a system of signs as mediators in a learning situation, these systems of signs influence the subjects' interactions and the concepts that emerge from these interactions. This is demonstrated when the use of different systems in the same situation leads to different conceptual schemas. To illustrate this point, I refer to an investigation on children's concept of area (Nunes, *et al.*, 1993a; Nunes, Light and Mason, 1994).

There are at least two ways in which the area of a plane figure can be calculated. The first one uses the height and the width of the figure in a formula. The area of the rectangle is height times width. This way of calculating the area corresponds to the schema of *product of measures* (see Vergnaud, 1983). Here two linear measures, in centimetres, when multiplied yield a third and new measure, the area, in square centimetres. The second schema involves starting out from area units. These area units are arranged in rows and columns on the figure, the area is calculated through multiplying the number of units in a row by the number of rows. This approach is equivalent to a schema in multiplication termed *isomorphism of measures* (Vergnaud, 1983). The two conceptions differ in a crucial way: the product of measures involves three variables, whereas the isomorphism of measures involves only two. This analysis led us to hypothesize that children develop different schemas for area depending on whether they meet either linear or area units. In a series of studies about area (Nunes, *et al.*, 1993a; Nunes, *et al.*, 1994), we investigated whether children would explain how they obtained the area of figures such as rectangles and parallelograms in different ways that corresponded to the type of measuring tool they were given. The measuring tools were systems of signs that would mediate their attempts to quantify area.

We asked pairs of children, 8 to 10 years, to solve area problems. The pairs were randomly allocated to one of two conditions. In the first, they were given rulers as their measurement tool. In the second condition, they were given 1 cm^2 bricks but not enough bricks to fully cover the figures so that a solution by covering and counting the bricks was not possible. The children were presented with two figures and were told that the figures were the drawings of two walls, painted by two friends, each one having painted one wall. The friends were then paid for the paint job together. Before dividing the money, they wanted to know whether they had done the same amount of work by comparing the area of the two walls. The children in our study had been taught to cover figures with area units and count them and were subsequently taught the height times width formula. We expected that children who had assimilated the formula would have no difficulty with the initial problems in our study, which involved the comparison of rectangles, but would still have to adjust their procedures when comparing a rectangle with a parallelogram.

The performance of the pupils in these problems differed as a function of the systems of signs they met in the experimental situations, rulers versus area units. Differences were observed both in terms of the number of correct responses and the type of conception used during problem solving. The children who had area units available performed significantly better than those who had rulers.

The pupils who had the rulers were more likely to add the measures than to multiply them. They either calculated the perimeter or the half-perimeter. Some pupils then proceeded to make a decision about the relative size of the figures on the basis of this information; others did not consider this information adequate and felt they could not take a decision about amounts of work done. These subjects' responses indicated that they conceived of linear measures as appropriate for linear evaluations. Previous teaching did not help them because the tool had not been appropriate for the situation from their viewpoint. A third group of children displayed a significant problem-solving strategy. They attempted to use the ruler as an area unit, placing it against one of the edges of the figure and moving it to the other side as they counted how many rulers fitted into the figure. The ruler as a conventional, linear measuring tool was disregarded and treated as a non-conventional area unit.

The pupils who had the area units as measuring instrument often discovered a formula to solve the problem: number of bricks in a row times number of rows. This formula was more easily modified to solve the problem of the area of the parallelogram than the height times width formula they had been taught. In contrast, the ruler users who had been successful in solving the rectangle problems did not figure out that the height and the side of the parallelogram differed. They used a 'side times side' conception which, when applied to the parallelogram, produced an incorrect solution.

To sum up, children's schemas of area in this series of problems were clearly influenced by the measuring tool they had been given. The children who received area units invented a formula 'number of bricks in a row times number of rows'. The children who had been given rulers may have used a previously learned or developed 'side times side' formula for calculating the area of parallelograms. Thus systems of signs provide the users with the opportunity to approach problems in particular ways, that relate to representations of situations. Because signs mediate the subjects' thinking and often also their actions in a learning situation, they become part of the elements that structure the subjects' interactions and their emerging concepts. Different systems of signs may highlight different aspects of a concept and therefore provide different frames for knowing in the situation.

It must be stressed, however, that the structuring role of systems of signs in concept formation cannot be viewed in a deterministic way. Subjects have their own ideas about what they wish to achieve and may make use of a tool in an unexpected manner when the mediating system itself is considered. In these experiments, children who wanted to rely on area units used the ruler as an area unit rather than an instrument for obtaining linear measures. Thus, systems of signs play a structuring role in the subject's interactions as mediators of reasoning but do not determine the outcome of learning without taking into account the subject's own role in the situation.

Literacy, Numeracy, and Other Frames of Knowledge

The influence of systems of signs on reasoning and knowledge is not a new topic. Whorf (1956) suggested that thinking was so influenced by language that we were led to see the world in ways that were determined by our language. Vygotsky (1978) and Luria (1973) also stressed the influence of systems of signs on our thinking. They suggested that all higher mental functions are mediated by systems of signs that function as mental tools which allow humans to surpass the natural limits of their perception and memory. There are, however, differences between these and the hypothesis proposed here. No overall or general effects of systems of signs are proposed here; the suggestion is rather that specific effects relate to the practices and activities in which the systems of signs are used. This hypothesis is consistent with the results obtained by Scribner and Cole (1981) with respect to the effects of literacy. We need not think that the mind changes but our reasoning can change when we use different systems of signs as objects to think with.

The mind uses a number of systems of signs. Language, literacy, numeration systems, algebra, graphs, diagrams, measurement tools all represent examples of systems of signs that can mediate reasoning. Systems of signs are rather more widespread in our everyday lives than one would initially assume. Different systems seem to throw light onto different aspects of our objects of thought and thereby change the nature of the relationship between our reasoning and the object we are thinking about. For example, a problem that is difficult if we only know arithmetic may be rather simple if we know algebra. If we had only one system of signs, we could hardly tell the nature of the system from the nature of the mind and the nature of the object. A new way of looking at systems of signs is to look at the variety of signs. What do the same people accomplish with different signs? What opportunities does the use of different mental tools afford the learner during learning? What does the tool enable or constrain? And when is it a good time to change to another tool?

To sum up, there is plenty of evidence to suggest that systems of signs work as frames of reasoning and knowledge in mathematics. They act as mediators, or mental objects, with which we reason. Both the characteristics of the systems of signs and the practices in which they are used constitute frames for our ways of knowing and reasoning. However, there is no need to make them into the hardware of thinking. They can be used or set aside in different circumstances and for different purposes. Similarly, different sorts of literacy practices seem to be associated with different frames for knowledge. Cultural variation can be observed even when the same type of literacy seems to be under consideration. For example, Goodnow (1990) has pointed out that different traditions of psychological analysis seem to result in different forms of academic writing when European and US productions are considered. Participation within particular traditions seems to be more enabling than participation across traditions. But a question that we have not yet asked with respect to literacies is whether the ownership of knowledge that comes with different forms of literacy constrains thinking in such a way that other frames for knowledge cannot be easily taken on.

Note

1 Portions of this paper are adapted from Nunes, T. and Bryant, P. (1995) *Children doing mathematics*. Oxford: Blackwell, in press.

References

COCKCROFT, W.H. (1982) *Mathematics Counts*, London: HMSO.

GAY, J. and COLE, M. (1967) *The New Mathematics and an Old Culture*, New York: Holt Rhinehart and Winston.

GOODNOW, J.J. (1990) 'The socialization of cognition: What's involved?', in STIGLER, J.W., SHWEDER, R.A. and HERDT, G. (eds) *Cultural Psychology: Essays on Comparative Human Development*, Cambridge: CUP, pp. 259–86.

HEAD, J. (1985) *The Personal Response to Science*, Cambridge: Cambridge University Press.

LURIA, A. (1973) *The Working Brain*, Harmondsworth, Penguin.

MORENO, C. (1994) 'The implementation of a realistic mathematics education programme in a special school for the deaf'. Unpublished thesis for MSc in Child Development, Institute of Education, University of London.

NUNES, T. (1993) 'Learning maths: Perspectives from everyday life', in DAVIS R.B. and MAHER, C.A. (eds) *Schools, Mathematics, and the World of Reality*, Needham Heights (MA): Allyn and Bacon, pp. 61–78.

NUNES, T. and BRYANT, P.E. (in press) *Children Doing Mathematics*, Oxford: Blackwell.

NUNES, T., LIGHT, P. and MASON, J. (1993a) 'Tools for thought: The measurement of length and area', *Learning and Instruction*, **3**, pp. 39–54.

NUNES, T., SCHLIEMANN, A. and CARRAHER, D. (1993b) *Street Mathematics and School Mathematics*, New York: CUP.

NUNES, T., LIGHT, P. and MASON, J. (1994) 'Children's understanding of area'. Paper presented at The International Conference on the Psychology of Mathematics Education, Lisbon.

SCRIBNER, S. and COLE, M. (1981) *The Psychology of Literacy*, Cambridge (MA): Harvard University Press.

VERGNAUD, G. (1983) 'Multiplicative structures', in LESH, R. and LANDAU, M. (eds) *Acquisition of Mathematical Concepts and Processes*, London: Academic Press, pp. 128–75.

VYGOTSKY, L.S. (1978) *Mind in Society*, Cambridge (MA): Harvard University Press.

WHORF, B.L. (1956) 'Science and linguistics', in CARROLL, J.B. (ed.) *Language, Thought and Reality*, Cambridge (MA): Harvard University Press.

8 Children's Formal and Informal School Numeracy Practices

Dave Baker

Mathematics is regarded pre-eminently as the discipline that is most abstract, culture-free and value-free. At the symposium Dave Baker posed the question as to whether 2 + 2 always equals 4. Despite participants' willingness to question the basis of their own knowledge and ways of knowing the initial response was that of course it is 4. When presented with the question about the temperature of a glass of water made up by putting together two glasses each at 2 degrees centigrade, that is 2 + 2 = 2, their responses varied from claiming the sum was not really mathematics to accepting that all problems are set in cultural contexts. The first claim is based on numeracy seen as abstract, autonomous knowledge, the mathematical canon. In contrast in this paper, Baker starts from the premise that numeracies are social practices, a premise encountered in other papers here especially those by Street, Burton and Joseph. Baker sets out to develop a theoretical framework through which numeracies can be viewed by comparing primary school children's formal and informal school numeracy practices. The research exposed the part that contexts and culture (values and beliefs) play in numeracy practices, and showed that learners' concern with their performance, in order to get praise, dominated their practices: yet as a motivating factor performance does not drive curiosity or fuel the desire to solve a problem. The paper concludes by urging teachers to move away from 'learning through practice' towards 'learning in practice' in order to value and exploit their learners' own cultural imperatives.

Introduction

The research discussed here is concerned with implications of the premise that numeracy is a social practice. The object of the research was to look closely at children's numeracy practices; to compare those that children use in a variety of domains; to find differences and similarities in order to set up frameworks within which children's numeracy practices could be viewed and analysed in order to inform educational endeavour. The investigation was stimulated by the awareness that some children move easily between formal and informal school numeracy practices whilst others who succeed in informal settings find formal numeracy practices problematic. There are many possible reasons for these difficulties and some of them have been discussed elsewhere — for example Nunes, Schliemann and Carraher (1993). However, the model of numeracy practices put forward in this article and the frameworks that resulted from the work provide a different means of analysis and a different perspective.

Background

Numeracy is a social practice. This is not a generally accepted position and debate about its validity continues (*cf.* Baker and Street, 1994). Here, numeracy is taken to be the numeracy practices in which individuals engage in daily life: the occasions when they do mathematics, be it at work, in school, in the community, wherever. These numeracy practices are part of the social fabric of their lives, that is, they are social practices. The phrase *numeracy practices* is used in preference to mathematical practices to alert readers to the parallels that exist between the work being undertaken here and that done under the title of literacy practices (Street, 1984, p. 1; Street, 1993, p. 12). Given common usage, it is much harder to replace the word 'mathematics' with 'numeracy'. The word 'mathematics' will be used wherever common usage makes it necessary. Another term that will be used in this study is *numeracy event*. This is based on a term used in the study of literacy (Heath, 1982). A numeracy event is any occasion where mathematics is integral to participants' interactions and their interpretative processes.

Children engage in different numeracy practices in different domains of activity. In this research the practices children engage in during mathematics lessons will be called *formal* numeracy. Other authors call this school numeracy (*cf.* Nunes *et al.*, 1993). During the school day children also engage in a variety of numeracy practices, principally in the context of non-mathematical disciplines. In this study these will be called *informal* numeracy practices: for example, the designing and making of children's topic books where the size, shape and number of pages of the book needed to be chosen. There are other numeracy practices which will not be the concern of this article, e.g., street numeracy (Nunes *et al.*, 1993). The boundaries between these different numeracy practices are not totally distinct. There are overlaps. There is no assumption here of a deficit model, that one practice is better or worse than another; they are seen as different practices. But focusing on the children's purposes in using them makes the boundaries easier to see, and it is expected that one of the outcomes of the study will be data that provide better understanding and clearer descriptions and definitions of these different practices.

The study compares qualities found in formal and informal school numeracy practices. For reasons of space, discussion of children's strategies to cope with the movement between formal and informal school numeracy practices will be left to future research studies.

It is useful at this point to look more closely at what constitutes numeracy practices. Drawing on the work in literacy of Reder and Wikelund (1993, p. 179) and applying it to numeracy, I wish to propose a model of numeracy practices that consists of three components: the content (skills, activities, kinds of mathematics); the contexts (occasions, purposes); and the culture (beliefs and values) that individuals draw on when doing or using mathematics.

The first component relates to the usually accepted or dominant view of numeracy which sees it as a list of skills, techniques and knowledge. The other two components are more problematic. The second concerns the occasions and contexts in which the mathematics is done and the purposes for doing that mathematics. Context is often noted in the rhetoric as important, yet the dominant pedagogical practice of teaching numeracy in the restricted context of the formal mathematics classroom belies this. The third component of numeracy practices concerns the beliefs and values of individuals doing mathematics. These will affect the numeracy practices they adopt. They will make decisions on the mathematics they do, on what they see as acceptable mathematics based on their beliefs about the nature of mathematics, and on a set of values about the best approach for them, the right way to solve a problem or the notion of the best argument or proof. Behind my thinking is not only Bishop (1988, p. 181), who states that mathematical education 'should make the values explicit and overt in order to develop the learner's awareness and capacity for choosing', but also Lerman (1989, p. 43) who argues that 'mathematics is as much a social construction as any other form of knowledge, it is culture-bound and value-laden'. This cultural component is not generally accepted and will therefore be looked at most closely in this research. The use of culture to label the third component stresses the centrality of culture in that component and does not imply that there is no cultural element in the first two. The data that arises in the research will be used to evaluate the validity and usefulness of such a model.

Research

The intentions of the study required a close look at children's numeracy practices. The data that were sought were the detailed ways in which children worked in different numeracy domains. This required close observation of individual children, their responses to a variety of situations, and their choices and decisions. This is in keeping with the concept of an 'Analytical Case Study' where general principles of children's practices in particular circumstances are being sought from 'telling cases' as outlined by Mitchell (1984, p. 239). These telling cases required careful selection of the children, to allow comparisons and to point up differences and similarities. They were not expected to be representative. To investigate children's numeracy practices they needed to be closely observed whilst engaged in formal and informal numeracy events within their school day. These days were therefore left as normal as possible. The teacher continued her usual programme of work. The researcher was a participant observer.

The study was undertaken with two Year 6 children, both girls chosen from the same class. This enabled decisions about which child to focus on at any one time to be determined by the potential research value of the work being done. The children could also be observed in similar circumstances, engaged in similar work with the same teacher. The children were selected by the teacher. They were chosen to show a breadth of numeracy practices — to allow depth of comparison and to suit the 'telling case' methodology. One of them was chosen as being significantly more successful at formal mathematics than the other.

The children were observed working in two kinds of activity: one was a numeracy event in a formal numeracy setting labelled by the teacher as 'mathematics'; the other was primarily a non-numeracy activity which involved numeracy practices, when the child saw them to be appropriate for the task. The non-numeracy activities were only of interest to the research when they were numeracy events. Whilst the children were working on their task the observer worked with them and kept notes on what they were doing and any relevant comments that were made. Data was also collected through discussions with the children and the teacher; through reactive, unstructured interviews with the children and the teacher separately; and, through analysis of the children's written work and school documents.

Data and Analysis

The first part of this section describes the children. This is followed by descriptions of selected numeracy events which present evidence of theoretical relationships within children's practices. Both formal and informal settings are described separately and interpreted within the terms of the study.

The children are referred to as M and L. The teacher saw M in a very positive light and L as deficient in her mathematical skills. She said that M 'has developed skills and understanding . . . (she) grasps new concepts easily and enjoys "what if?" questions. She is well organized and able to choose appropriate tools and methods.' On the other hand, L 'has difficulties with fundamental concepts and is unsure of the meaning of things like "times". She lacks confidence, is weak mathematically and does not like maths.'

Not surprisingly, the children's views of their own mathematical performance reflected the teacher's views. M said that mathematics was about 'sums and investigations — it's what we do in maths lessons'. She liked mathematics and liked to get sums right. She was curious about other ways of doing sums, and thought that using a calculator was cheating ''cos yer supposed to work it out yourself'. L said that mathematics was 'working in Cambridge;[1] sums and investigations'. She tended to work on her own in mathematics sessions and said 'copying is not good, you don't learn if you copy other people' and 'you won't properly learn from a calculator'.

The children's work in formal activities — for example, finding the area of a doll's house door as given in a textbook — showed that they saw mathematics as a body of knowledge with right and wrong answers. L, when faced with a rectangular door 10 cm by 6 cm, started by adding the 10 and the 6 and then looked for immediate confirmation from an adult. She wanted to get the right answers and to complete the task. She hoped that she would be praised for that and would avoid criticism; she was concerned with her performance. I propose to call the values that underlie her concern 'performance-driven', in line with Lave (1988a). M, when finding the area of the outer framework of a four-panel door in the same textbook task, sought a different, quicker method. She mentally merged the four panels, worked out that area in one step and subtracted it from the total door area. She could explain her approach, and understood her work relationally. She was able to pursue a better method. She saw mathematics as something useful and interesting. In this instance she was 'mathematically-driven'.

In other work, M was not happy to share her results with others because 'that would be cheating'. In the same way, when L was asked to find cuboids with a volume of 36 cm^3 and found a possible answer, she hid it so that no one else could copy it. These are social values which affected their numeracy practices. Such a set of values I propose to call 'personal/social' values.

In an informal setting L wanted to make a puppet out of papier-maché. She decided to add a pair of fangs to her puppet animal and wanted these fangs to be exactly the same length. The fangs were to be made out of straws and, instead of simply matching them, she decided to measure each one to the nearest millimetre, using a ruler. This task was purposeful to her and the technique she chose depended upon how she wanted the puppet to look. The technique solved her problem, though it might appear inappropriate to an outsider given the inaccurate method of attaching the fangs.

Both L and M were asked to make a folder to hold their topic work. They had to decided how many A3 sheets, piled flat and then folded once would make the necessary number of 'nested' A4 folders. Each sheet therefore made four pages and could take four inserts. L did not count her inserts. She took five sheets of paper and tried to fit hers into them. As she had eleven inserts, five sheets proved too many. She removed the outer sheet and repositioned all her inserts. She then found she had to do the same again. M, on the other hand, counted her inserts first and worked out that for nineteen pieces of work she needed five sheets. The children were successfully solving problems and choosing their own techniques and approaches.

On another occasion M was asked to allocate her team of children to sports day races. She had fourteen children to place in sixteen races. Each race required several children from her team resulting in a total of fifty places to be filled. Initially she used a practical approach to allocate her team to races but this resulted in an unequal and unfair allocation. She realized that to be fair she needed to know how many races children could expect to be in. She tried having four children in three races each and ten in four races. This gave a total of 52. She said 'I need to take two off.' After some thought she tried six in three races and eight in four giving her a solution. She then returned to a practical allocation to ensure that no one child appeared twice in a race. Later she realized that she had unequal numbers of boys and girls, and yet the same number of girl and boy races. She was then able to modify her theoretical numbers of fair races to solve the new problem. This task was clearly purposeful to her and she chose mathematical techniques to solve the problem. These came from both formal and informal practices, but the values behind her choices were her desire to have a fair allocation rather than a winning team. The former led her to try for an equitable allocation which relied on her awareness of relationships between numbers in her problem. The latter would have led to a practically based allocation.

Interpretation

In these data there is clear evidence to support the proposed model of numeracy practices with its three components (content, context and culture). The content component was present by definition. In each case the context and purposes were apparent, some being purposeful for the child and others for the teacher. The cultural component was the most problematic. The dominant view of mathematics (*cf.* Baker and Street, 1994) is that it is an agreed value-free body of knowledge. Yet from the activities described above there were differences in the ways the children reacted to the numeracy events based on their values and beliefs, for example, the social values that M's practices were based on in the sports day allocation and the performance values that drove L's methods with the dolls house. These values are grouped below to provide a framework for analysis. This is followed by an analysis of the children's beliefs. The model is then used to identify differences between values in formal and informal practices.

The proposed framework for the values has three types: performance; personal/social; and mathematical. They are not necessarily mutually exclusive and some or all can be involved in numeracy practices at any one time. They are described below in terms of the behaviour of the children seen in this study.

- Performance values were seen in the children's desire to get the right answers; to complete work; to receive praise or to avoid being blamed or criticized.
- Personal/social values were evident in the children's desire for equity and fairness; their desire to win at games and avoid losing; their response to peer group or friendship pressure; their rejection of cheating; their attitude to collaborating; their aesthetics; their need to be satisfied and pleased with what they had done.
- Mathematical values arose in the children's desire to understand the mathematics in a situation; their attempts to find not only a solution to a problem but a better solution; their curiosity about a situation and their desire to continue to pursue a problem.

Within the formal domain, the values that drove the children were mainly performance-based. There were, however, instances where a child sought to understand the numeracy practices she was engaged in or where she sought a better way of solving a problem. Generally the children did not want to share their formal work.

Mathematical and personal values, therefore, also appeared within formal numeracy practices in some circumstances.

Within their informal numeracy practices the children were largely driven by personal or social values. Thus, when making straw fangs for a puppet the child L was aesthetically motivated when she decided that the fangs should be exactly the same length. For her that meant that she had to measure them to the nearest millimetre before cutting the straws individually rather than simply estimating or cutting them side by side to get the same length. Sharing and helping and getting help from others were seen as not only acceptable but helpful. For example, in the allocation of children to athletic teams, the captains of two of the teams worked together to get the most effective method, making the predominant values personal/social.

The data also suggested that the children's beliefs about mathematics depended on the domains in which they were working. Within formal numeracy practices the children saw mathematics as an activity they only did in a classroom, working through a textbook or in an investigation, and as one always involving right or wrong answers. They were aware the activities were directed towards specific areas of mathematics which they saw as separate and not interconnected. They were chosen by the teacher for reasons that were not transparent to the children. For them, learning mathematics here was often seen as an activity to do on their own. The children learnt a skill and technique through practice, practising it after the teacher had introduced it to them. They were seldom motivated or enabled to make connections between techniques.

Within informal settings the children denied that they had used mathematics. They therefore viewed the numeracy practices they used there as part of the larger task, integral to what they were doing elsewhere. Mathematics was then part of their ongoing experiences. The children had to select for themselves the approaches or techniques to use. To do that, they had to see the techniques in relation to lots of others. As the task was about solving problems within a larger classroom context it was seen as an activity to be done with others. Moreover as the larger task did not involve only one right answer the children had the space to use and develop their own ideas. In this way they met and extended their numeracy practices. They were learning in practice.

The three component model for numeracy practices was then used to compare the children's formal and informal numeracy practices by looking at their responses to numeracy events. Differences were clearly visible but were not always there nor were the boundaries between them precisely formed. There are, however, distinct differences of emphasis on, or a predominance of, certain qualities within that practice. Four main categories of difference between formal and informal numeracy practices were identified: choice of content; learning in practice; purpose; and values.

In formal settings the content was well defined and prescribed, whereas in informal settings the child actively choose the content for herself and as such had to understand it relationally. She could therefore explain her approach and method. In the latter, the numeracy event was not the focus of the activity. The numeracy practice that the child selected had a purpose for the child beyond the numeracy event itself. As such it was purposeful for the child, unlike the formal task that was set by the teacher and the purposes for the child were neither immediately obvious nor relevant. This meant that within the informal task, when the child needed help with a technique new to her she was meeting it in a practical context which had purpose and could be said to be *learning in practice*, in line with Lave (1988b). The formal setting, on the other hand, tended to be of the type where the new idea was introduced by the teacher and the children learnt by practising that skill. I term that *learning through practice*. The values in the two situations had a different emphasis. In the formal situation the children were usually performance driven and occasionally they were mathematically driven. In informal settings the children were mainly personally/socially driven. Moments of mathematical curiosity were not in evidence.

Conclusion

The proposed model of numeracy practices — with its three components of content, context and culture — has proved a useful way of understanding and viewing children's numeracy practices. It shed light on the different ways that children perceived and undertook their school numeracy activities. The place and importance of context and culture in their numeracy practices were easier to see once the different components had been teased out and provided evidence of the value-laden nature of mathematics. It enabled the research to consider the relationship between the formal practices, ones that are recognized as numeracy within the education system, and informal ones, which usually are not. By contrasting the numeracy practices in these two settings the four main differences in practices of choice of content, purpose, learning in practice and values were identified.

The most useful analysis arose from a close examination of the values that drove the children's numeracy practices, resulting in a framework for these values. The framework when applied to their work revealed the ways that the children are predominantly driven in their formal numeracy events by concerns about their performance and not by interest or curiosity in the ideas per se. In their informal events they are mainly driven by personal/social values.

The absence of active choice and purpose for the children engaged in formal numeracy events, coupled with their preoccupation with their performance and lack of curiosity may be a real concern for teachers. The power and drive of personal and social values, so evident in their informal practices, suggests that schools should move away from formal numeracy events towards the use of informal numeracy events, or at least towards breaking down the barriers between formal and informal numeracy practices. Efforts to provide classroom structures where this is encouraged have been made (*cf*. Baker, Semple and Stead, 1990).

A note of caution does need to be raised here. The present educational and political climate has led to demands for tighter curricula, with a greater emphasis on the use of formal activities. The shift of emphasis suggested by the research may therefore have to wait for the development of an appropriate political and educational atmosphere. In the meantime, further research is needed to explore ways of harnessing children's personal and social values, and of encouraging the development of their mathematical curiosity.

Note

1 She refers here to her class mathematics textbooks called *Cambridge Mathematics* published by CUP, Cambridge.

References

BAKER, D., SEMPLE, C. and STEAD, T. (1990) *How Big is the Moon?*, Melbourne: OUP.

BAKER, D. and STREET, B. (1994) *Literacy and Numeracy: Concepts and Definitions*, The International Encyclopaedia of Education Oxford: Pergamon Press.

BISHOP, A. (1988) 'Mathematical education in its cultural context', *Education Studies in Mathematics* 19(2) pp. 179–93.

HEATH, S.B. (1982) 'Protean shapes in literacy events', in TANNEN, D. *Spoken and Written Language: Exploring Orality and Literacy*, Norwood NJ: Ablex.

LAVE, J. (1988a) *The Culture of Acquisition and the Practice of Understanding*, Palo Alto: Institute for Research on Learning.

LAVE, J. (1988b) *Cognition in Practice*, Cambridge: CUP.

LERMAN, S. (1989) 'A social view of mathematics — implications for mathematics education', in KEITEL, C., DAMEROW, P., BISHOP, P. and GERDES, P. (eds) *Mathematics Education and Society*, Paris: UNESCO.

MITCHELL, C. (1984) 'Typicality and the case study', in ELLEN, R. (ed.) *Ethnographic Research: A Guide to General Conduct*, ASA Research Methods in Social Anthropology 1, London: Academic Press.

NUNES, T., SCHLIEMANN, A. and CARRAHER, D. (1993) *Street Mathematics and School Mathematics*, Cambridge: CUP.

REDER, S. and WIKELUND, K.R. (1993) 'Literacy development and ethnicity: An Alaskan example', in STREET, B. (ed.) *Cross-cultural Approaches to Literacy*, Cambridge: CUP.

STREET, B. (1984) *Literacy in Theory and Practice*, Cambridge: CUP.

STREET, B. (ed.) (1993) *Cross-cultural Approaches to Literacy*, Cambridge: CUP.

9 'How Can You "Discuss" Alone?': Academic Literacy in a South African Context

Lynn Hewlett

Lynn Hewlett's interviews with her undergraduate students at the University of the Witwatersrand in Johannesburg reveal how narrow and inexplicit the conventions of academic literacies can be for those who are not familiar with them. For Hewlett's students the difficulties of academic literacy acquisition are compounded both by the fact that the medium of instruction, English, is not the students' mother tongue, and by the cultural assumptions hidden within academic texts — hence the title of her paper. Brian Street's paper, which follows Hewlett's, also discusses exposing the hidden assumptions of academic writing, particularly in terms of the power relationships between readers and writers. Such power relationships are central to the situation that Hewlett describes here, where most white lecturers know little of African languages, and black students are evaluated in terms of their competences in English. Hewlett's quotations from her students are unusually illuminating in communicating what it feels like to be using an alien language in a genre not one's own.

Her paper also links with another important theme of this book, the relationship between literacies that are about learning academic subjects, and literacies used for more personal, playful, and affective purposes — 'expectations of terminological conciseness and precision inhibit students from using these risk taking and word play strategies to "try on" new ways of using language'. We know that in learning to read risk taking and self-correction are positive strategies, and there is now abundant evidence of the benefits of stories, poems, and word play of all kinds for developing reading. Creativity in word play is seen by Hewlett as characteristic of black South Africans' use of English. Her paper should be read alongside the one by Alan and Viv Kenyon in Part One and Peter Esterhuyzen's in Part Three. Both testify to the literacy gains of using the imaginative genres as part of reading for learning — a theme of the papers by Meek and Heath, too. Hewlett's paper raises the question of whether exposing the hidden cultural and authority assumptions of academic texts is a means of empowering readers who are new to their conventions, or whether it is the power structures themselves that need transforming — a question for

South Africa and elsewhere that extends well beyond the subject matter of this book.

In this paper I discuss some of the issues involved in becoming academically literate for students in a South African context. The material for this paper is drawn from interviews with fifteen black first year students at the end of their first year (1994) of an academic literacy course at the University of the Witwatersrand (Wits) — a 'historically' white institution. The students, seven women and eight men, were selected to reflect a range of ages and backgrounds, both urban and rural and, as they did not wish to be tape-recorded, their comments are taken from notes made during interviews. Focusing on this group, I have attempted to locate patterns in the students' comments in socio-cultural terms, particularly in the university context. A brief summary of one of the interviews appears in the appendix to this chapter.

The Context of Academic Literacy in South Africa

Across and within institutions, approaches to academic literacy are broadly *functional*, *cultural* and *critical*. Within a South African tertiary institution, academic literacy is seen as the mastery of technical skills and the surface features of English and academic discursive practices. *Cultural* approaches emphasize that becoming literate in the university 'involves learning to "read" the culture, learning to come to terms with its distinctive rituals, values, styles of language and behaviour' (Ballard and Clanchy, 1988, p. 8) and are often assimilationist in intent. A *critical* literacy perspective questions assimilationist views of academic literacy and advocates pedagogical practices and content that enable students to challenge the 'ways of knowing' and the ways of presenting knowledge. Such approaches may also include a critical functional perspective — aiming simultaneously to teach the features of academic discourse and examine their role in supporting the interests of dominant groups.

At Wits, academic literacy courses are mainly intended for black students. These students are often institutionally positioned as 'disadvantaged', 'under prepared' and/or 'ESL'. The focus of student development is on the language and cognitive skills they are assumed not to have developed from prior learning experiences. While prior learning has systematically under-prepared them for the demands of higher education, institutional assumptions are that this 'under-preparedness' can be remedied by a year's course (often compulsory for certain students) or through adjunct classes in mainstream departments.

Because academic development initiatives are not seen as an institutional responsibility and have focused on student deficit most of the work is done on the margins by staff in insecure positions. This situation probably protects the dominant mainstream from adjusting to the needs of diverse groups of students. The pressure to assist students who are based in departments that are resistant to change often undermines attempts to address student and staff developments holistically.

The factors that influence academic literacies relate to previous language learning experiences and competencies, literacy and language socialization, contested social meanings of English, self-esteem, 'reading' the culture of the institution, and cultural clashes with words and meaning making.

Becoming Academically Literate — What's Involved and What's at Stake?

Language Learning Experiences and Competencies

Black South African students enter the university with considerable language competencies, often speaking more than three or four languages. They have mostly learned languages in order to accommodate speakers of other languages and to be accepted into new domains and communities, as their lives have mostly been characterized by geographical movement and shared, crowded space. Geographical movement was largely for reasons associated with job scarcity, political upheavals and poverty. Language has largely been acquired informally, often mediated by peers or the children of family friends and relatives.

In students' accounts of their language learning practices they describe strategies of 'risk taking', creativity in word play — particularly the use of code-switching — and mediation by peers. Such creativity in word play is characteristic of black South Africans' use of English, e.g., 'I was born, bread and buttered in Soweto' (from a student autobiography).

The institutional focus on students' competencies in English, lecturers' lack of competencies in African languages, and expectations of terminological conciseness and precision, inhibit students from using these risk-taking and word play strategies to 'try on' new ways of using language. Instead students feel pressure to plagiarize.

> We don't have the ability to play with words in English. We students don't know how to put those words into our own words. We think the lecturers won't know if we copy — they can't read all those books. (*Student 1*)

Students also commented on the use of code-switching to facilitate understanding in informal settings and some mentioned its use in formal settings.

> At college [nursing] if my lecturer was a Tswana he will try to say it in Tswana — 'I'm trying to say this. . . .' It was a help. (*Student 3*)

In a context where many lecturers speak no African languages, the use of code-switching as a scaffold for teaching literate discourses is neglected. In examining code-switching by Xhosa-speaking students in discussions, Peires (1994) comments on how code-switching takes the focus off grammatical correctness and allows students to 'put it in my own English' (*Student 2*) — a way of addressing anxieties about not speaking for fear of getting it wrong.

Some students, however, found the issue of code-switching problematic. This student's comment reflects both the hegemony of English in the South African society and the negative pressure that this exerts on views of African languages:

> They [teachers] would use North Sotho to make sure we understood. This causes problems for us in the exams. We're disadvantaged because they have to make sure we can express ourselves in English. (*Student 14*)

Literacy and Learning Experiences

In order to succeed at university, students have to unlearn strategies that have previously made them successful and to develop a sense of ownership of writing.

In talking about their prior learning experiences, students commented on rote learning, copying from the board (often the only form of expository writing encountered) and the textbook as *the* dominant knowledge authority. The gap between course expectations and students' school literacy experiences is often deeply unsettling.

> When we started we used to copy a lot, we thought we were doing the right thing. (*Student 14*)

> Taking facts from different books — I did not expect this — the views are contradicting. (*Student 11*)

Prior academic success, measured by passing the matriculation exam, involved memorizing and repeating teachers' notes or sections of textbooks. Being successful at university involves having to unlearn many of their earlier cognitive strategies and learn deeper processing activities by gaining insight into and monitoring cognitive processes (Moll and Slominsky, 1989). In addition, the disrupted schooling experiences of many of these students in the 1980s means that some have hardly any experience of formal schooling.

Many students commented on their difficulties in developing a sense of ownership over written modes. Their exposure to written English was often through textbooks and a limited range of school genres. Access to books is a major problem in South Africa where there are few public libraries and high taxes on books. Both school and higher education literacy practices shape and limit students' conceptions of what counts as 'reading'. Some students commented that they didn't read or rarely read until I specified that I was asking about any text types. Students' reading material included detective novels, love stories, popular magazines, Bibles and daily newspapers. Schooling has also shaped conceptions of 'writing':

> This problem of writing — it's tangled with high school writing where you use the words to impress your teacher. (*Student 15*)

Before, I'd say things for the sake of writing. I didn't have the knowledge of things I was saying . . . Now I get the light of what is happening. (*Student 6*)

Mainstream curricula rarely give students the time to unlearn these past practices, draw on their former literacy experiences, or develop a sense of ownership over written discourses. Whilst students are struggling to express new insights they are also expected to have gained control over formalized, condensed uses of written language.

Social Meanings of English

In South Africa the social meanings of 'English' as a language and the discourses associated with it are contested. Student comments on English express resistance to some of the meanings, and ownership of others.

Many black South Africans perceive that adequate access to the English language was denied to them. Proficiency in English is associated with power, learning and social advancement. The school curriculum has operated with strong first language/second language distinctions. While white English students wrote English First Language, black students and white Afrikaans students would write English Second Language matriculation examinations, largely regarded as yet another device for providing them with an inferior syllabus. Consequently some students are resistant to their teachers' understandings of composition studies/English as a Second Language (ESL) as areas of practice and enquiry. They feel they are receiving something inferior — only for black students. Programmes operating with a dominant view of students as 'ESL' learners rather than as bilinguals/biliterates are likely to be operating a form of subtractive bilingualism, possibly affecting students' performance and self-esteem.

The stresses of learning through a language in which one is insufficiently competent have been documented elsewhere and are echoed by some of my interviewees.

You don't approach [to ask for help] because of the language — you don't know what you want to say — you want to have a well-structured speech. They [students] evaluate themselves before they speak. (*Student 4*)

I couldn't write notes. I couldn't hear the way of saying the words. I thought I'd just lose something so I only try to hear. (*Student 5*)

Most students mentioned the importance of English in their former experiences of political discourse. Their writing sometimes shows strong traces of the oral political discourse of the mass rally and political meetings. In the interviews, some students were angry at comments on essays that questioned the relevance to a given topic of political comments. The marker's comments may have been related to expectations of different discourse and register patterns, but, if these are not made explicit, students perceive them as the suppression of voice and the denial of their oppression. This is a particular issue where the marker is white and unfamiliar to the student.

Self-esteem

A recent study of students on academic support programmes at Wits confirmed the observations of many tutors: that students perceived motivation and anxiety as causing the greatest difficulties for learning (Agar and Knopfmacher, 1994). These difficulties may in part be related to feelings of alienation, pressure to assimilate, and institutional racism.

Some students expressed strong feelings of alienation which they attributed to the impersonality of the university environment, family pressure to perform, and a lack of peer-group support:

> I remember there was a time I thought I was going to have a nervous breakdown. You just feel like an ant. (*Student 8*)

> Comments from the other students make you feel like you won't make it. (*Student 7*)

> When it gets really tough you just go for the people's mark (50% — just a passing mark).

These comments, all made by women, reflect the pressures of trying to adopt 'white' ways of doing and knowing, as a route to success:

> If you try to retain your culture you become a minority. You have to end up being like a white. (*Student 8*)

Reading the Culture of Academic Literacy and the Institution

In an institution where undergraduate teaching takes place mainly through large group lectures, students comment on their difficulties in distancing themselves sufficiently from the 'story' of the lecture in order to perceive the aims of the lecture as a whole.

> It was hard — at school. Everything you read is in the book. [Now] the lecturer sort of told a story. You can't understand what is the main message. They don't repeat the things. (*Student 4*)

The students are left to impose some order and sequencing on the content. Their difficulties may be related to experiences of different narrative structures, and a lack of explicit scaffolding to signal sequencing — what Cope and Kalantzis (1993) and Delpit (1988) associate with progressivist pedagogies largely developed with middle-class groups of students in mind.

When I queried the problem of lack of repetition, Student 4 elaborated that the main message wasn't said strongly or often enough for her to follow. Another student commented on 'doing the recitations to learn how to say the words' at school (Student 2). These were mainly repetitions of oral narratives. Research on students' use of narrative and expository structures elsewhere (Ball, 1992; Gee, 1990), suggest that these 'repetitions' are an important feature of oral storytelling, serving socializing functions as well as the 'learning how to say the words' the Student 2 articulated.

Becoming academically literate involves understanding academic discourse as a form of argument. For some students 'argument' evokes 'win-lose' dichotomies. Further, the rules about what counts as acceptable evidence in different disciplines often remain implicit. Student difficulties in relation to use of evidence also reflect struggles with cultural views of knowledge:

> It [acknowledgment of sources] has to do with respect for individualism and individual thought — my culture doesn't entertain such thoughts. (*Student 1*)

Other comments reflect tensions with the models of writing they encounter, and their discomfort at questioning the power of the written text.

> When you must argue on the basis of two people you become a non-existent entity. You're just there as a non-existent entity and you feel inferior. (*Student 10*)

Some students found that a turning point in addressing these difficulties had come when they asked teachers for help and established individual relationships with them. When I asked why these students had not sought help earlier they saw patterns of language socialization, staff unfamiliarity with them, power inequalities and racism as key inhibiting factors.

> Access is a problem. You don't know what to do — knock, go in. You can't just stand outside. When they just say 'what's your problem' you feel angry. You don't know if it's cultural or what. (*Student 8*)

> We need more African people — where you can go to them in their language. (*Student 10*)

Words and Meaning Making

Most of the students saw 'lack of vocabulary' as a major limitation on their control over literate discourses in English. 'Vocabulary' operates as the visible expression of attempts to make meaning, what students can see and name, and a place where visible improvement can be seen. For some students 'vocabulary' is the means to work quickly, the expression of a need for enhanced language processing fluency, and multiple understandings of words.

> I had lots of problems with my vocabulary. I wasn't aware of modalities — now I'm aware that I'm putting a certain meaning if I use a word. (*Student 14*)

> Before I understood revolution as fighting and bloodshed — I now see it can be peaceful. (*Student 6*)

Other students are grappling with a less visible sense of words — 'the sum of all the psychological events aroused in our consciousness by the word' (Vygotsky, 1986, p. 245). The quotation in the title of this paper is an example of this. A lecturer at a recent South African Association for Academic Development (SAAAD) Conference delivered a paper on student writing, describing how in an assignment question Xhosa-speaking students translated the word 'discuss' to 'chaza' which means 'explain' rather than to its correct translation of 'xoxa' — 'discuss'. He commented that 'in defending their answer the students argued that one cannot "discuss" (or "xoxa") alone' . . . and continued . . . 'I suppose students associated the word "xoxa" with its cultural interpretation, i.e., having more than one voice' (Mabizela, 1994, p. 355). The students may not have been initiated into the academic tribal practice of holding a conversation with other written viewpoints drawing on a body of 'acceptable' evidence to support their side of the dialogue. However for these student it is also culturally impossible for a voice to discuss alone.

The ownership of words is also contested. At the opening session of the SAAAD conference, questions were raised about what 'academic development' means and who defines it. These questions highlight several tensions. Is academic development defined as a discipline with its own discourse (and therefore gaining legitimacy and funding)? What are the exclusionary effects of the emergent discourse of academic development and the assumptions underlying that discourse? On the subject of these exclusionary effects, a delegate asked why it is not possible to use the word 'talk' instead of 'discourse'. Cazden (1992) uses Bakhtin to help explain a parallel example where a student resists using the word 'discourse' and substitutes 'talk' because she feels she does not 'own' the term 'discourse'. The word is 'overpopulated with the intentions of others' (Bahktin, 1986).

> Sometimes when I write it's not my voice — these words I've never used before and some that you find have a different way — English terms, law terms, political terms. I feel they are mine when I'm saying them out — but not on paper. The things that you say are with you at that present moment. When on the paper, it can be changed by anybody. (*Student 6*)

Another way of reading the question of the conference delegate may be to look at it from the perspective of access into a discourse 'community' whose members operate with different epistemological assumptions and methods of analysis, and where there is often no consensus on what words mean.

Issues for Pedagogy

The tensions highlighted in the previous section have implications for, and raise questions about, pedagogy and its limitations. If being successful, according to dominant literacy practices, involves understanding how to know in different disciplines, then a central issue is how teachers from diverse pedagogical traditions can help to make dominant discursive practices explicit, while simultaneously giving students a sense of security, and developing flexible and critical competencies. The notion of 'explicitness' as well as the limitations of a focus on explicitness are examined in the rest of this chapter.

Recent discussions on academic literacy focus on how acquiring such literacies involves learning the cultural rules, ways of knowing, limits of knowing, and notions of evidence that members of a discipline share (Bizell, 1992; Taylor *et al.*, 1988). There is a tendency to assume homogeneity in the discursive practices into which students are being acculturated. Different and sometimes contested notions within disciplines, different intended audiences, and the increasingly interdisciplinary nature of disciplines complicate the question of what it is students are being acculturated into. Where there is no homogeneity, access to a discipline may partly depend on practitioners being both willing and able to spell out those contested positions and, to make transparent the epistemological premises of their own 'dialects' within the discipline. This heterogeneity suggests that working with monolithic notions of academic literacy rather than plural literacies is misleading, particularly in South African universities where skirmishes are taking place over the nature and content of curricula, the canon, admissions policies, assessment practices, staff composition, and beliefs about the ideal full-time student. Negotiating academic literacy initiatives between and within disciplines may depend on engaging in such dialogues and spelling out these differences to students.

What of the pedagogic practices through which students are expected to gain access to these academic literacies? Teaching refugees from a range of different cultural and linguistic backgrounds in Further Education in the UK was my first experience of applying the progressivist pedagogies of my own teacher education to my classroom. Many of the students I taught were clearly uncomfortable with deductive methods of teaching and learner-centred styles. I realized that it was not the practices themselves but the lack of explicitness about their purpose that students found confusing — how to activate metacognitive strategies (and which ones) and the masked power relationships and rules of accountability between student and teacher (Bernstein, 1990). Such pedagogic implicitness is reflected in the following comments:

> Here you are left to discover most of the things on your own. You don't know what's important. (*Student 15*)

It [teaching] must be more personalized. It's unfair to leave students to find the way. (*Student 8*)

Another dimension to explicitness is the relationship between lecturers and students. Some black students comment that they find it difficult to read the intentions and motives of white lecturers. This is exacerbated by white lecturers not speaking the student language/s, lack of cross-cultural awareness and social contact, ongoing tensions between students themselves and between students and administration, and low self-esteem. In such a context — without clear acknowledgement of the 'discourse stacking' in the institution and its consequences (Delpit, 1993, p. 294) — it is difficult to establish the kinds of cooperative learning environments that may give greater access to dominant literacies and greater awareness of the epistemic foundations on which those literacies rest.

There are, however, dangers in arguing for a focus on explicit pedagogy in an untransformed institution. Past learning experiences of students and staff mean that such a focus on explicit pedagogy also needs to be careful not to uncritically reinforce the powerful position of the teacher and, therefore, work against the development of more collaborative learning. Also, the traditionalist pedagogy of the classical canon has been regarded as a form of visible pedagogy, so designing tasks with an explicit pedagogical focus could be seen as an invitation to retreat into traditionalist practices (Brookes and Hewlett, 1993). To challenge both traditionalist pedagogies and multicultural tokenism, the discourses of power and the relations that shape and maintain those discourses need to be acknowledged and critiqued in the classrooms. However, teachers need to consider the implications of overprivileging students' voices and of not challenging them to examine the assumptions underlying their own discourses, even though they acknowledge the gatekeeping role of powerful institutional discourses. Educators like Delpit (1993) argue against teachers' concerns that acculturating students into dominant discourses might lead to further oppression. They urge teachers to teach explicitly the 'superficial features' of middle-class discourse — grammar, mechanics and style — whilst validating students' home discourses in order not to limit their potential.

While some initiatives are attempting to shift the focus from student under-preparedness to staff under-preparedness, such initiatives in academic development and in the mainstream operate within the constraints of fragmented, content-heavy curricula that work against collaborative learning and a holistic focus on student development. Academic literacy development is still seen to be needed by black students, a position that fails to recognize that the whole South African education system was framed within the discourses of apartheid and the philosophy of Christian National Education. While many black students are disadvantaged by their school experiences and social conditions, most South African students have been disadvantaged by an uncritical acculturation into dominant 'ways of knowing'. They lack strategies to question old understandings and create the ones required for a new South Africa.

Bizell's (1992) comments on how, as yet, no one has articulated a truly collaborative pedagogy of academic literacy — one in which the canonical knowledge of the teacher can be integrated with the literacy practices of the students. Discipline-specific courses, and academic literacy and language classes are rich contexts for investigating such a pedagogy, particularly in areas such as language use, translation, language socialization, and language learning. In these areas, because of their multi-lingualism, the student competencies could be harnessed for empowerment. The challenge is whether it is possible to move those initiatives from the margins to the mainstream without wider institutional change.

References

AGAR, D. and KNOPFMACHER, N. (1994) 'The learning and study strategies inventory: A South African application', Paper presented in the Academic Support Programme, University of the Witwatersrand.

BAHKTIN, M.M. (1986) The Dialogic Imagination, Holquist, M. (ed.), Austin: University of Texas Press.

BALL, A. (1992) 'Cultural preference and the expository writing of African-American adolescents', *Written Communication*, 9(4) pp. 501–32.

BALLARD, B. and CLANCHY, J. (1988) 'Literacy in the university: An anthropological approach', in TAYLOR, G. *et al.* (eds) *Literacy by Degrees,* Society for Research into Higher Education Milton Keynes: Philadelphia/Open University Press.

BERNSTEIN, B. (1990) 'Social class and pedagogic practice', in BERNSTEIN, B. *The Structuring of Pedagogic Discourse Volume IV: Class, Codes and Control*, London: Routledge.

BROOKES, H. and HEWLETT, L. (1993) 'Curriculum change and explicit pedagogy.' Unpublished paper presented at the South African Association for Academic Development Conference, 1–3 December.

BIZZELL, P. (1992) *Academic Discourse and Critical Consciousness*, Pittsburgh: University of Pittsburgh Press.

CAZDEN, C. (1992) *Whole Language Plus*, New York: Teachers' College Press.

COPE, B. and KALANTZIS, M. (eds) (1993) *The Powers of Literacy: A Genre Approach to Teaching Writing*, London: Falmer Press.

DELPIT, L. (1988) 'The silenced dialogue: Power and pedagogy in educating other people's children', *Harvard Education Review,* 58(3) pp. 280–98.

DELPIT, L. (1993) 'The politics of teaching literate discourse', in PERRY, T. and FRASER, J. (eds) *Freedom's Plough: Teaching in the Multicultural Classroom*, London: Routledge.

GEE, J. (1990) *Social Linguistics and Literacies*, London: Falmer Press.

PEIRES, M. (1994) 'Code-switching as an aid to L2 learning', *Southern African Journal of Applied Language Studies*, 3(1).

MABIZELA, M. (1994) 'Killing three birds with one stone: A tutorial system to challenge the status quo', South African Association for Academic Development Conference Proceedings University of Natal, Durban. 30 November–2 December.

MOLL, I. and SLOMINSKY, L. (1989) 'Towards an understanding of cognition and learning in the academic support context', *South African Journal of Higher Education*, 3(1) pp. 160–6.

TAYLOR, G. *et al.* (1988) *Literacy by Degress: Society for Research in Higher Education*, Milton Keynes: Philadelphia/Open University.

VYGOTSKY, L. (1986) *Thought and Language*, Cambridge, M.A.: MIT Press.

Appendix

Lazarus

Lazarus is a male student in his early twenties who is studying law. His mother is a teacher and his father a middle manager working for a newspaper. Xhosa is his mother's language and the language of his maternal relatives. Although his father is Swazi, his mother's language dominated the home. He started his schooling through the medium of Xhosa until standard three (Year 5). During the state of emergency in the mid-1980s and the student-led school boycotts, he was sent to live with relatives in the Western Transvaal where, he says, because of the 'negative environment of the school' the influence of older boys and the reluctance of relatives to have him there he started getting into drugs and a culture of disrespecting teachers. He completed high school in 1991 but did not obtain a pass that qualified him for university entrance so he repeated matric in 1992 and went on to do one year at Vista University in Soweto before being accepted at Wits.

In describing language, teaching and learning practices in his secondary school, he highlights the lack of use of textbooks and the 'endless copying notes from the board'. 'English wasn't much used except for school work.' The move to the Western Transvaal meant that he had to learn to speak Sotho and Tswana in order to speak to people from that area. These languages he learned from friends. He talks proudly of his abilities to switch between languages. With close friends he uses Isicamtho (a Zulu-based urban language variety mostly used by young people) where he says 'we just speak anyhow' and he also code-switches between the languages he knows. With religious friends he says he uses language 'in a formal and respectable way'. He sometimes uses English to speak to peers at university but says he feels he doesn't identify with African culture when he speaks English.

He reads detective novels, novels by African writers and sometimes newspapers — when he has time. He describes academic writing as 'some kind of formal writing in a tradition'. In talking about plagiarism (the concept is stressed in written departmental requirements) he comments that 'it has to do with respect for individualism and individual thought — my culture doesn't entertain such thoughts'. He also comments 'we don't have the ability to play with words in English. We students don't know how to put those words into our own words. We think the lecturers won't know if we copy — they can't read all those books.'

In response to my question on factors that he feels influence his performance, he commented particularly on financial problems. He talks passionately about his feelings about 'the racial thing' — his resentment because he is unable to afford the residence fees that would enable him to study in more conducive circumstances (than having to spend time and money commuting and trying to study late at night in cramped living conditions), of perceived racism in relation to marking practices — 'if you get 50 and you're black, you know it's really 60' — and his confusion about the hostility of white students — 'their rude manner, they don't know how to talk to black students . . . they just grin and think that's sufficient to greet me — in my culture that's not acceptable.' He feels that these feelings of alienation will not change until the university admits more black students and has more black staff. He says he feels that by the end of his first year he's learned to adjust to this: 'Now I just don't care — I just try to get on and keep involved in student politics.'

10   Academic Literacies

Brian V. Street

Brian Street's paper is unusual in that its message is communicated in part by the style and form of its presentation. It begins from the same premise as several other papers in the book — that literacy and numeracy are social practices — and then considers the implications of this for academic literacies. Students in higher education are expected to be able to write effectively. Institutions usually offer students help with academic literacy through study skill components which Brian calls a 'technicist fix'. In her paper Lynn Hewlett looks at what this means in the South African context. Street's own response to students' needs has been to unpackage and make explicit the bald and often unhelpful comments students receive from tutors, such as 'analyse', 'elaborate' and 'tease out the meanings'.

Street sought a dialogue with colleagues on this pedagogical analysis, and their written responses are included in their original form within his paper, attempting to avoid the homogenization which is inherent in traditional academic literacies. Their critiques of the 'make explicit' position were that although it can be helpful to students it ignores power relations (including Street's own position and authority), embedded authority statements, hidden cultural and class structures, and issues of epistemology. His colleagues help to identify hidden, shared assumptions within the academic literacy community, for example, the convention of using an impersonal style which could be used by insiders to restrict access to the community. This dialogue, which Brian expects to continue and which might one day affect mathematics and science, has resulted in a growing awareness that there are multiple academic literacies and that access to them is more complex than providing alternative pedagogical approaches. They are about deeper issues of ideology, power and discourse. However, engaging higher education institutions in a debate about such issues may well flounder on exactly the same analysis: that underlying their positions are ideology, power and discourse which will work towards maintaining the status quo.

Brian V. Street

Preface

This is an unusual 'paper' for an academic book: it does not follow the rules of the academic 'essay' that have come to dominate academic discourse in the West. Where the 'proper' essay consists of an argument supported by theory and (usually) data, written by a single person or a group adopting a single authorial voice, this contribution consists of a series of disparate comments linked by their reference to a common stimulus — that is, a short piece by me 'Academic Literacy'.

This piece was originally written as a result of my experience of trying to make explicit to students my own assumptions about 'academic literacy'; it was circulated amongst colleagues and at workshops on the subject and some people responded in writing. I asked if their responses could be included in a conference paper I was planning, and received general agreement. It would have been more conventional in my paper to refer to these responses within quotations or through reported speech. That I have not done so was intended to draw attention to the genre and to force myself and the reader to reconsider the conventions we take for granted — in proper anthropological fashion 'to make the familiar strange'. Those who find the attempt irritating, perhaps factitious or just plain lazy are asked to consider the source of such sentiments and to treat themselves as ethnographic evidence for the contemporary academic 'reader': are we so imbued with the principles of the classic essay text that we cannot accept other forms, at least within a larger text already inscribed with the signs of that genre — the academic imprint, title page and cover, contents page, and referencing paraphernalia?

At the Brighton symposium, there were responses from a different direction, particularly from feminists more accustomed to challenging such conventions, and critical that I was concealing my own power position. It was disingenuous of me to cite my own academic background as Oxford in passing without acknowledging the power implicit in such an institution. In the UK, even now, the term 'Oxford' itself is not innocent in any discussion of academic literacies. Moreover, my own right to pronounce, both to students and readers, and to challenge the canonical essayist text, comes from a position at a prestigious university and from having earlier publications that did conform to the norm. I have tried, therefore, to make more explicit the conditions of production of my own text and to be more reflexive in the concluding section.

Ultimately, however, the test of this experiment seems to me to rest on two criteria. Firstly, does the argument within the piece as a whole come across as clearly and as fully as it would in a single composition? And secondly, does it really help us to reflect usefully on the genre as a whole? In my view, if the answer to both questions is positive, then the exercise will have been worthwhile. I shall address these issues in a postscript after the reader has had an opportunity to read the initial short piece and the various responses to it.

Academic Literacies: A Case Study

Brain V. Street

There is a growing literature (*cf.* Taylor, 1988; Lea, 1994; Ivanic, 1993) on the gap between faculty expectations and student interpretations of what is expected in student writing. Mary Lea, for instance, notes that faculty frequently put comments on essays such as 'make explicit', 'this needs expanding', 'elaborate', 'put more structure', etc., without making clear to student writers what is involved in doing this. As a faculty member myself, I think faculty assume that these ideas will be learned over the years through constant interactions between tutors and students so that we can make these comments without having to make explicit the underlying assumptions. Recent accounts of students' own perspectives (Cohen, 1993; Ivanic, 1993) have brought it home, however, that this is not necessarily the case. This may happen at all levels, from first year students to doctoral candidates: in a recent doctoral hearing in which I was involved it became apparent that the candidate did not share the meanings of key phrases being used by the examiners when we asked her to 'tease out' the meanings of her statements in the thesis, to 'elaborate', to 'analyse', to 'follow through' an argument. We were also at cross purposes regarding the notion of 'making generalizations', 'pitching it at a more abstract and analytic level', of 'making themes more explicit' and 'pulling them out from the embedded text' — as the examiners struggled to communicate our meanings the student felt we were either asking for 'repetition' and 'redundancy' or that she had already done everything we were referring to.

I thought it might be helpful, therefore, to provide an example from another text that is not so close to home of what I think we mean by the expectations above; to make explicit my own conception of 'academic literacy' as an anthropology lecturer. To do this I analyse a passage from a book by Godfrey Lienhardt (1964) called *Social Anthropology* (see pp. 107–110). I use this passage with students applying to do anthropology at Sussex University, to give them an idea of the kinds of things we are trying to do in seminars and what we expect in essays and also as an example of the kind of analysis of text, its authority and its relationship to the reader, now current in much research literature — which is why my title is 'Academic Literacies' and not just 'academic writing' (Street, 1993).

The passage from Lienhardt begins with a number of general abstract statements on which the subsequent concrete examples hang: *viz. positive social functions of customs* and the *interdependence of social institutions*. I would argue that the rest of the text is an attempt to explicate these abstract claims about the nature of social life and, conversely, that the detailed descriptions of exchange, gift giving, etc., are made sense of through relation to these abstractions. On their own the descriptions that follow are interesting but do not provide a basis for comparison from one culture to another: we could just list such examples forever without gaining any great insight into their significance. By relating them to the abstract claims of the two sentences at the beginning, Lienhardt gives us a basis for making generalizations, for seeing the more general significance of these local activities. Once we have seen the principle, we can begin to apply it in other circumstances.

I find that students with whom I use the text quickly begin to make comparisons with gift giving in their own experience, such as Christmas cards, parties, etc. They are aware that the concrete details and social contexts of Indian potlatches and of British Christmas card giving are very different; and yet there are principles they may have in common and that we can test for by further exploration. They also see ways in which the original analysis could be extended — by noting that in Britain, for instance, it is often women who do the work of managing card distribution. 'Is this part of a wider analysis of gender roles, e.g., that women manage family relations; could Lienhardt have brought out the gender implications in his own examples?' And so comparison and analysis proceed . . .

What we mean by such terms as 'analysis' and 'tease out the meanings', then, is what is going on here. 'Analysis' here means 'link the immediate concrete examples to more general, abstract claims'; 'tease out' means 'show how the particular example does or does not link the generalizations', perhaps by also bringing in further examples; what 'follow through' means in this context, is 'consider whether the general principles discovered in one case could be applied to another' (such as the gender example above).

It is helpful to notice the ways in which Lienhardt does this in his text. Having set out his general, abstract principles, he then provides detailed concrete descriptions of gift giving, but he keeps making reference back to the initial points: e.g., '. . . was the basis of a complex social organisation that could not be maintained without it' (p. 80); 'The patterns of social interdependence which the Indians had created . . .' (p. 81); 'modern industrial society [is] in some way comparable to that found among the Indians'.

This is the sort of writing we are frequently asking students to do. We ask them, firstly, to set out, as Lienhardt does, one or two basic claims of an abstract kind and then to provide ethnographic examples that illustrate, elaborate or challenge these claims. To take an example from a thesis I recently examined; the abstract proposition was 'that there are different models of literacy — professional workplace/schooled/community — that may come into conflict'. Then in the text as the writer is describing particular literacy practices, e.g., parents' concern with grammatical correctness, she could make reference back to these abstract principles (as Lienhardt does) and briefly remind us how the specific case is an illustration of the general principle (or not). A comparison with concrete examples of teachers' views of learning literacy could then provide a way in to a more general, comparative point in which the author draws attention to the underlying principles and to differences — at the level of conceptions or models — between this case and others. The relationship of concrete examples to abstract propositions, then, provides both deeper insight into this particular situation and a broader basis for comparison with others. As these points of abstraction weave their way through the text, they will add texture and depth to what otherwise would be simply a list of events and comments. The writer can then go back over the thesis or essay and pick out the passages where these more abstract points are made, then pull them all together and write a conclusion that outlines her current position in the light of all the conflicting evidence and argument. Finally, that conclusion goes to the beginning of the thesis or essay and becomes an initial assertion: 'this thesis argues that x, on the basis of y, and I will take you through how my data and my analysis of it (from particular research perspectives) led me to those conclusions'. The reader can then make up their own mind and make their own comparisons and the writer will have added to the ongoing conversation.

I am acutely conscious that this is my own interpretation of 'academic literacy' as a Social Anthropology tutor who has been teaching at Sussex for the past 20 years and also as a researcher in literacy looking for these issues in texts. Also, that I have used examples from doctoral theses as though they could be applied directly to first year essays. The differences obviously need exploring more closely, but my point is that the same principles and problems occur across the range and the same general expectations — of abstraction, structure, analysis — are being used to define 'academic writing'.

At a recent workshop on this material, colleagues pointed out some of the problems with my over-positive approach to Lienhardt's text. The opening sentences, for instance, which I revere as a model of good academic writing, could be seen as simply a means of establishing his authority *vis à vis* the reader/student by opening with a complex and unfamiliar set of abstractions. Throughout the text Lienhardt provides proof of his own wide reading and knowledge, again establishing authority. More interesting from a 'literacy' perspective, his distancing strategies — use of noun phrases, impersonal style — serve to hide the (real) social relationship being established between him as writer and the student as reader: that relationship is the dominant social feature of the interaction, and yet it is disguised here as the author hides behind the text. This becomes apparent when we reach the long quotation from an 'Indian chief' where he addresses the listener directly: 'And now, if you are come to forbid us to dance, *begone*, if not you will be welcome to us.' It might be objected that this is spoken language whereas Lienhardt's text is written, but the point is that both are socially constructed according to specific, culturally-embedded assumptions — the medium itself does not determine the discourse. What the example points up for me, through the directness of address in the imperative '*begone*', is that Lienhardt does not give us such explicit clues to his own character and relationship (although a further reading suggests that he does implicitly present himself as a 'goody' up against either less radical anthropologists or against 'developers', who would 'abolish' the potlatch through lack of the kind of understanding he is advocating). The lack of explicitness about the author/reader relationship in texts such as this is a feature of 'academic literacies' that many students — especially mature students — find hard to accept. As Lea (1994) points out from her study of mature students, many were already skilled in writing before they came to university, but the demands of 'academic literacy' seem to de-skill them — 'I thought I could write until I came here'. As Ivanic points out (1993), many students see this academic literacy as a 'game' in which they are being asked to take on an identity that is 'not me', that is not true to their image of their 'true' self. It is at this level — identity, self-hood, personality — rather than simply at the level of writing technique, skills, grammar, etc., that the conflict and miscommunication around academic writing often occurs between students and tutors.

It has been argued that students are simply being exposed to a new 'genre' (Franklin, 1993; Cope and Kalantzis, 1993) — one that has considerable power in society at large and in the institution to which they have chosen to come, and they can learn to use it just as they have developed other genres in other contexts (business letters, personal writing, school tests, etc.). Indeed, being conscious of the styles required in different genres is an important part of reading any text. Lienhardt's, for instance, involves a number of 'voices' — his own authorial authority as academic and writer; that of the Indian chief; the phraseology adopted from Veblen as a secondary source. Such mingling of texts and voices — often referred to as 'intertextuality' (Bakhtin, 1981) — is a key part of how we communicate in both oral and written mode, and university should be a prime site for the elaboration of such skills and the analysis of them. Students, however, have argued that this process mostly remains hidden (Taylor *et al.*, 1988). Few tutors make explicit that this is what is happening and is expected of them, and they are seldom given the basis for analysing genres and voices for themselves. In the absence of explicitness, variety becomes a problem rather than a resource, especially when different voices are not just a 'game' to the student but a central aspect of their identity. This is an argument, then, for more than just study skills as a kind of technicist solution to problems that students encounter in doing academic writing: the issues involved are those of epistemology (who controls knowledge and how; who has the right to give voice) and of identity (what version of self is being expressed in different forms of writing, *cf.* Street, 1994). This represents a different challenge to tutors than simply sending students with 'difficulties' to a study skills unit, whilst they get on with the job of 'teaching' academic knowledge.

References

BAKHTIN, M. (1981) *The Dialogical Imagination*, (ed) M. Holquist Austin: University of Texas Press.

COHEN, M. (1993) 'Listening to students' voices: What university students tell us about how they can learn.' Paper to Annual Meeting of AERA: Atlanta, GA.

COPE, B. and KALANTZIS, M. (1993) *The Powers of Literacy: A Genre Approach to Teaching Writing*, London: Falmer Press.

FRANKLIN, S. (1994) 'Sounding the right words', *Special Children* (72), February.

IVANIC, R. (1993) 'The discoursal construction of writer identity: An investigation with eight mature students.' Unpublished PhD, University of Lancaster.

LEA, M. (1994) 'I thought I could write till I came here: Student writing in higher education.' Paper to Pennsylvania. Ethnography Forum, February.

LIENHARDT, R.G. (1964) *Social Anthropology*, Oxford: OUP.

STREET, B. (ed.) (1993) 'The new literacy studies', *Special Edition of Journal of Research in Reading*, 16(2).

STREET, B. (1994) 'Struggles over the meaning(s) of literacy', in HAMILTON, M., BARTON, D. and IVANIC, R. (eds) *Worlds of Literacy*, Clevedon: Multilingual Matters.

TAYLOR, G., BALLARD, B., BEASLEY, V., BOOK, H., CLANCHY, J. and NIGHTINGALE, P. (1988) *Literacy By Degrees*, Milton Keynes, SRHE and Open University Press.

Academic Literacies

Social Anthropology

Godfrey Lienhardt

In the very nature of their material, social anthropologists have been forced to draw attention to the positive social function of customs which, if looked at from a purely economic point of view, appear irrational and sometimes ruinously wasteful. This approach does not, as is sometimes supposed, spring from any anthropological desire to conserve exotic customs, but from experience of the interdependence of social institutions. As those who have official responsibility for directing social change have sometimes found out to their cost, institutions of which they approve are often inseparably connected with customs which they would prefer to abolish, and an ill-considered measure which appears to be for the good may produce effects quite other than those intended.

One of the most familiar anthropological examples of the non-economical use of wealth was to be found among the Indians of the coasts of British Columbia in an institution called *potlatch*. These Indians, immensely rich by the standards of even the wealthiest subsistence economies, had a most elaborate system of rank and status. This was largely maintained by display and competition in gargantuan feasting and entertainments, where from time to time persons of distinction would *potlatch*—that is, give away or even destroy vast quantities of their possessions. Of these the most highly regarded were plaques or sheets of copper, of no intrinsic utilitarian value, but counted worth great numbers of blankets and other useful goods. Though blankets, cloth, fish oil, and other commodities dispensed on a wildly extravagant scale in *potlatch* were, unlike the 'coppers', potentially useful, they were accumulated by the rich in such quantities that their owners had little use for them outside the *potlatch* situation.

The purpose of this entertainment and distribution of gifts was to assert relative social standing and compete for higher and higher prestige. The recipients at a *potlatch* 'party' were required by custom to accept the gifts; and in order not to lose face they 'fought' to outdo their previous host when, after perhaps a year, their turn to *potlatch* came round. A good indication of the scale of this obligatory gift-exchange is to be found in Helen Coderë's monograph *Fighting with Property* (1950), where *potlatches* are recorded in which thousands and tens of thousands of blankets, as well as many other commodities, have been given away. The Indians' enthusiasm for the non-utilitarian copper plaques is conveyed by a traditional account of a very large copper, which had come to represent, in terms of exchange, more or less limitless riches:

... there was nothing that was not paid for it. It made the house empty. Twenty canoes was its price; and twenty slaves was its price; and also ten coppers tied to the end was its price, and twenty lynx skins, and twenty marmot skins, and twenty sewed blankets was its price; and twenty mink blankets was its price; and one hundred boards was its price; and forty wide planks was its price; and twenty boxes of dried berries added to it and twenty boxes of clover. ...

and the list continues, giving a very direct impression of the nature of the wealth of that Indian culture.

The Administration made strong efforts to forbid and discourage *potlatch* on economic and other grounds, and in some cases indeed it reached such a pitch of wastefulness, in manic competitions by the actual destruction of property—breaking coppers or throwing them into the sea, and burning blankets and oil—that it is easy to see the administrative point of view. Yet the Indians clung to their custom, as when one Indian chief said to Boas:

We will dance when our laws command us to dance, we will feast when our hearts desire to feast. Do we ask the white man, 'Do as the Indian does'? No, we do not. Why then do you ask us 'Do as the white man does'? It is a strict law that bids us dance. It is a strict law that bids us distribute our property among our friends and neighbours. It is a good law. Let the white man observe his law, we shall observe ours. And now, if you are come to forbid us to dance, begone, if not, you will be welcome to us.

Helen Codere has shown that the *potlatch*, from the European point of view a form of madness, was the basis of a complex social organization which could not be maintained without it. The heavy expenditure it made necessary could not have been undertaken without an intricate system of loans, credit, and interest. Indebtedness, as anthropologists have often pointed out, is a form of relationship with many integrating social functions. To abolish *potlatch* then was not merely to abolish an isolated wasteful custom, but to destroy the system of ranking in the society, the relations between tribes and their chiefs, even the relations between friends and kinsmen. The pattern of social interdependence which the Indians had created and valued would have been radically altered. Further, as some of the people themselves recognized, the destructive *potlatch* was a substitute for warfare, proscribed by the Administration, and certainly even less acceptable to those responsible for government than the *potlatch* itself. An Indian said: 'When I was young I have seen streams of blood shed in war. But since that time the white man came and stopped up that stream of blood with wealth. Now we are fighting with our wealth.' He might well have understood some of the international loans and gifts made by the Great Powers in our own time as they bid for influence.

Extravagance and display in the use of wealth in modern industrial society, and competition for power and prestige there in some ways comparable to that found among the Indians, engaged the interest of the nineteenth-century American sociologist and economist Thorstein Veblen. Veblen introduced the expression 'conspicuous consumption' for the competitive use of wealth to establish and validate social status. His *The Theory of a Leisure Class* (1899) is a wider-ranging survey and analysis of the relation between wealth, labour, social prestige, and power, based upon his observation that activities economically and practically unproductive—fox-hunting might be an example—often carried high social prestige, while productive labour was often a mark of lower social status. So in his own American society useless objects (comparable to the coppers of the North-West Coast Indians) were frequently accorded higher value, and conferred greater prestige on their owners, than merely utilitarian articles. With much attention to details of social behaviour in the America and Europe of his time, Veblen argued that the highest social prestige was accorded to those who did not need to work in order to live. In the economic competition for power (which he attributed to a surviving predatory instinct) those were most likely to succeed who had the marks of inherited wealth and leisure.

Comments on Academic Literacy: a case study. Brian Street.

It seems to me that there is a problematic concerning academic texts, or more specifically, with the practices surrounding the uses of academic texts, which makes it impossible to separate the relationships of power and authority, created through interpreting the text, from the organisation of knowledge and ultimately the validity of "ways of knowing". I think this is why the "genre" approach is an incomplete model for learning academic disciplines. I had an interesting conversation at a workshop at Lancaster last week with Andy Northedge, from the OU -the author of the Good Study Guide, on this same issue. He believes that if you introduce the discourse- as he described it to me- to students, then you enable them to understand the discipline and ultimately academically accepted ways of presenting the discipline. I would argue that this approach has some benefit but one must also consider the constraints of learning a discourse: "genre" and "discourse" are being used interchangeably here as I understand them. The constraints are a result of the ways in which texts are read, understood and replicated at different level in the academic institutions.

When you refer to the doctoral candidate who did not appear to share the same meanings as the examiners, there seems to be an expectation that these meanings could be created through shared ways of knowing. Academic texts are not shared ways of knowing but are read or heard in contrasting ways by students and staff at different levels within the university hierarchy. The author/reader relationship is problematised for students because they are frequently exposed to texts which are addressed to academic staff. I would suggest three problematic relationships within the text and your example of Lienhardt's text could be used to illustrate this. Firstly, the relationship between the author and the student could be read as " I am an authority on this subject and I intend to set out, within the conventions of anthropology, an interpretation of this event which can be abstracted and used to understand other phenomena which are traditionally understood to fall within my discipline." Secondly, the relationship between the author and other anthropologists: "I believe that this is a useful and valid interpretation of knowledge within our disciplinary boundaries and this publication is intended to maintain my standing as a recognised academic authority." The third relationship exists with readers of other disciplines:"This is the way in which knowledge is organised within anthropology to enable us as anthropologists to make abstract claims about the nature of social life."

Academic texts -spoken and written- cannot be understood as impartial bearers of specific ways of organising knowledge. If students are replicating a genre then which relationships within the text are they replicating? Embedded within a first year undergraduate essay, a doctoral thesis, a paper for publication, an academic book are -as you elaborate -different relationships of authority between the author and the reader. Yet all these authors may have drawn on the same texts for the creation of their own texts. I think that it is impossible to separate the multi-faceted power relationships embedded within the text from the organisation of knowledge. If students attempt to replicate features of disciplinary texts within a different set of power relationships i.e. within their own texts, then their interpretation and organisation of knowledge may appear inappropriate and incomplete. Additionally, for many students their own more familiar ways of representing knowledge feels invalid within academic settings.

I think your own article is a good example of what I am suggesting. Early in the paper you introduce a description of the problems encountered by a doctoral student. You use this to elaborate on your own theoretical position. I wonder how many undergraduates would feel comfortable using personal anecdotal material e.g. about a personal incident of card giving. Those students who have little experience of reading academic articles may find it difficult to use anecdotal experience within the academic model. They are constrained by the relationships of authority which exist within their own texts: the tutor as the reader; can I do this in anthropology? The illustration of an abstract concept through descriptive or anecdotal material may not appear to follow in the logical order that you suggest. How can a novice student understand the relationship between abstractions and a particular personal incident? This way of organising knowledge is for recognised authorities. The recognised authority does as you suggest" hide behind the text", but the student has no authority with which to do that.

Traditional study skills approaches are not designed, or equipped, to address the dialectic between the relationships which are surfaced by different individuals processing and producing academic texts, and the "ways of knowing": the organisation, presentation and interpretation of knowledge.
I hope this adds a little more to your debate on genres and voices.

MARY LEA
23/2/94

GOLDSMITHS COLLEGE
New Cross London SE14 6NW
Telephone 081 692 7171

10th May 1994

DEPARTMENT OF ENGLISH
Head of Department **Professor Chris Baldick**
Direct fax 081 694 8911

Brian Street,
School of Social Sciences,
Arts Building,
University of Sussex,
Falmer,
BRIGHTON,   BN1 9QN.

ENGLISH LANGUAGE UNIT
Co-ordinator **Joan Turner** MA

Dear Brian,

I was very interested to read your article on Academic Literacy which was sent to me by Roz Ivanic. I am particularly interested in what you have to say about underlying assumptions because a lot of my own work is taken up with finding ways of making such assumptions explicit to students from other cultures. I am currently doing some research on cross-cultural pragmatics with a Japanese colleague, Masako Hiraga, and one area which we have highlighted particularly is "elaboration". We are looking particularly at elaboration in spoken interaction between Japanese students and British tutors and hoping to make comparisons with British/British interaction and Japanese/Japanese.

We have found that what are formally produced as yes/no questions are treated as simply that and not expanded upon whereas the implicit expectation on the part of the British tutor is for greater elaboration. For example, a tutor asking a Fine Art student "Are you particularly interested in the work of X?" might just receive the answer yes. Other question types which seem to embody the implicit demand for exploration or elaboration are hypothetical questions and these too tend not to meet with appropriate responses. This seemed to me to tie in with what you described as "at cross purposes" in doctoral hearings.

I feel that both spoken interaction in academic contexts and academic writing are subject to a specific value system underlying academic culture which needs to be made more explicit. My own work is primarily with international students but I have in the past worked with mature students returning to study and feel that the problems in terms of getting to grips with academic culture are similar.

Best wishes.

Yours sincerely,

Joan Turner.

GOLDSMITHS IS A COLLEGE OF THE UNIVERSITY OF LONDON INCORPORATED BY ROYAL CHARTER

A RESPONSE TO "ACADEMIC LITERACY: A CASE STUDY".
David Howes.

Brian Street's paper, "Academic Literacy: a case study" (1994), raises the questions produced by the study of all and any literacies: what constitutes this literacy?; why is it so constituted?; and how is it acquired? Some answers to the first two of these questions have been suggested to me by recent personal experience.

Last year, in Melbourne, I carried out a quantitative study into the effectiveness of a particular teaching methodology. It was an unusual study in that it brought together two previously distinct fields: the teaching of writing (from the domain of the teaching of English) and the question of individual differences in cognitive style (from the domain of psychology).

When I initially designed the study, I discussed my ideas with an academic friend. She was enthusiastic but pointed out that the study involved many contested areas: marker reliability, trait scoring and the subjects of the study were just some she listed. Her advice, later reiterated by my supervisor, was, "Make sure you have a reference to support every decision you make".

The study progressed well but my supervisor, whose academic background is psychology, was horrified when I presented my first write-up. I had blithely written in the manner to which I am accustomed - for an audience of those within the "English" domain. Phrases such as, "I think", or, "This, to me, is a clear indication ..." littered the text. Red circles filled the pages: "All this has to be de-personalised!" was the emphatic response.

This year in London I happened to mention this experience to an academic and writer. She responded in something like these words:

> "I write as a feminist on feminist themes for a feminist audience. I have to use the
> 'I' form if I am to have any hope of communicating with my audience. I have to be
> very careful not to be seen as taking too authoritarian a stance as a writer."

What do these three responses say about academic literacy?

The most obvious is that, contrary to the position implicit in Street's paper, they reveal there is no such thing as a generic "Academic Literacy". Rather, there are different academic literacies for different academic audiences. Writing for an audience of psychologists, for example, requires the personal element in the presentation to be excluded in order to maintain the status of scientific inquiry as an objective process that can be conducted uninfluenced by a researcher's individual history. Writing for a feminist audience, on the other hand, requires the authorial self to be foregrounded to reduce the notion of authorial status and authority, to present the writer as just one voice among many. There is, however, a certain element of sleight-of-hand in this technique. The writer uses a strategy such as foregrounding herself in order to apparently reduce her authority as author, which in fact is the most effective way to establish her authority in the particular context in which she writes.

The common pursuit in each of these strategies is, of course, the search for textual power. My anecdotes suggest one way to achieve such power is by the promotion or diminution of the authorial voice, while another is the use of references.

The injunction I mentioned earlier, "Make sure you have a reference ..." is particularly revealing. Note the injunction is not, "Make sure you present a *rational reason* supported by evidence". The use of references in academic literacy has become a system of self-evident proof of an argument and hence of power. The dangers of this are obvious, as exemplified by the self-referential nature of much of the writing produced by early genre literacy theorists in Australia. Propositions supported by earlier work (published, unpublished or even "work in progress"!) assume an authority derived without any examination of the actual arguments that led to the conclusions of such work. Those who construct academic literacy now rely on their reader sharing this assumption that reference = proof. This shared assumption now constitutes a prime source of textual power in all academic literacies and therefore the rules of the game that students are asked to play, as the students cited in Street's paper so accurately perceived. Should the game continue to be played according to these rules?

*

A broad answer to the third of my questions ("How is academic literacy acquired?") is hinted at in Street's paper. Street cites two studies that show that at least some students do not understand what it is that constitutes academic literacy. He then discusses an example of academic literacy he uses with his own students to "make explicit" his own understanding of academic literacy. The conclusion the reader seems to be asked to draw is that this will help his students acquire academic literacy.

But what does "make explicit" actually mean? In the conclusion to his paper Street rejects any interpretation of this phrase that would lead to a search for a "technicist solution". By this he presumably means the kind of strategy that would focus on explicitly teaching students how to write "academically". Street goes on to identify what it is that constitutes academic literacy (the ability to discern "who controls knowledge and how") but does not propose a method for making this knowledge knowable.

This is characteristic of the discipline of "literacy" as presently practised. The arguments on which so much current thinking about literacy is based, that is, that "form is meaning" and its corollary "process is indistinguishable from product", have led to the assumption that a statement of what literacy is includes a statement about how it should be taught. The process of teaching and learning is presented as implicit in the identification of the product. For example, when Street writes that the issues in helping students overcome problems encountered in "doing academic writing" are those of epistemology and identity, he has presented an implicit answer to the question, "How do you overcome these problems?", which is: "By helping students learn how to work out who controls knowledge in a social situation and what 'version of self' an author presents in a text". But this has not answered the unfashionable question, "*How* do we best help students learn how to work out etc. etc."

It is not surprising that it is unfashionable given the unproductive nature of so much of the literature that has been generated in response to this question. These responses have generally fallen into two categories: those who propose what Street terms a "technicist" approach, and those who have proposed what might be termed the osmosis approach.

Street is right to reject the "technicist" approach. It is an approach which posits the answer to the question of what constitutes literacy as determined rather than constructed. It is, in any case, as my own study I referred to earlier eventually showed, ineffective. It is, I think, also time for the necessary rejection of the romantic vision that universities or schools can reproduce the learning environment of a literate home which is the argument central to the osmosis approach. Leaving aside the question of whether all students do learn by osmosis, the economic order under which we presently live and which we will continue to suffer for the foreseeable future has ensured the destruction of that vision.

Instead, we need to propose and trial new ways of helping students learn. It is no longer sufficient to identify what we mean when we speak of academic literacies or any other kinds of literacies. What is needed is a clear understanding of how all students can be helped to share this understanding. This may emerge from a renewed interest in the ways students represent knowledge and therefore how they can best be helped to acquire knowledge. It is likely that the answer will be not be found in any of the traditional academic disciplines alone but will require a synthesis of the study of semiotics, language, culture, linguistics and psychology.

What is certain, as the experience of the students cited in Street's paper makes clear, is that in a time of ever-increasing education the task is an urgent one.

Notes on your "Academic Literacy: A Case Study"

One of my current projects is to collect and analyse case studies of academic literacy in American higher education. Because of the Writing-across-the-curriculum movement in US higher education and because the field of composition studies has gained some academic respectability (and research funding) in the last decade, there are quite a few of these studies. I've found over 100 so far.

Yours takes us to some common themes in these studies: that "academic writing" is not a single thing but a aggregation of literacy practices that make and are made by the epistemologies and practices (including the use of power) of specific disciplines and other institutional formations; that it mediates identity struggles; that it is largely transparent to instructors socialised in a discipline, assumed; that technical solutions such as "study skills" do not get at the problem.

But what interests me the most is your relating these issues to wider literacy concerns. Academic literacy is not "autonomous," to use your term. Thus, it cannot be studied as a ding an sich, whether in composition courses, as in the US, or in "study skills" courses as in Australia and England. One must go to those involved in the activities that give rise to textual practices a group of students wants to learn to participate in and ask to spend time learning what is involved.

For example, I would like to know what Lienhardt (and his "core set," as the sociologists of science call those researchers who acknowledge each other as participants in the research dialogue) thinks those textual practices you refer to are doing. From his (their) perspective, the "author/reader relationship" might be quite "explicit": one member of the core set to another.

As sociologists of science have found out to their pain, it's quite difficult to become an ethnographic observer in academic contexts because of the potential threat to the work of the "culture." I wonder if social anthropologists would be amenable to having a social anthropological study done of their practices!

David R. Russell
English Department
Iowa State University
Ames, IA   50010   E-mail: drrussell@iastate.edu

Response to "Academic Literacy: a Case Study" by Brian V.Street

Shirley Franklin (M.Phil. student at Institute of Education, University of London).

I enjoyed reading your interpretation of "Academic Literacy", because you have are addressing the issue of Genre, but particularly, because, in so doing, you are using the work of our late teacher and drinking companion, Godfrey Lienhardt. However, I am not in agreeement with your interpretation of my viewpoint on Genre.

I like your idea of using Godfrey's method of writing about the *potlatch* as useful in establishing for students a model for writing anthropologically. But this example could only be used for specific academic writing. Does all academic writing necessarily follow this structure, incorporating this empathetic approach? Does empathy have a role to play in Scientific Report writing? Surley not. Godfrey's writing is a model for anthroplogists and perhaps historians writing about people's practices in other cultures or other times within a particular, perhaps academic, setting.

I do not think there is one Genre called "Academic Literacy". Life as an academic reader or writer would be quite simple, and perhaps boring, if this were true. A multiplicity of social factors affect the genres we use. Genres reflect the purpose for writing. Thus the staging which Godfrey used in this text, starting with his position of the importance of understanding the importance of the social function of customs, rather than interpreting them through Western economic perspectives. His purpose, then, is to explain how the *potlatch* is integral to social relationships amongst the Indians. .

The problem of difference, which you pose, between the interpretations of the student writer and the academic faculty. is true of most student/teacher literacy experiences across the educational strata. Students of all ages come to education ewith their own literacy experiences (Street 1984,1992, Cole and

Scribner 1981, Heath 1983) and therefore have to be taught the genres used for the varying academic purposes they meet. In schools, the "S"treet literacy experiences of students are insufficiently extended to meet the demands of cross-curricular genres. Writing appropriately to reflect understanding, to put forward an argument, or to write a scientific investigation requires a familiarity with styles of writing appropriate to these textual tasks.

These styles or genres have been shaped socially mainly by those in power: those academics in the particular field of study who have an effect on shaping appropriate genres to their field, those who mark examination or test papers, teachers, and of course increasingly the Government through their dictates on Standard English or "correct" forms of writing.

Thus the somewhat inpersonal or "not-me-ness" (Ivanic,1993) of writing in academic genres is not about identity, beyond the identity of being an academic "anthropologist" or a "Sociolinguistic PH.D. student". Students do not have to be "exposed" to the academic genre, but to succeed in their acdemic writing, to be taken seriously, they need to be able to understand and to use the appropriate genres.

Once empowered by an ability to be able to write in the "acceptable" form, to be able to express new understandings in ways that are acceptable within the disciplinary area, students and academics are closer to a position from which they can reconstruct and create their own generic structures.

References

COLE,M and SCRIBNER,S. 1981, *The Psychology of Literacy*. Harvard University Press.

HEATH, S.B. 1983, *Ways With Words*. Cambridge University Press.

IVANIC,R. 1993, *The Discoursal Construction of Writer Identity: an Investigation with Eight Mature Students.* Unpublished Ph.D. University of Lancaster.

STREET,B. 1984. *Literacy in Theory and Practice.* Cambridge University Press.

STREET,B. (ed.) 1992. *Cross-Cultural Approaches to Literacy.* Cambridge University Press

(Please correct this draft for appropriate genre/linguistic usage!)

To Brian Street
Some Thoughts in Response to 'Academic Literacy: a case study'

It seems to me that identifying mismatches between teachers and students in the way academic writing is used and interpreted is an important first step in overturning a deeply engrained, rather circular, assumption in higher education; put crudely, that good students do well because they are good and that less good students do less well precisely because they are less good. Putting the assumption like this may sound extreme, as if denying the influence of teaching on an individual's success. Yet assumptions such as this do influence the way students are enculturated more or less successfully into academic disciplines. What they do is to naturalise the process of academic learning and sustain the emphasis in teaching on content and the coverage of topic areas rather than on the literacy practices/discourses through which that content is given disciplinary specific meaning. The emphasis is identifiable also in the way teaching is described in, for example, promotional material and course handbooks, where it is plainly the *what* rather than the *ways* that are presented as substantial. One consequence of regarding disciplines as receptacles rather than practices is the creation of study skills or induction programmes, which are conducted as additional extras to the main business of learning. In my experience the instrumental – what you call technicist – aims of these programmes fall short of allowing students greater access to 'knowing in' their discipline (since they are not based on authentic experience within that discipline) and also shy away from 'knowing about' – in the sense of having a critical perspective on – the discipline.*

Overturning assumptions and changing emphases is not simple and does not lead to easy solutions, but it seems to me that effective (itself a debatable term in this context) approaches need to incorporate an understanding of teaching and learning which is based on discourse rather than knowledge and which breaks down such unhelpful dichotomies as form and content, knowledge and argument and replaces them with more rhetorical notions such as authority, persuasive purpose, use or strategic value. These are aspects of literacy which are very much dependent on understanding of and orientation (whether positive or negative) towards specific contexts.

There are difficulties and dilemmas with this approach however – as I think your case study illustrates. It is discourse, not knowledge, that is powerful in academic contexts and a condition of power is invisibility. The implications of making discourse visible and exposing the means by which it configures the world are not straightforward. If those who are seeking to acquire the discourse are simultaneously in the process of undermining it, how does this affect their access to the position of power that it embodies? Is the power they gain, as one teacher put it to me, simply that of the cynic? There is something of a chicken and egg situation here, for if discourse remains hidden behind

---

* 'knowing in' and 'knowing about' are distinctions made by James Gee (1989) who describes discourses as 'ways of being in the world', *'saying-(writing)-doing-being-valuing-believing combinations'* (p.6-7)

the visibility of content, then belief in the naturally selected 'good' student is upheld and for many access to transactions of power remains elusive.

In that it signals the discourse of the discipline as something which can be discoursed about, I would consider your use of the anthropology text with students to be an example of the approach I am suggesting. Equally your case study illustrates the more radical ground to which such an approach might tend. As you acknowledge, your 'meta-discourse' on the text operates in accordance with a specific agenda, that of the teacher who exposes to his students (whether through discussion or instruction is not clear) exemplary modes of argumentation within his discipline. The mechanism of the text (as a manifestation of the discipline) is apparently laid bare, but, as your conversations with colleagues suggest, this mechanism is constructed as much by the hidden assumptions of the reader as it is inherent within the text itself. Another type of meta-discourse, another set of interpretative tools produces a very different set of meanings for the text – ones which challenge rather than endorse the conventions of academic literacy. By selecting these alternative tools the investigation is moved beyond 'successful' practice towards reflexivity and critique; tipping from the positive to the negative mode of interpretation (Ricoeur, 1970 p.27).

This is where those unsettling questions start. What are the aims of making discourse visible? Where do the parameters lie? How does the balance of power shift in the process? How is it distributed between teachers and students? Are they equally empowered to endorse or critique what they read and how they write? What are the actual consequences of critique in terms of the assessment and examination systems by which institutions operate? What would be at issue, for instance, if students brought the charge against the academic thesis (as you describe it) that it excludes or subsumes dissident voices and alternative interpretations, that its expressions of certainty enact a kind of violence – and what if they, as a consequence, refused to write in this way?

In the research I have recently completed on argument in post-sixteen academic education (Mitchell 1994), the objective of finding ways in which students could become better arguers was continually hedged by questions of this kind. The research's focus on *argument* caused me to think inevitably beyond the delivery of content and in terms of process, ways of organising and operating upon given material (through reading, writing and in speech) as well as in terms of authority, legitimacy, spaces and boundaries, ways of showing deference and orientation towards others and ways of creating identity for oneself. It seemed to me that not only was argument used within the relatively closed world of a discipline to make new knowledge in certain conventionally sanctioned ways but that it frequently also had the potential to cross the boundaries of these worlds, to critique them and to make possible new connections (such as with personal identity or experience). This transgressive tendency seemed altogether a more risky business, but one to which I was drawn sensing that it might ultimately enrich the disciplinary worlds or (which is perhaps not the same thing) help students to find their way more meaningfully within them.

Below I give two examples of how students might both be given access to what Sheeran and Barnes (1991) call the 'ground rules' of academic literacy and at the same time how they might be given space to reflect on these. What I hope these exercises create is some kind of tension between reproducing the given and reforming it, between consolidation and change.

The first example is based on an extract from the writing of a first year undergraduate Sociology student in which she reflects on her experiences of taking on the 'role' of student. The aim of the writing task was to move the students from their personal experience towards sociological explanations: a goal which is only marginally realised in Kate's writing. When I read the piece I started thinking how it might have been more successful; what, that is, it lacked 'sociologically'. From this I developed an approach similar in some respects to yours.

The exercise consists in taking one text and, in trying to 'spell out' what it is saying using particular criteria, developing a new and different text. The activity is neither 'translation' nor 'paraphrase' – though it may involve attempting to rewrite in other words – rather it is a kind of 'transformation'. The aim is not to preserve original meaning but to extend and develop it to create new significances.

This is the extract from Kate's writing:

> Certain aspects of behaviour were spelled out quite literally – how to not appear as a freshman. For example, freshmen women tend to want to carry purses – college students just don't do that. Also, only freshmen would be seen wearing high school jackets, sweatshirts or other paraphernalia - within a few weeks these signs were completely gone as the new students adapted to their new environment.
>
> I remember not knowing the procedure for getting course syllabi and buying books. By observing and asking, I acted as if I knew what I was doing, but I was merely going through the motions. In subsequent semesters, I did indeed know exactly what I had to do. This is when I became the student.

And these, my reflections upon it:

> Kate's writing is largely descriptive, though she registers the change from conscious adoption of the role to living the role. What does writing like this need in order to become sociological? Is it a degree of abstraction higher; a systematic way of characterising the observations; an interpretation of rules which are implicit, so that what is now description becomes illustration? Would a sentence such as 'The student conforms to certain dress codes which are picked up within the first few weeks of term' be sufficient? This is a general statement which introduces sociological categories. It might be improved by an indication that groups achieve identity also by being different from others: so 'The student conforms to certain dress codes which are picked up within the first few weeks of term and which differentiate him or her from other roles.' This seems to me to be a level of description which is sociological. I could strengthen my comment by

introducing some parallel examples to show that I am talking more widely about role adoption.

From here, it might be possible to formulate a hypothesis: 'Becoming a college student involves putting aside certain other identities and the outward appearance that signals them. Specifically the student puts aside both the signs of belonging to an earlier group (high school) and the signs of impending adulthood (purses?). These rejections suggest an identity which has side-stepped conventional paths of development.' To make this hypothesis I have looked at the particular illustrations as evidence from which to infer and then with which to support a broader statement. I have had to ask myself why the purses and the high school jackets were unacceptable, rather than simply to register that they were. Beyond this I've begun to wonder whether I want to differentiate student role adoption from other kinds of role adoption?

My text very obviously contains two elements or voices; the actual rewriting of Kate's text and a kind of meta-commentary on the tentative process of rewriting. These two voices could quite easily be prized apart and worked into separate texts and, for the purposes of the discipline, the sociological text would most likely represent the final outcome.

My second example is related to the first. It utilises the difference between texts as a discursive space in which the reader/writer's voice might come to be heard in a more reflective and critical mode than closed and monologic forms tend to allow. In this example two texts are configured side by side on a single page, so that the self-containedness of each is disrupted to create in the interplay a third dialogic text. The example is given by Meyer (1993) as an exercise for students whose thinking was, she felt, stifled by the 'illusion of mastery' demanded by academic convention.

ASSIGNMENT: Double Trouble

Fold a piece of paper in half. On one side, tell me what you think the sentences say. Be declarative, stating your reading as though you're sure of yourself and the author's intentions. Begin your writing with a description of the text and what it "means" or represents.
Now on the other side, begin your statements with, "But something bothers me". On this side be hesitant, questioning your assertions and certainties of the "right" side. Think about contradictions, about "what ifs", about what the sentences don't say directly. Explore double meanings and alternative conclusions. Relate what is said to personal experience and to subjective responses. Don't censor the outrageous or the improbable.

Higgins: Pickering! Nonsense: she's going to marry Freddy. Ha ha! Freddy! Freddy! Ha ha ha ha ha!!!! [He roars with laughter as the play ends]. (Pygmalion 100)

SAMPLE RESPONSE

I know that Higgins is laughing at Eliza and Freddy. Shaw shows that Higgins has not changed at all and is still scornful of others. The tone expresses his continued sense of superiority and Shaw's in relation to other human beings. He is laughing at their weaknesses, compared to his own strength.	But what if the joke is on Henry? Perhaps his laughter has a slight edge of hysteria to it. Maybe Shaw is suggesting that Henry is not the Superman he thinks he is but is vulnerable to the same emotions such as jealousy as everyone else. I'd like to believe in a more sympathetic Higgins, one who is not fully in control. But then, maybe Shaw has the "last laugh", showing me how much I want a different ending.

(Meyer , 1993, p.60)

I don't consider the voice of one side to be more 'authentic' than the other, nor that one side of the page has the greater claim to truth about the literary text. One side may indeed be more authoritative, but this authority is thrown into relief by the other, questioned by the context in which it finds itself. The split text creates spaces in which to discover not a true self so much as to create different roles and voices and through these to explore opportunities both to acknowledge and critique authority and discourse.

Both of the exercises I've described use difference to make discourse visible and therefore the object of discussion and reflection: what kind of writing is this? who and how does it seek to persuade? what claims to authority is it making and how? By basing such questions around more than one text dialogue is created. The dialogic principle in the Bakhtinian sense operates on sameness and difference and this is how the identity of the reader/writer is conceived of here, opening spaces in which she can both place herself within the dominant discourse and outside it.

These texts offer, then, rather different roles for writers and readers than those inferred from the text you used. This is not to say that your text could not play a useful part in such a multi-vocal process. It might form the initial text an a three (or more) columned page, the subsequent columns containing alternative interpretations of the academic literacy it exemplifies and forming the basis for further dialogue and reflection.

References

Gee, J. P. (1989) 'Literacy, Discourse and Linguistics: introduction' in *Journal of Education*, Vol. 171 No. 1 pp. 5-17.

Meyer, S. L. (1993) 'Refusing to Play the Confidence Game: the illusion of mastery in the reading/writing of texts' in *College English* Vol. 55 No. 1 (January 1991).

Mitchell, S. (1994) *The Teaching and Learning of Argument in Sixth Forms and Higher Education: Final Report Hull*: University of Hull, Centre for Studies in Rhetoric.

Sheeran, Y. and Barnes, D. (1991) *School Writing*, Buckingham: Open University Press.

Sally Mitchell, July 1994

Academic Literacies: Postscript

Brian V. Street

In the Preface to this article I set out two criteria for assessing the value of the unusual format represented here. Firstly, does the argument within the piece as whole come across as clearly and as fully as it would in a single composition? And secondly, does it really help us to reflect usefully on the genre as a whole? I argued that if the answer to both questions is positive, then the exercise will have been worthwhile. I shall address these issues in this Postscript now that the reader has had an opportunity to read my initial piece and the various responses to it.

The initial piece *Academic Literacy* with which this 'article' began, was an attempt to reflect upon my own experience as a university lecturer faced with students' difficulties in mastering academic discourse. In particular, I was concerned with their encounter with academic writing and reading in which many quite able people experience debilitating and identity-shattering problems. I used a case study of an essay text by my former tutor in Oxford, Godfrey Lienhardt, in order to make explicit my own assumptions about what 'good writing' is. On the basis of these assumptions, I would help students to read such texts both as a means of learning anthropology and as a model for learning to write their own anthropological essays.

My faith in Lienhardt's writing was already called into question by colleagues who read early drafts of my piece and argued that his writing could be used more critically to reveal the sources of students' difficulties with such discourse. For instance, the text contains embedded statements about his own authority which may deter students with different experiences and who may be resistant to its academic claims. Already there is a tension around the text, but there are power relations at play too: in Lienhardt's relationship to his readers; in my relationship to Lienhardt's text and my uses of it; and in the power of colleagues to question my approach in ways that students might find more difficult. In this case, I incorporated those comments into my text, reporting them at second hand and responding to them in my own voice so that they are encapsulated. This is in keeping with the traditional academic genre and I could have continued to do this as responses came in from other colleagues. However, by reproducing these responses in their original format — letter heads, full text, signatures and address conventions — I believe that I have made transparent the nature of the different voices, their own writing styles and conventions, and the subtleties of their argument. This matches my first criterion for the value of this mode of presentation. If I now respond to them I must do so in the full glare, as it were, of the reader's acquaintance with them and the possibility that my reading will differ from theirs. This will fulfil, I would argue, both the first condition I set out in the Preface and also the second one by drawing attention to the genre itself.

What do I think the commentators have said and what do they add to the original piece? If I comment on each one in turn I will make explicit what, in much academic discourse, remains implicit. The dialogic nature of reading and of writing is frequently disguised in the essay text genre; by the separation of texts in time and space; by the incorporation and re-presentation of secondary commentary into an author's, account, so that it can serve their purposes rather than those of the original commentator; by the detachment of the authorial voice from personal responsibility (it was the experiment or the theory that 'spoke'); by the homogenization of text production (a source's comments appear in the same type face and text type as those of the author who cites them). Students may well find it bewildering, but they lack the confidence to point out, that it is contradictory; they are being asked to comment critically on texts and yet to disguise the conditions of difference between those texts and their own; to reduce the whole discourse to a common genre; to de-personalize their texts when it is they themselves who are the source of critical commentary.

By considering each of the commentators on my text I hope to uncover the implicit debates and multiple interpretations that occur in any reading and writing. Students feel disempowered from acknowledging these implicit debates in their own literacy practices. This, then, may be a source of many of the 'writing blocks' that apprentice academics experience. Such problems tend to be dealt with as though they were technical issues to be resolved by mechanistic training pro-cedures.

Mary Lea extends my critique of such mechanistic procedures to the 'genre' approaches to teaching literacy. Writing herself in a direct and personal voice — 'I had an interesting conversation at a workshop at Lancaster last week with Andy Northedge' — she immediately sets up a dialogue, with both the reader and with Northedge, as she describes his view. She then addresses me directly — 'when you refer to a doctoral candidate' — and criticizes an implication of my argument that I had not made explicit. This is that shared ways of knowing would enable exam-iners and students to overcome their miscommunication. Academic texts, she ar-gues, are 'not shared ways of knowing', at least not as far as students are concerned: writers frequently address other writers, or academics and the student is simply listening in. These relationships, she believes, could be made explicit by deconstruction of Lienhardt's text, exposing the power relationships involved. She lays out her own theoretical proposition in abstract form, though with some per-sonal mitigation: 'I think it is impossible to separate the multi-faceted power rela-tionships embedded within the text from the organization of knowledge'. It is this that often makes student writing seem inappropriate; if they adopt the 'wrong' or unexpected power relationship, use the conventions of a different discipline, present themselves in unacceptable ways, then their texts are invalid. That could also be happening to this text, as readers from other disciplines approach it with different expectations and challenge my attempt, indeed right, to present discourse in this manner. But Lea is not only agreeing with me, but also using my text to bring out the hidden nature of my own power position. I can use anecdotal material, but students are disallowed from doing so by their authority relations with their tutors. Lienhardt may do this (he uses anecdotes too); I may (attempt to) do this; but may a student writing a term essay? Lea is not, I think, arguing against the convention that students should avoid anecdote in such essays, so much as arguing that the right to do so or not is hidden in the text. When students learn to write as academics they are learning about authority, and about disguising it, not simply about abstraction and what counts as evidence. I, as author of this text, cannot claim to stand on a separate platform from the subject of my inquiry. If I am right about the hidden power relationships in text, then they are there in my text too but, as Lea points out, I find it easier to notice them in others than in myself.

Joan Turner addresses the point about tutor expectations in terms of different cultural views of 'elaboration'. Where I had commented that students do not always understand what a tutor means when they are asked to 'elaborate', she points out that such expectations are sometimes implicit rather than explicit. They can be embedded in such apparently simple questions as: 'Are you particularly interested in the work of X?' to which Japanese students might answer 'yes', whilst British ones may know that fuller accounts are expected. This may help explain the nature of certain examinations, such as the Oxbridge Entrance examination where questions like: 'Art is in the Eye of the Beholder' may appear bland to the non-initiate, whilst those trained to the convention will expect to write for three hours on the basis of an elaborate structure of rules. Similarly, in the International Baccalaureate, a French professor once set as a 'question', 'La Nature', on which he expected a lengthy disquisition, whilst English students and tutors did not even recognize that it was a question. The hidden structures are carried by cultural and class groups, whose ability to satisfy examiners rests as much on knowledge of conventions as on cognitive skills.

Hill and Parry (1994) have recently argued that tests are prime examples of claims that certain texts are 'autonomous'. They elaborate the 'autonomous' model of literacy to demonstrate that it applies not only to autonomy of texts but also to autonomy of institutions, individuals and skills. The person taking the test is expected to use only information elicited from the text provided and any reference to knowledge derived from their real-life experience is likely to disadvantage them. Those who know this convention can play the game of test taking successfully whilst those who do not may inadvertently bring in background knowledge or personal reference that rules out their answers as invalid. Again academic literacy represents a barrier, and the reasons for failure may not be apparent to those many able people who fall at the gate. Turner seems to believe, in contrast to Howes and in keeping with my own initial argument, that making the 'underlying academic culture more explicit' can help overcome many of these problems. I am now less certain of this and wonder what its implications are for her own work, both cross-culturally and also with mature students.

David Howes similarly calls upon personal experience to elaborate the questions raised in my text. He provides an intellectual biography of a project he designed (a convention becoming more acceptable now that process as well as product are on the agenda, partly perhaps as a result of the more critical and social view of literary represented here). As Lea pointed out, his supervisor would not be happy with anecdote. More precisely, a supervisor from a different discipline, psychology, was resistant to the conventions now emerging in literary studies, and required de-personalization of the text. The contrast between this and the equally dogmatic conventions of personalization in some contemporary feminist discourse, leads him to criticize my implicit assumption that there is a single genre, academic literacy. There are, he argues, as did Lea (*cf.* also Chiseri-Strater, 1991), 'academic literacies for different academic audiences'. Both the use of references and the use of personal voice may be ways of pursuing, if not always achieving, textual power. Such power can be acquired partly through shared assumptions. The assumption that reference equals proof, for instance, may operate as a kind of privileged intertextuality that includes those who know these texts and excludes others. But whereas I had argued that students could be helped to learn these processes by focusing on their form, Howes argues that simply making explicit who controls knowledge, etc., does not tell us *how* to help them. I think he is suggesting here a similar argument to that used by radical black educators in the US, such as Delpit (1988), who argued that the process approach to learning, privileges those from middle-class and academic-style homes where such discourse is already taken for granted. She suggests that black children who arrive at school unfamiliar with this learning style, may be disadvantaged. She claims that some of the product-oriented, rote learning and fact-based styles critiqued by radical educators, may be more empowering for such children than the writing-process, whole-language approaches advocated by liberals. This is what I take Howes to mean by his critique of the 'osmosis' approach: there is a gap in my account at the level of pedagogy. My project of identifying academic literacies and their underlying assumptions and then making them explicit will not in itself, he argues, achieve the pedagogic aim of helping students to learn.

David Russell looks at work on the writing-across-the curriculum movement in the US and implies that it is culturally specific and may hide the underlying epistemologies and identities on which it is premised. Applying this argument to my original anthropological text, that by Lienhardt, he notes, like Howes, that the way in which researchers 'acknowledge each other as participants in the research dialogue' is central to the issue of academic literacy and the barriers it creates. Like Howes he too sees the members of the core believing themselves perfectly explicit to each other. Again those outside the circle are not being addressed: they may either try to listen and understand from outside the dialogue, or spend years in apprenticeship in order to enter it. How they learn to do so remains problematic since the text only encodes its shared conventions, not the methods for acquiring them. Russell seems to go further and argue that insiders have a vested interest in restricting access: indeed, that anthropologists might be resistant to having anthropology done on them because that would represent a threat. In this somewhat conspiratorial view, it appears not to matter what the particular conventions are since those in power may simply alter them if too many outsiders learn the rules.

This is the argument being put forward by Gee in criticizing the genre approach to literacy learning currently popular in Australia. Some there would argue that children cannot learn to question the power structures of the society they inhabit until after they have learned these genres. The teacher's task, then, is to impart knowledge of the traditional forms of reading and writing — the dominant literary forms, the genres of expository prose and essay text writing, the ways of composing letters to business organizations — in order to empower their students. Only then can those students be in a position to question whether these forms are biased against their particular backgrounds, in gender or ethnic terms for instance, and work to change them. Gee (1990) points out a number of problems with this 'wait for critique' approach. Much of the linguistic triviality that goes to make up such genres and to mark social groups as separate (phonology, spelling, surface grammar, punctuation, etc.) is learnt in 'socially situated practices' (p. 149) not in the classroom: hence 'they cannot be "picked up" later, outside the full context of an early apprenticeship (at home and at school)'. This is the problem with J.D. Hirsch's much publicized notion of 'cultural literacy', which is strikingly similar to that proposed by those at the other end of the political spectrum as the 'genres of power'. Hirsch is right, says Gee, 'that without having mastered an extensive list of trivialities people can be . . . excluded from "goods" controlled by dominant groups in the society; he is wrong that this can be taught . . . apart from socially situated practices incorporated into their lives' (Gee, 1990, p. 149). Furthermore, if the markers of separation are often trivial, then it is not very difficult for those in power to change them as new cohorts of outsiders learn the spelling, grammar and phonology of the dominant groups. Treating academic literacies simply as genres and assuming that anyone can gain access once they have been made explicit, is problematic not only in terms of pedagogy, as Howes points out, it also runs counter to current understandings of power relationships and of the role of discourse in them.

Shirley Franklin also addresses the relationship between academic literacies and genres. Like Howes, Lea and others, she is critical of my title: there is not one 'academic literacy' but many. Most students arrive in the education system with a limited repertoire of literacy genres and need to be taught a range of them, across different disciplines and functions. She appears to suggest that these genres do not run as deeply as I implied: student identity may not necessarily be bound up in learning new ways of writing, they may simply acquire them whilst maintaining their own identity. This is rather like Ivanic's data on students regarding the whole process as a game. However for many students playing those sort of games is itself a moral issue that challenges their identity as honest and straightforward. The writing process is not just a set of technical skills but is implicated in other domains — moral, ideological, political. Franklin argues that learning the genres is a form of empowerment in that, once students have learned them, they can 'reconstruct and create their own generic structures'. This is an intriguing idea and might provide an answer to Howes' question about *how* students learn: once literacy practices are modelled for them, they are in a position to use the rules of construction like Levi-Strauss's *bricoleur* to create new ones.

Sally Mitchell's response develops the notion of learning and argues for a focus on learning based on discourse rather than on knowledge. Like Lea and many of the other contributors, including myself, she locates literacy learning in issues of authority and adds other rhetorical notions such as persuasive purpose and strategic value. She concurs with Howes in noting that merely making discourses and their underlying authority explicit is neither simple nor necessarily effective. The meta discourse that I constructed for helping students deal with Lienhardt's text, for instance, is not innocent: one reading of it might simply help students become cynics, challenging this and every text; another might help select the already good student thus reproducing the very discourse and power structure I set out to oppose. Other meta discourses would have other results.

So what are the aims of making discourse visible and does it make any difference to the balance of power? Like Lea, she is suspicious of my implied claim that students can simply take on critical discourse. They already know implicitly, and frequently explicitly, just what the boundaries of their own critical rights really are and soon learn the penalties of overstepping them. Mitchell's own research on *argument* raised similar issues. Transgressive as opposed to reproductive uses of argument — that is argument across disciplinary boundaries to make new connections — is a risky business. Nevertheless, she seems to believe that training in exercises which reveal both potentials of specific literacy practices can help students reflect and change as well as merely consolidate. Like me, she attempts to use a text 'transformatively', to extend and develop its original meanings and help students learn to accomplish this. This responds to Howes' question about the ways in which students learn but does not necessarily resolve Gee's point about the arbitrariness of power over discourse forms.

A few themes, then, emerge from these responses. Most contributors agree that academic literacy is multiple, varying across disciplines and contexts; that the rules for acquiring it are often hidden and arbitrary, and that they involve assumptions about authority, legitimacy and power. But some responses challenge the notion that simply making these implicit conventions explicit will contribute significantly to empowerment. Firstly, the ways in which students learn need to be addressed. Learning may be transformative if it includes dialogic and alternative views of text but the boundaries of such views are still held by tutors rather than students and by institutions rather than individuals. Secondly, power may reside precisely in the arbitrariness of the conventions; learning them may not by itself provide access to power positions if those in control can alter them relatively easily. Thirdly, those of us attempting to help students reflect and comment critically need to recognize our own boundaries, at one extreme simply producing cynics and at the other reproducing the good student as one who does like we do.

If these are the issues raised by a closer look at the question of academic literacies, then, as in the study of literacies more generally, we find ourselves quickly moving away from the surface issues of reading and writing and becoming involved in deeper issues of discourse, ideology and power. That the academic world should be one of the last to see that this is what is involved in addressing literacy may seem ironical to those who believe its claims to scientific and critical authority: but as with any institutions, applying our insights to ourselves rather than others is frequently the last and most difficult task we face. It is that recognition of the mote in our own eye that, I believe, finally justifies the novel form taken by this article: the multiple voices, styles, genres, formats, taken by the short pieces reinforces the theoretical argument about multiplicity in a way that would be lost if one author simply summarized in a single format text all of the contributions.

It thereby fulfils, I believe, the condition I set myself at the outset of drawing attention to the genre itself; it allows the dialogic nature of all discourse to penetrate more evidently into academic discourse from which it has often been excluded —or disguised — and it makes a whole that is greater than the sum of its parts. I look forward to further responses . . .

References to the Postscript

CHISERI-STRATER, E. (1991) *Academic Literacies: The Public and Private Discourse of University Students*, Portsmouth, NH: Heinemann.

COPE, B. and KALANTZIS, M. (1993) *The Powers of Literacy: A Genre Approach to Teaching Writing*, London: Falmer Press.

DELPIT, L. (1988) 'The silenced dialogue: Power and pedagogy in educating other people's children', *Harvard Educational Review*, 58(3), pp. 280–98.

GEE, J. (1990) *Social Linguistics and Literacies: Ideology in Discourses*, London: Falmer Press.

HILL, C. and PARRY, K. (eds) (1994) *From Testing to Assessment: English as an International Language,* London: Longman.

HIRSCH, E.D. JR. (1987) *Cultural Literacy: What Every American Needs to Know,* Boston, Mass: Houghton Mifflin.

STREET B.V. (1995) *Social Literacies: Critical Approaches to Literacy in Development, Ethnography and Education,* Longman: London.

Part III: The Role of Texts in Literacies and Learning

Introduction

Part Three, which looks at printed materials published for didactic rather than pleasurable purposes, brings together problems found both in the majority world and minority world contexts. While Alan Peacock outlines the enormous difficulties of producing educational science texts for the countries of Southern Africa, Peter Esterhuysen shows us, aided by illustrations from his highly imaginative comics, how a simple popular medium can provide part of the solution, particularly when the readers become writers of their own texts. Both papers implicate the publishers of the dominant form — textbooks — in literacy practices that are costly, disempowering, and inaccessible for all but a few. However, with a few adjustments, their critique of dominant literacies in Southern Africa also applies to countries with long-established education systems like the UK and the USA. Esterhuysen's science comics, *Spider's Place*, with their lively narratives of learners learning, could find a home in both the township classrooms where the Kenyons teach and in the British schools where Leone Burton, in Part One, calls for the use of new and plural narratives in the mathematics curriculum.

Staying with reading for learning, rather than fiction or imaginative genres, Margaret Meek asks us to examine the kinds of reading imposed upon learners by the current spate of information and topic books. Again the question of authority is raised, since the authors of information texts rarely take the responsibility for communicating with their readers that writers of fiction do. How then can the authority behind the 'facts' be identified or challenged particularly in an age when, as Heath pointed out in Part One, the facts and what there is to be found out about have multiplied beyond the capacity of single learners to know them? Like Heath, Meek sees computer literacies encroaching upon and changing traditional ways of knowing. We urgently need to study the practices of these new literacies to ensure that the old dominant authorities and canons are not further strengthened by them.

11 An Agenda for Research on Text Materials in Primary Science for Second Language Learners of English in Developing Countries

Alan Peacock

In this paper, Alan Peacock explicates the difficulties of producing appropriate primary science materials for learners for whom English is a third, fourth or fifth language. The particular challenges faced in teaching primary science in Southern and East Africa are carefully explored. In recognizing the unavoidable centrality of textbook material, he identifies six main factors as having a crucial bearing on it: three are particularly relevant to developing countries, and three have a wider application. Included in the former are issues of language, culture, and economics; while the latter have to do with the discourses of science education themselves, and will be familiar to readers from outside South and East African contexts. His critique of the limitations of textbooks as a dominant mode of science literacy needs to be read alongside Peter Esterhuysen's ensuing paper and the paper by Alan and Viv Kenyon in Part One. Their innovative approaches to the production of science materials for schools may be part of the answer to the problems Peacock talks about here. Peacock's paper makes an important contribution to the debate about the use of textbooks produced in accordance with the impersonal, non-narrative structure of the dominant scientific literacies, in a language that is unfamiliar to teachers as well as learners.

Introduction

The centrality of textbooks to learning in primary schools in most cultures has been referred to in many contexts. Text material is crucial to the process of teaching and learning in schools.

> . . . most teaching is initiated by some form of 'text': a textbook, a syllabus, or an actual piece of material the teacher or student wishes to have understood. The text may be the vehicle for the accomplishment of other

educational purposes, but some form of teaching material is almost always involved. (Shulman, 1987)

In the USA, Yore and Denning (1989) point to the 'overwhelming reliance on textbook teaching' in science, and believe that it is likely to remain dominant. In teaching primary science in developing countries, text material assumes greater importance because of the specific problems encountered. These can be summarized as:

1. Teacher quality
2. Cultural appropriateness of textbooks
3. The language of instruction
4. Linguistic textual and structural complexity
5. Science content
6. Learning context

The purpose of this article is to define an agenda for research which will identify the problems within existing science text material and its use by teachers and pupils in primary schools in developing countries. This may lead initially to the development of better strategies for teachers to deal with existing texts, and ultimately to the development of improved materials for science learning by children. The agenda will be defined by reference to existing understanding as it relates to the six main areas of difficulty set out above.

Text and Primary Science Teaching

Teacher Quality

Many teachers are poorly qualified and untrained. Primary teachers themselves often have little science background, and frequently have poor command of the language of instruction. They rely to a great extent on texts as their main source of ideas about teaching.

In 1976, Kenya introduced a new and radically different primary science syllabus based on problem-solving skills, supported by high-quality materials developed with the aid of international expertise in science education. At the same time, the primary teaching force was being expanded to cope with the introduction of free compulsory primary schooling. The report of the National Committee on Educational Objectives and Policies (Republic of Kenya, 1976) noted that there were then 35,000 untrained teachers, of whom 12,000 had only primary or junior secondary education and were not trained in methodology or science. Most of these teachers had no access to inservice training and were dependent on their understanding of the philosophy of the new materials. Many found the concept of problem solving and process skills too difficult to internalize from the new text alone and therefore reverted to a focus on factual content. For many teachers, it was simpler to use the old syllabus and its implied didactic approach. Hence, the new text material was not used as intended by its authors. To compound this problem, most science tutors in primary teachers' colleges had an academic science background but no experience of teaching in primary schools or of using a process approach, hence they were not successful in training teachers to use the new text effectively.

The importance of teachers' subject matter knowledge, particularly their pedagogical knowledge of a subject, has been increasingly emphasized in recent research (Shulman, 1987; Ball and Feiman-Nemser, 1988; Kennedy, 1991). In the USA, where much of this research has been carried out, and where teachers are relatively well qualified and trained, this research has shown that texts often conflict with young teachers' beliefs about the pedagogy of a subject, and present concepts that young teachers cannot understand. How much more difficult for primary teachers in developing countries, therefore, to know how best to represent science ideas to children when the pedagogical science knowledge (through its textual representation in the teachers' second or third language) is not clearly understood by the teachers themselves. The difficulty is one both of method and also of belief, since training has at least made teachers aware that their culturally constructed approaches to teaching do not coincide with the methods that their superficial understanding of the text appears to require.

Cultural Appropriateness of Resources

Most schools have few resources for science and texts are often perceived as their only resource material. The rapid expansion of primary education in most developing countries has meant that expenditure per capita on resources has been universally low. Development of textbooks has usually been carried out with the cooperation of international publishing houses. Ministries have set the specifications, but authorship has often been in the hands of expatriate writers. In several countries, economic stringency has meant that both the quality of writing and illustration, as well as the durability of the books themselves, has suffered in recent years. Usually there is no alternative, or supplement, to the approved text. Commercial publishing by multinationals dominates textbook production.

Language of Instruction

In many countries, children are learning science from a text which is written in a language different from their mother tongue, hence the quality of text is crucial. This has been a major political issue in most developing countries, and continues to be so today, particularly in Africa, where research on the question continues (Bamgbose, 1991; Rubagumya, 1990; Hyltenstam and Stroud, 1993). In the great majority of developing countries, children's primary education begins in the mother tongue but soon changes to a lingua franca or English.

Recently independent Namibia, for example, has adopted English as the language of primary schooling largely for political reasons, despite the fact that it is not spoken outside school by the vast majority of children or their teachers. It would have been impossible for the newly elected SWAPO government to adopt Afrikaans as the official language of instruction in schools. Indeed, Swilla (1992) has argued that political factors rather than educational ones shape decisions about language of instruction. Mozambique, for example, continues to provide all its primary education in Portuguese, whilst Kenya has several times proposed and debated changing from English to Kiswahili in primary schools on educational grounds, only to remain with English for reasons of expediency.

Major problems arise for most children in science at the age of transition from mother tongue to second language, often around the fourth year of primary school. At this stage, children who have up to then learned English only as a second language are suddenly confronted with texts in all subjects in English, written for first language readers. Hyltenstam and Stroud (1993) have indicated how in many cases reading instruction via text material has usually ceased by this stage and how the texts often take no account of the linguistic differences between the children's mother tongue and the language of the text.

Science text material is also very different in structure from the narrative text in the second language which children have so far experienced. This makes dealing with the comprehensibility of science texts much more than a matter of analysing readability, since readability indices say nothing about causes. The widespread and uncritical application of readability measures has been criticized by many researchers (Woodward, 1987). Cleghorn (1992), in a study of teachers' use of English and vernacular languages when teaching science to primary children in Kenya, has concluded that 'code-switching' by teachers from second to first language helps to make the input more comprehensible. She argues for purposeful maintenance of the mother tongue in school to assist with the development of learning in the second language, especially where the teacher is also a second language speaker of English.

The most detailed research into the linguistic difficulty of primary science texts for second language learners has been undertaken in South Africa by the Threshold Project (Macdonald, 1990). This project investigated the effects of 'delayed immersion', the transfer into English as a medium of instruction (EMI) after several years schooling in mother tongue. One strand was a detailed linguistic analysis of two primary science texts for standard 3 children (the first year of EMI) alongside a comparative analysis of the English schemes used with the same children up to standard 2. Tests of comprehension of text material were also carried out. The evaluation found that there were marked disparities between the demands of the science texts and the English taught through the English schemes. Amongst the samples of science text analysed, 38–55 per cent of the vocabulary used was not taught in the schemes; children had sentence comprehension problems in 27–60 per cent of sentences depending on the passage analysed; the logical connectives (e.g., conjunctions) used in the texts were not taught in the schemes; and coherence conventions (headings, visual material, etc.) were used but not taught in either the science texts or the English schemes (van Rooyen, 1990). The evaluation noted that children in standard 3 were coping not only with a second language, but also with the transition from narrative to expository text. All these constraints are recognized as features of science learning in most Anglophone African primary schools. The author concluded that textbook writers should know which structures and conventions the target group has internalized, so that these structures can be used and built upon; new vocabulary should be introduced in thematic clusters to help form schemata and should be explained where it is used; cohesive ties should be easily retrievable and made clear by explicit conjunctions; and argument should be well structured, headings predictive and reinforced, summaries provided and visual material integrated into text (van Rooyen, 1990).

Textual and Structural Complexity

Science text material is expository, exploits illustrations and graphics and uses language for a complex range of functions such as giving instructions, describing phenomena, explaining ideas and hypothesizing. It is more difficult to interpret than narrative text. Many researchers have drawn attention to this in developed countries. Cummins (1983) has elaborated three dimensions of text material (abstract-non-abstract: elaborated-situated: informational-involved) and has pointed out that written science text material is highly literate in relation to these dimensions. It makes great demands on learners, particularly second language learners. Literateness, Cummins argues, is a symptom of the author's orientation to subject matter. Examples of these structural aspects of science texts are the high proportion of new vocabulary (Yager, 1983); the use of analogy, simile and metaphor (Gilbert, 1989); word order, subordination and contracted prepositions (Hyltenstam and Stroud, 1993) and use of headings (Dansereau, 1982). It is not surprising that researchers in various countries have found that the demands of science texts are often above the level and capabilities of the primary school children for whom they were intended (Staver and Bay, 1989; Fatt, 1991).

If this is so in developed countries amongst first language speakers, how much more serious the problems are likely to be for second language learners in developing countries. Roth (1985) has suggested that all readers have difficulty learning from science texts which use ineffective text-processing strategies. Such strategies are rarely taught to primary children in developing countries, since in the main the teachers themselves have not mastered them and English language schemes tend not to teach them either.

Illustrations are widely used in science texts in both developed and developing countries to aid understanding. Research on visual literacy suggests that the actual function of illustrations may be much more complex and often ineffective. Reid (1990) has shown that literacy is a precondition for making sense of illustrations. Reid and Beveridge (1986) have suggested that pictures in themselves provide no motivating effect, and whilst the more able benefit more from pictures, the less able are more often distracted by them. Yet in a developing country context,

Berenschot-Moret-Basboom Consultants (1980) found that 34 per cent of Kenyan 10–18 year olds did not understand pictures presented to them. Cultural factors related to readers are crucial. Several authors have shown how previous experience of pictures is related to the ability to interpret them, rural children faring worse than urban (Colle and Glass, 1986). Environmental factors can lead to confused interpretations and misunderstanding, particularly with such features as perspective and symbols (Berenschot-Moret-Basboom Consultants, 1980). Pictures facilitate comprehension for some text material, but only if visual additions are specifically designed to complement printed instructions (Dwyer, 1988). A number of researchers have strongly emphasized the collaborative development of text materials, involving an understanding of local 'visual languages' and illustrators with an intimate knowledge of the contexts in which learning through texts takes place (Gerlach and Ely, 1986; Fetter, Clark, Murphy and Walters, 1987). The implications of this for developing countries and for the role of commercial publishing are considerable.

The complexity of text format is closely related to assumptions about the way in which learning occurs and is organized in many western classrooms where the teacher fulfills numerous roles; in the course of one lesson the teacher may give direct instruction, ask questions, mediate in group tasks and conversation, provide and manage materials, monitor and assess learners. There is virtually no research evidence as yet on the way in which teachers actually use text material in primary science. Clarke (1994; 1995) has begun some work in South Africa and has reported that effective use of text material does not simply depend on readability but is affected crucially by such matters as teacher mediation. What is essential is further research into the difficulties encountered by second language learners and their teachers with the text material of science itself, and into the way such material is used in primary classrooms, as a prelude to developing new forms of text material in science for primary schools particularly in developing countries.

Science Content

Science learning involves acquiring and using a wide range of concepts which are often not part of children's everyday experience and which are only encountered in school science lessons through text material.

A large and expanding body of research evidence exists relating to children's acquisition of science concepts, much of it related to constructivist theory. In relation to primary children's science learning, the most comprehensive body of evidence has been put together by the SPACE Project (1991 onwards). In Africa, effective text material is often the only vehicle for developing conceptual learning. And yet many of the concepts when presented in a second language such as English are inaccessible to pupils, not only because of their difficulties of comprehension but also because vernacular languages do not have comparable concepts or terms equivalent to the concept in English. For example, in Botswana, the majority vernacular language, Setswana, has only two categories within which all animals are classified (Russell, 1991).

Learning Context

In most developing countries, primary teachers have large classes of 50–80 children and few resources other than textbooks. In science, the problem is often exacerbated by lack of access to running water, electricity and even flat surfaces on which to place equipment for experimental work. Teachers are often poorly qualified and untrained. A combination of factors has meant that primary teaching throughout the developing world has continued to be based on methods which heavily emphasize teacher talk, recitation and repetition, rote learning and copying of text material. Group work, practical activity and investigation are extremely uncommon; teachers occasionally demonstrate experiments in science, but the vast majority of children never design or carry out investigations. Such ways of teaching are still seen as not feasible in practice. Science teacher education in a number of developing countries has made strenuous efforts to alter this situation without as yet a great deal of success (Peacock, 1993; 1995 in press).

Conclusion

The most urgent and appropriate focus for further research would be the stage in children's schooling where they presently first begin to learn science in their second language. This may vary somewhat from country to country, but in much of Africa the transition to English as the medium of instruction currently takes place at around the fourth year in primary school. South Africa is now considering a gradual approach to transition spread over the first few years of schooling, as distinct from the delayed immersion approach practised in many other African states. The implications of gradualism for textbook production are likely to be even more complex, as dual or parallel texts would probably be required during the early years of schooling.

Further detailed desk research analysing specific texts is needed. At the same time, research needs to focus on the links between language schemes used to teach the second instructional language and the expository texts used to teach subjects in that language. Much research also needs to focus on meta-textual factors, particularly the way in which learners use text when working independently, and the mediation of text by teachers in a classroom context. And in a developing country context, this mediation process cannot be separated from a study of the specific pedagogical-cultural features of the environment in which science is being learned through the use of text material. This will need to include studies of the learning culture of initial teacher training provision for primary teachers and the way textbooks are dealt with during training.

Finally there is a need for enquiry into the way science textbooks are commissioned, written, produced and adopted by education systems, regions or individual schools in developing countries. Costs of such research will be high, but the benefits in terms of the improvement in children's learning are potentially enormous.

References

BALL, D.L. and FEIMAN-NEMSER, S. (1988) 'Using textbooks and teachers' guides: A dilemma for beginning teachers and teacher educators, *Curriculum Inquiry*, 18(4).

BAMBGOSE, A. (1991) *Language and the Nation: The Language Question in Sub-Saharan Africa*, Edinburgh: Edinburgh University Press.

BERENSCHOT-MORET-BASBOOM CONSULTANTS (1980) *Report on the Visual Literacy of Kenyan Primary School Leavers*, Tilburg: BMB.

CLARKE, J. (1994) 'An ethnographic investigation into the development and trialling of more accessible text materials for second language teaching and learning in science.' MEd thesis, University of Cape Town.

CLARKE, J. (1995) 'Sister can you spare me a book I can understand? The second language reader and her secondary school science textbook', paper presented at the Annual Conference of the South African Association for Research into Mathematics and Science Education, Cape Town, Jan.

CLEGHORN, A. (1992) 'Primary level science in Kenya: Constructing meaning through English and indigenous languages', *International Journal of Qualitative Studies in Education*, 5(4).

COLLE, R. and GLASS, S. (1986) 'Pictorial conventions in development communication in developing countries', *Media in Education and Development*, 19(4).

CUMMINS J.J. (1983) 'Language proficiency and academic achievement', in OLLER, J.W. (ed.) *Issues in Language Testing Research*, Rowley, MA.: Newbury House.

DANSEREAU, D.F. (1982) *Effects of Individual Differences, Processing Instructions and Outline and Heading Characteristics on Learning from Introductory Science Texts* (Three Sections) Fort Worth, Texas Christian University.

DWYER, F.M. (1988) 'Examining the symbiotic relationship between verbal and visual literacy', *Reading Psychology*, 9(4).

FATT, J.P.T. (1991) 'Text-related variables in textbook readability', *Research Papers in Education*, 6(3).

FETTER, K., CLARK, M., MURPHY, C. and WALTERS, J. (1987) *Teaching and Learning with Visual Aids*, London; Macmillan.

GERLACH, V. and ELY, D. (1986) *Teaching and Media: A Systematic Approach*, London; Prentice Hall.

GILBERT, S.W. (1989) 'An evaluation of the use of analogy, simile and metaphor in science texts', *Journal of Research in Science Teaching*, 26(4).

HYLTENSTAM, K. and STROUD, C. (1993) *Final Report and Recommendations from the Evaluation of Teaching Materials for Lower Primary in Mozambique: (II) Language Issues*, Stockholm: Stockholm Institute of Education.

KENNEDY, M. (ed.) (1991) *Teaching Academic Subjects to Diverse Learners*, New York: Teach.

MACDONALD, C.A. (1990) *School-based Learning Experiences: A Final Report of the Threshold Project*, Pretoria: Human Sciences Research Council.

PEACOCK, A. (1993) 'The in-service training of primary teachers in science in Namibia: Models and practical constraints', *British Journal of In-Service Education*, 19(2).

PEACOCK, A. (1995 in press) 'Access to science learning for children in rural Africa', *International Journal of Science Education*, 17(2).

REID, D.J. (1990) 'The role of pictures in learning Biology' (Two articles), *Journal of Biological Education*, 24(3 and 4).

REID, D.J. and BEVERIDGE, M. (1986) 'Effects of text illustration on children's learning of a school science topic', *British Journal of Educational Psychology*, 56.

REPUBLIC OF KENYA (1976) *National Committee on Educational Objectives and Policies*, Nairobi: Government Publication.

ROTH, K.J. (1985) *Conceptual Change Learning and Student Processing of Science Texts* Michigan: Michigan State University, Institute for Research on Teaching.

RUBAGUMYA, C.M. (1990) *Language and Education in Africa*, Clevedon: Multilingual Matters.

RUSSELL, A. (1991) 'Primary science and the clash of cultures in a developing country', in PEACOCK, A. (ed.) (1990) *Science in Primary Schools: The Multicultural Dimension*, Basingstoke: Macmillan Education.

SHULMAN, J. (1987) 'Knowledge and teaching: Foundations of the new reform', *Harvard Educational Review*, 57(1), pp. 1–22.

SCIENCE PROCESSES AND CONCEPT EXPLORATION PROJECT (SPACE) (1991 onwards) *Research Reports: Evaporation and Condensation, Growth, Light, Sound, Electricity, Materials*, Liverpool: Liverpool University Press.

STAVER, J.R. and BAY, M. (1989) 'Analysis of the conceptual structure and reasoning demands of elementary science texts at the primary (K-3) level', *Journal of Research in Science Teaching*, 26(4).

SWILLA, I.N. (1992) 'The relation of local and foreign languages to national needs in Africa', *Journal of Multilingual and Multicultural Development*, 13(6).

VAN ROOYEN, H. (1990) *The Disparity between English as a Subject and English as the Medium of Learning (Final Report of the Threshold Project)*, Pretoria: Human Sciences Research Council.

WOODWARD, A. (1987) 'Textbooks: Less than meets the eye', *Journal of Curriculum Studies*, 19(6).

YAGER, R.E. (1983) 'The importance of terminology in teaching K-12 science', *Journal of Research in Science Teaching*, 20(6).

YORE, L.D. and DENNING, D. (1989) 'Implementing change in secondary science reading and textbook usage; a desired image, a current profile and a plan for change'. Paper presented at the 62nd Annual Meeting of the National Association for Research into Science Teaching, San Francisco, March 1989.

12 'Focusing on the Frames': Using Comic Books to Challenge Dominant Literacies in South Africa

Peter Esterhuysen

Graphic literature has been a rapidly developing genre in recent years, but Peter Esterhuysen's paper shows how wide its applications can be in the hands of a highly original team whose knowledge of their readers' needs is embedded in creative collaborative partnership. Although the reported figures for illiteracy in South Africa are as high as 60–70 per cent, Esterhuysen, like others in this volume, claims that most of those regarded as illiterate in fact engage in literacy practices in their everyday lives. In a country where books are neither affordable nor accessible to large groups of the population the Storyteller Group comics are nevertheless not merely cheaper educational resources, or substitutes for books. So skilfully wrought are the comics that the practices of reading and writing are woven into the stories they tell in ways that help readers to reflect on what their literacy practices are and might be. Books and stories, reading and writing, play a critical role in the narratives, so that those who read them learn how specific literacy activities can be materially, psychologically and socially transformative. In this respect, the comics described by Esterhuysen are examples of what Barthes (1974) calls 'writerly' texts, that is texts that foreground the processes of their own construction rather than concealing them. (Street's paper in this volume could also be read as writerly in this sense.) Esterhuysen's paper belongs not only with the other South African contributions to this book, but also links with the papers of Barton and Jenkins on community literacy practices in Part Two, and with Clay's paper, in Part Four, on the need for new scientific literacies to meet the environmental crisis facing the planet.

A Story about Reading

A few years ago I attended a comic story workshop at a community centre in Soweto, along with two colleagues from the Storyteller Group. We arrived at the centre before the other participants and sat outside, savouring the late morning sun. In the distance we could hear two church services taking place. Groups of small children were playing in the quadrangle. After a while three young girls — no older than six or seven — approached us timidly. They had spotted the pile of comics we had brought to show the workshop participants. One of the girls leaned over and began to read the words '99 Sharp Street' aloud. '99 Sharp Street' is the series title of a children's comic we created in support of the International Year of Literacy. I had a few extra copies which I gave them.

The three girls retired to a corner, opened a comic, placed it on the ground and began to read the first page. Their reading consisted of pointing at a picture and engaging in some discussion in their mother tongue. Then one of the girls would attempt to read the English speech bubbles while the others corrected her English. Thereafter, the text in the speech bubble seemed to be the subject of further discussion — even negotiation. A short while later, the other participants arrived and we moved inside. When I walked outside an hour later I noticed that the girls were still sitting in their corner reading the comic. They were on page four.

Introduction

The Storyteller Group is a South African publishing company that specializes in popular visual literature. Since our inception six years ago, we have created and distributed about four million comic books. In this chapter I shall describe three of our comic projects to show how we have used the conventions and format of popular media to promote reading and writing. Although often shaped by the constraints of client or funder, budget and deadline, our approach to popular media has been consistent in the assumptions it makes about literacy practices and the ways in which readers can engage with texts. And in different ways our comics have set out to challenge two kinds of literacy that are extremely influential in South Africa.

The first is the 'essay-text' kind of literacy — the model of literacy that funders, academics and NGOs (Non-Governmental Organizations) usually have in mind (Street, 1984). This kind of literacy is associated with English or Afrikaans in South Africa and is 'embedded in a host of social practices that are the unthought-about assumptions of middle-class people living under conditions of modernity' (Robbins and Prinsloo, 1994). The pervasiveness of this model with its narrow, rather decontextualized view of literacy and its sweeping generalizations about the consequences of being literate has, in my opinion, caused actual literacy practices and real needs to be overlooked.

The second kind of literacy is enacted daily in the majority of South African schools. In these classrooms students are treated as passive recipients of teacher-transmitted information and texts (usually textbooks) are turned into artifacts to be memorized, or copied verbatim. Textbooks, like the teacher, are invested with an authority which does not brook challenge.

Both kinds of literacy bear very little relation to the everyday needs and literacy practices of the majority of South Africans and, in this sense, are disempowering. In our popular media we have tried to challenge the assumptions of the first and subvert the assumptions and practices of the second. As time has gone by, our comics have begun increasingly to focus their own frames both in a literal and metaphorical sense: to talk about their own production and the limits of what they can say as popular educational media. They also paint pictures of contexts in which they and other texts interact in meaningful and critical ways.

Books and Reading in South Africa

In South Africa much use is made of literacy statistics. Government officials, NGOs and the mass media frequently point to levels of illiteracy as high as 60 or 70 per cent (Robbins and Prinsloo, 1994). In 1994 many pundits of doom predicted that certain political parties would suffer because their supporters were illiterate. However, on election day — surely the most momentous literacy event in the history of South Africa — the greater majority of the adult population turned out to vote. The low percentage of spoilt papers can, in part, be attributed to successful voter education, but also suggests that many people who are labelled illiterate can and do engage with texts in their everyday lives. However, research does suggest that millions of South Africans, particularly people living in rural areas and squatter settlements, do not have access to and are not habitual readers of books and other forms of print media (Robbins and Ammon, 1995). Aside from the Bible, a hymn book or a clothing catalogue, few children from those communities grow up with books in their homes. Most will have their first experience of books when they go to school. Sadly, many of the textbooks that will form the basis of their formative reading experiences are dull and unattractive, inaccessible and unrelated to their lives; texts not to be interacted with nor enjoyed but to be copied, learned off-by-heart and recited.

The River of Our Dreams

The Storyteller Group began publishing its comic books as a response to this perceived lack of a reading culture. From the start we argued that the power of the story in promoting reading for pleasure and in consolidating literacy skills was being overlooked both within the formal schooling system and in adult literacy classes. When we began to look for funding we marketed comic story to funders, companies and NGOs as a resource that would promote and consolidate English literacy and second language skills. International funders bought into this vision and we received support to originate and print a comic as part of the International Year of Literacy, which, we hoped to show, could be used as a powerful educational tool in formal and informal classrooms while serving as a popular resource to promote reading for pleasure. This comic, called *The River of Our Dreams*, was published early in 1991 with a print run of 320 000 copies.

One of the challenges we faced when developing a comic story to promote reading was to find ways of drawing on the power of popular fiction while moving away from the 'lost in a book' image of reading and the nuances of solitariness and

Figure 12.1 A campfire scene in The River of Our Dreams

passive consumerism that such an image often evokes. We wanted to draw on the power of popular conventions, but also create a reading resource that could show and validate multiple literacy practices and relate literacy skills to real life and real needs. One of the themes of the story should be literacy itself, we decided, and the comic should refer to and even contain a range of other texts.

Briefly, *The River of Our Dreams* tells the story of a group of school children who attend a rather unorthodox inner-city school in Johannesburg — Stride Universal College. Their eccentric headmaster, Sidney Mabaso, organizes a fieldtrip to an 'idyllic' stretch of a river which he knew as a child. After a chaotic journey in an old dilapidated bus, the children arrive at the spot in Paradise Valley only to discover that it is severely polluted. The children stay at a nearby school where they find a beautiful unpolluted tributary. A teacher tells them that this river was cleaned up by local schoolchildren after an outdoor biology lesson. The children, with their newfound friends in the rural village, decide to form an action group to clean up the other river. The story ends with their return to Johannesburg leaving behind a community galvanized to carry out civic action. As the story unfolds, we show characters using, sharing, enjoying and forging friendships (see Figure 12.1) around a number of different written and oral 'texts': a comic, a novel, a booklet with pictures of water animals, a book of recorded urban legends, a praise poem and a letter which concludes the narrative.

The role of the water booklet in the story is to show a different example of textbook usage and to challenge the idea that reading materials, to be of value or to have an impact, need to be produced by outside experts and packaged between glossy covers (see Figure 12.2). It is through their use of the water booklet that the children, who are able to discover for themselves how devoid of life the polluted river has become, decide to form an action group. And the water booklet which they use had been created by other schoolchildren both in the story and in real life. With the support of a teachers' manual, a library pack, a literacy pack and an environmental pack the comics were used widely throughout the country, mostly by NGOs and in the formal schooling system to meet a number of needs. The distribution was most successful in the areas where the comic was mediated (Bahr and Rifkin, 1992). Today, five years later, there are still pockets of teachers and students throughout the country using *The River of Our Dreams*.

Figure 12.2 Using the water booklet in The River of Our Dreams

Responses from readers and educators confirmed that *The River of Our Dreams* is a very powerful tool for promoting reading and writing. In some instances we even received reports of children being inspired to carry out 'action' in their communities. Moreover, the water booklet and an accompanying water slide, published by the Natal Park's Board, have been used quite extensively by environmental groups. However, no indepth research was conducted to determine whether the comic shaped the general reader's thinking about texts and literacies. Copies given to libraries for use in library programs were simply given away without any mediation, and feedback from the comics' distribution through mass media was not very enlightening. But interviews with students suggest that the comic helped to shape their talking about reading in one fundamental way: they no longer insisted on making such a firm distinction between reading and having fun (Bahr and Rifkin, 1992).

Towards a Dialogic Approach to Popular Communication

The distribution of *The River of Our Dreams* took place in 1991, at a time when the Nationalist Government was beginning to dismantle the Apartheid State and negotiate with its newly unbanned rivals. This brought about a new urgency to communicate with the millions of people usually excluded by mainstream media and a new sensitivity to literacy and post-literacy needs. The success of Sharp Street inspired a wide range of companies and NGOs to consider comics as a medium of communication for adult readers. Since 1991, we have been commissioned to create a range of comics, often in a number of languages, to communicate with adults. There have been comic stories about electricity provision, negotiated local authority accords, retirement funds, unit trusts, political violence, the breakdown in schooling, AIDS, voter education and democracy — all contested and controversial areas.

As I have written elsewhere, 'easy readers' created for adults often simplify their content along with their language. Like school textbooks, many texts designed for easy reading, and not so easy reading, exclude the broader context of their production: the policy debates, the struggle for ownership and meaning that have raged around them. The texts become authoritative 'monologues' which homogenize conflicting voices (Esterhuysen, 1992). To avoid this, we have tried to fuse the spoken dialogue of the comic medium with the concept of dialogue as explored in the writings of Mikhail Bakhtin. Our comics set out to make accessible the broader context in which the authorial voice is part of an ongoing conversation where multiple voices are rejoining, interrupting, mimicking, contesting, agreeing and disagreeing.

Our dialogic approach has been successful to varying degrees. In one comic dealing with political violence, for instance, our characters are cast as a group of actors who have come together to create a play based on the communication brief that we, the Storyteller Group, had been given. In fictionalized form, we re-enact many of the discussions, arguments, challenges and frustrations experienced by the real-life team researching the issues explored in the comic. But it is mostly in our own work that we have been able to explore different ways to confront the authority with which texts are invested. Linked to this has been our continuing exploration of the tensions between using popular conventions and challenging the values they often represent. These concerns converge in our recent venture into the romance comic genre in a comic called *Heart to Heart*.

Heart to Heart

The comic, *Heart to Heart*, had its beginnings in 1991 when Patricia Watson, a student teacher from Wits University, elected to do her teaching practice in a rural school in Gazankulu. As part of her language teaching she introduced her students to *The River of Our Dreams*. The comic proved to be an overwhelming success in the classroom, and the students asked for a comic story that would explore the lives of rural youth like themselves. Patricia approached the Storyteller Group with the idea of developing a rural comic story, assisted by the students of Magwagwaza High School. She was commissioned to carry out further research and returned with a story outline, called 'Dream Love', which focused on teenage pregnancy and relationships between young men and women. In 1993 we held a workshop with a group of students from Magwagwaza, intending that the students should add flesh to the bare bones of the story. Although the students accepted the theme of love relationships, they made fundamental changes to the central character, Tintswalo. During the workshop, Tintswalo, originally conceived of as fun-loving and assertive, with interests and a voice of her own, became transformed into a passive, hardworking and compliant young woman. The group also simplified the conflicts, doubts and feelings between Tintswalo and her boyfriend, Magezi (Watson, 1994).

In the students' version of 'Dream Love' Tintswalo becomes pregnant and leaves school, willingly giving up her dream of being a social worker. The story ends with a conventional happy wedding although it is clear that Magezi will continue to womanize — a reality all too common in rural areas like Acornhoek. We were faced with a dilemma. The story was undoubtedly realistic and authentic, but it conflicted with our own values and the perceptions of ourselves as educators who wanted to challenge patriarchal gender stereotypes, not confirm them! On the

Figure 12.3   The love scene in 'Dream Love'

Figure 12.4   The same scene re-worked for 'True Love'

other hand to manipulate the students' voices and recast the story would have been dishonest. After much searching of soul (and searching for funds) we decided to take a draft of the story back to the students and to use it as the basis for further workshops. We were particularly interested to see how the girls, who had been very quiet in the first workshop, would respond to the character of Tintswalo now that she had been brought to life.

In the 1993 workshops, which included about half of the original participants, Trish made use of a number of drama-in-education techniques to access the different voices within the group and to encourage critical reflection. Some members of the group, mostly girls, decided to change the characterization of Tintswalo while other members, mostly boys, resisted this fiercely. Heated debates about the role of men and women in rural society ensued. We teased out the second story line to create another version of 'Dream Love' called 'True Love' and decided to publish them side by side in a comic book entitled *Heart to Heart*. The plot, the set of characters, and the situations are the same in the two stories, but the second Tintswalo has a stronger personality and responds differently to Magezi (see Figures 12.3 and 12.4). While story one is resolved in a marriage, the problems of Tintswalo are not

Figure 12.5   *Tintswalo on her wedding day in 'Dream Love'*

Figure 12.6   *The open ending of 'True Love'*

as easily resolved in story two and are left open for our readers to decide (see Figures 12.5 and 12.6). To present the two narratives as possible variations of the same story, without further commentary, might have been the post-modern thing to do, but would not have told the whole story. Both stories are shot through with the conflicting values, assumptions, experiences and cultural meanings that characterized our dialogue with the students and their dialogue amongst themselves. So we decided to document our responses, some of the students' debates, and the process through which the second story was created in a third comic story. To separate out

Figure 12.7   Storyteller writers and artists expressing their opinions

the two levels of reality, and to remind readers that our 'documentary' although about real people and events was still a construction, we had the artist draw ourselves and the students in a caricatured style (see Figure 12.7).

When *Heart to Heart* was published some educators dismissed it as being too intellectual, particularly as the comic's target audience are rural youth who are often described in deficit terms which go beyond simply describing their English language skills. Certainly the comic stories are rather fragmentary and the lack of space means that the reader barely has time to settle in to either of the two texts. Despite these qualities, however, the rural and urban youth who read the comic and took part in follow-up focus groups interacted enthusiastically with its complicated and open-ended form (Watson and Esterhuysen, 1994a). Many participants expressed an interest in developing the dialogue by making their own plays; one group has already begun to do so. The focus groups suggested that the comic succeeds in making students grapple with important issues. In the words of 16-year-old Queeneth Mathebula:

> The *Dream Love* is so nice! It's how I dream. But when I first read the comic I didn't finish the students' story, but after I read 'True Love' I was really confused. I went back and finished the students' story . . . Shoo, this book makes me to think.

Spider's Place

I shall conclude this chapter by describing a series of comic books which we are developing to complement a puppet television series called *Spider's Place*. Unlike *The River of Our Dreams* and *Heart to Heart*, the *Spider's Place* comics are specifically designed for the classroom, with each episode covering topics from the school syllabus (see Figure 12.8). In this series our challenge to classroom literacy practices lies at the heart of children's experience of authoritarian teaching and authoritative texts — the science lesson. The *Spider's Place* series consists of thirteen puppet videos which have been made for national broadcast. Each video has a corresponding comic book which can be used without the video and a student

Figure 12.8 Spider and her friends tracking down a thief in Acids and Bases

workbook illustrated by the comic characters which contain activities and exercises suitable for the standard 3 to 5 classroom. The comic book consists of two comic stories, *Spider's Place* and *Class T Spider's Place* which is adapted from the video. The stories show an urban, multi-racial group of children using problem-solving skills and science concepts in their everyday lives, usually to get out of tricky situations. The series draws on social constructivist research to explore and challenge children's conceptions of the world.

The second story, *Class T*, frames the *Spider's Place* story. *Class T* is told from the vantage point of a group of children in a primary school with overcrowding and few resources. School is boring until a new innovative teacher called Miss Lineo arrives with the TV and tries to prove that science can be exciting. The students soon learn to look forward to the screening of the puppet video which is the catalyst for becoming engrossed in a new topic and a whole new set of activities including trips out of the classroom to, for example, a scrapyard, a power station, or a fossil cave. *Class T* shows examples of a classroom where students interact with media, share ideas and carry out activities, even if this means making a noise. The comic also challenges the existing practice of forcing children to speak English in the science classroom. Many of the comics are multilingual and will be printed in clusters of three languages, one for each province, without translations being given (see Figure 12.9). We also use the comic format to sensitize children to the differences between everyday language and the discourse of science (Figure 12.10). Given the context of most South African schools, perhaps the most radical aspect of the *Class T* series is the way in which we depict the teachers and explore approaches to teaching and learning. Using gentle humour and a positive, albeit slightly eccentric, role model, we try to suggest that real learning is not the same as learning by rote. Miss Lineo's approach to teaching is contrasted with that of Miss Unisa (Yawn!) and Mr Dambuza. Mr Dambuza is a stern disciplinarian who does not like Miss Lineo's methods, but cannot fire her because she has succeeded with a difficult class (T stands for Trouble), where others have failed. He is nevertheless a constant background threat (Figure 12.11).

Figure 12.9   Negotiating a language plan in Plants

Figure 12.10   Class T play soccer and learn about science in Force

Figure 12.11   Different responses to Miss Lineo on her first day

Figure 12.12   Class T learning about paleontology in Acids and Bases

Can you answer Noni's question?
On a piece of paper, draw something that could apply enough force to the wall to make it fall down.

Figure 12.13   An extract from the workbook on Force

Unlike teachers who need to uphold their authority, Miss Lineo is not ashamed to admit that she doesn't know all the answers (Figure 12.12). And unlike other textbooks, our comics do not have all the answers either. Often characters ask questions which are never directly answered, but are picked up as workbook activities (Figure 12.13).

The *Spider's Place* multimedia package speaks directly to children in their own language and in the context of their world both in and outside the classroom. The comics are conservative by science education standards because they necessarily carry a lot of content demanded by the syllabus. But they are also potentially subversive in the way they try to encourage children to think and nurture expectations about the nature of learning and thinking in relation to the school.

Last year an implementation evaluation was carried out in a number of classrooms. Although the evaluation was very limited, one sobering pattern emerged.

Teachers seemed quite capable of slotting the material into a traditional curriculum and mode of teaching (Perold and Jansen, 1994). It was beyond the brief and scope of the evaluation to discover whether the material had any impact on pupils' perceptions of science and the classroom or inspired them to carry out activities outside the classroom, as seemed to happen during the testing of some of the comics in pencil form. As is the case with so many of our comic materials, the *Spider's Place* comics raise many questions about the possibilities and limitations of popular, potentially subversive print media. Hopefully, current indepth ethnographic studies will point to some of the answers and inspire us to find new ways to focus on the frames.

References

BAHR, M. and RIFKIN, C. (1992) *The River of Our Dreams: Interim Research Report*, Johannesburg: Storyteller Group.

BARTHES, R. (1974) *S/Z*, New York: Hill and Wang.

ESTERHUYSEN, P. (1991) *The River of our Dreams*, Johannesburg: Storyteller Group.

ESTERHUYSEN, P. (1992) *Towards a Dialogic Approach to Communication*, Storynet Newsletter, Johannesburg: Storyteller Group.

ESTERHUYSEN, P. (1994) *Spider's Place Vols 1–4*, Johannesburg: Handspring Trust.

PEROLD, H. and JANSEN, J. (1994) *How Do Teachers use Innovative Science Material? A Report on an Evaluation of Spiders Place*, Johannesburg: Handspring Trust for Puppetry in Education.

ROBBINS, S. and PRINSLOO, P. (1994) '"The fortune is in the sky! both black and white worship one god!": Representations of homogeneity and the assertion of difference in the 1994 South African elections.' Paper presented at the Fourth International Conference on Oral Tradition, Natal University.

ROBINS, S. and AMMON, C. (1995) 'Literacy and Cultural Contexts: A Study of Communicative Practices in Cukutown Squatter Settlement.' Unpublished paper. University of Cape Town: Department of Adult Education and Extra-mural Studies.

STREET, B. (1984) *Literacy in Theory and Practice*, Cambridge: Cambridge University Press.

WATSON, P. (1994) 'Comics and rural development', *Matlhasedi*, 13(3) pp. 28–31.

WATSON, P. and ESTERHUYSEN, P. (1994a) 'Does *Heart to Heart* work as an effective resource in sexuality education?.' Unpublished research report.

Watson, P. and Esterhuysen, P. (1994b) *Heart to Heart*, Johannesburg: Storyteller Group.

13   Book Learning: Literacy and Information

Margaret Meek

*Readers will be familiar with Margaret Meek's argument, set out elo-
quently and succinctly in* How Texts Teach What Readers Learn, *that we
learn our literacy practices, what the processes of reading are, from the
texts that we do our reading from. In this paper she turns her attention to
books of information used for topic work in primary schools, the subject
of a new study of reading to learn called* Book Learning. *Nowadays publishers compete with one another with glossy, massively illustrated books
in a highly lucrative educational market. Meek asks us how much we know
of the reading lessons these texts give their readers, and how children
know and understand the information in these texts. She asks us too to
reconsider fiction as a way of knowing 'facts', a theme visited in different
ways in several parts of this book. She uses the history of reading-to-learn
to illuminate our current understanding of the practices of reading information texts, texts which she sees are already imbued with the literacies of
the computer, and which she foresees, like Heath in the opening paper,
will be more computer driven in the future.*

The making of books for children to learn from is founded on a series of assumptions that are rarely tested or even scrutinized: that when readers read 'non-fiction'
they remember what they are told as 'facts'; that adult writers and illustrators not
only know *what* children are bound to learn but also how they are to do it; that
subject matter for primary school readers needs more pictures than texts so that the
books can be made more attractive; that non-fiction is important, serious and instructive, while narrative fiction is purely recreative. That is, information books are
to meet the demands of the curriculum and to supplement the knowledge teachers
lack. 'Book learning' has an ancient solid ring about it. The history of literacy
assumes this purposiveness (Clanchy, 1993). Nowadays, after their initial tussles
with written language in print, children's next step, commonly acknowledged as
progress, is to acquire and understand knowledge about the world written and
stored in books. Books exist and are organized for them to do that.

Public debates about which books are best for learning to read concentrate on
the first two years of schooling. The social convention is that boys are likely to pay
more attention to books of 'non-fiction'. Girls can read what they like as they are

'faster': the expectation is that they will read stories, although the evidence for this is less certain than it was. The distinction between the two kinds of text appears fixed and immutable, both in the National Curriculum Orders for English and elsewhere, as 'literature' and 'reading for information'. The latter includes IT-based reference materials and newspapers, encyclopaedias and dictionaries — that is, information as a 'quick fix' in inquiry or communication. The alphabetic principle, taught and learned at the first stage, is pressed into book use as an organizational device. The search for information is then divided between books and information technology, both assumed to be generally available. By distinguishing the contents page, index, chapter headings in books and the search systems of computers, children are expected to 'retrieve' information they are said to need for the purposes of learning. Those who determine these purposes are teachers, who also form the largest group of purchasers. Publishers consult teachers about the books they want. Primary school teachers ask for books on topics they are expected to teach but have little knowledge or experience of.

Since the eighteenth century it has been possible to distinguish 'printed works produced ostensibly to give children spontaneous pleasure, and not primarily to teach them, nor solely to make them good, nor to keep them *profitably* quiet' from 'all purely moral or didactic treatises, all reflective or adult-minded descriptions of child-life, and almost all alphabets, primers and spelling books' (Darton, 1932, p. 1). Nowadays, the division of books, in libraries as in lessons, into 'fiction' and 'non-fiction' is a storage convention not a content description. Over time, this separation has acquired other significations: that fiction is mostly narrative, therefore 'made up', [lies even], while non-fiction is factual, therefore true and important. Many adults and most middle school children assume these distinctions to be more stable than they are.

Before examining children's information books it is worth pausing to consider 'children's literature', a term which Peter Hollindale says 'asks for subtle and flexible definitions' (Hollindale, 1996 in press). In its long, rich English tradition, this is a body of important texts, important, that is, in the social history of childhood and literacy, and in the individual lives of those who read them and study them. There is also an oral tradition, which runs alongside: children's own sayings, riddles, games and other 'lore' (Opie, 1959). Over a lifetime, adults remember the books that made reading significant in childhood. Literary biographers pay special attention to early influences. Modern children recognize certain books as theirs and soon distinguish their preferred texts. Parents reading to their children discover in new picture books subtleties that change their view of reading for pleasure. Some have contributed significantly to detailed studies of the part this literature plays in early literacy (Scollon and Scollon, 1981; Crago, 1983; Wolf and Brice Heath, 1992; Fox, 1993). Despite its long established history, children's literature has only recently, over the last twenty-five years or so, been part of significant reading in school. For longer than that it has been underwritten by adult reviewing and criticism. It is now the subject of an increasing amount of research and academic interest (Rose, 1984; Hollindale, 1988; Lewis, 1990; Lesnik-Oberstein, 1994), but it is not regarded as integral to 'book learning'.

In contrast to books designed to give children pleasure, and to let them experience the literary possibilities of alternative worlds, the tradition of books in school is emphatically about learning. As textbooks, part of whose function is to define the subject to be learned, they have a long history. An edict of Henry VIII decreed that a book of Latin grammar, written in 1510 by Colet of St Paul's and extended by William Lily in 1527, was to be the only authorized text for use in 'grammar' schools. As *Lily's Grammar* it went through at least three hundred editions, having become *The Eton Latin Grammar* in 1758. State public schools, which inherited the utilitarianism of the nineteenth century, provided textbooks written in the same mode. For each subject I studied in secondary school in the late 1930s I had such a textbook. The solitary novel in my schoolbag was for English lessons. In many areas of educational learning, textbooks are still alive and well.

The distinctive 'topic book', my main concern in what follows, is designed to be as unlike a textbook as possible, although in recent years its didactic intent has been just as visible. Topic books arrived abundantly in schools in the wake of the Plowden Report (HMSO, 1967), which criticized rote learning in primary schools and proposed 'discovery' inquiry by children into the world around them. About the same time, a publishing revolution made it possible to produce attractive 'non-net' books, that is, they were not subject to the Net Book Agreement and could therefore be sold by educational suppliers at a discount to schools. The most conveniently teachable part of this new dispersed reading was 'looking up', so encyclopaedias and dictionaries for children, together with contents lists and 'resources' —pictures, posters, wall-charts and the like — became part of classrooms and school libraries, which were now extended to primary schools. For publishers the satisfactory aspect of these short books was the promise of continuous renewal. Out-of-date textbooks were expensive to recommission: information books, as recensions of longer works, less demanding to read and requiring less expertise in the writing, were easier and cheaper to produce. The book covers were attractive to both children and teachers. Children gratefully turned pages to look at pictures; teachers were sought out by publishers to say what they wanted the books to be about.

'Information books' is a convenient but inexact way of describing books for school learning. They present a slice of a 'topic of interest', a general introduction or a single instance. A series of six books might be *The Way We Used to Live*; single volumes of thirty-two pages, each presenting a period of social history — houses, food, transport and the like — in double-page spreads. The readers are to be 'attracted' to learning, hence the distinct appearance of the books on shelves. As for 'interest', it could mean that the reader already had some knowledge of the subject and wanted more information, or that the books would help him or her to become interested in it. Most information books designed for the learners' first experience of topic work are about beginnings, the naming of things in the world. Only exceptional volumes are reviewed at any length. Theoretical concerns with reading and learning scarcely appear in considerations of these texts; they are regarded as 'difficult' for readers to understand.

The current assumption is that, as they read topic books, children are to distinguish the discourse peculiar to the subject matter in its written form. That is, they take the first steps in learning to *write* about history, geography, science and technology in ways that identify learning. The teachers' book that accompanies a science series produced recently for beginners is emphatic that the children should be discouraged from using chronological narrative in their 'reports' of their investigations. Just how these things contribute to what Michael Clanchy calls 'a literate mentality' and to later 'knowing' is what puzzles me and impels the impressionistic speculation of the rest of this paper.

The history of words and pictures usually begins with *Orbis Pictus* (Comenius, 1659), although the history of comics is said to begin with Greek vases (Carpenter and Pritchard, 1984). Interest in early interpretations of 'the book of nature' has increased with studies of literacy (Olson, 1994). A thorough search might reveal other commentators besides Richart de Fournivel, a canon of Amiens cathedral in 1240, who designed a bestiary which became very popular. He explains in his preface that the learning about animals took place by means of 'painture' (pictures) and 'parole' (words read aloud). 'The visual presentation of a text was considered, at least by the learned, to be a part of its meaning, not limited to its themes or subjects but necessary to its proper reading, its ability-to-be significant and memorable' (Carruthers, 1990, p. 224). Through all my considerations of illustrated information texts, I have had Richart much in mind.

Memory, remembering, memorizing and recalling are part of all learning. They also link information books with the latest technologies designed for storage and 'retrieval'. Schools and classrooms are already part of the networkings and transmissions of the most that has ever been known and thought about. Much of the potential of this banked information may be beyond the grasp of individual school learners, but the control of the machines is not, and in time children in school will have their own accounts. Publishers of information books want a share in these technological futures, both in the new systems of printing and design and in the domain of interactive CD-ROM. One of the most acclaimed books of information for the young, *How Things Work*, a product of great imagination and drawing skill, demonstrates the principles of physics and mechanics by exposing the workings of machines in everyday use. It is a pleasure to read, skilfully adjusted to both adults and children, and a *tour de force* of book production. Now the text is available on CD-ROM, where not only are the workings visible but the machines move; they 'actually' work (Macaulay, 1990).

So what does reading to learn as part of literacy look like at this penultimate point in the millennium? How do new means of information retrieval relate to what schools still call 'study'? What constitutes a reading act when linear print is replaced by designs and diagrams? My view of the future is, like my sight, short. However, as a kind of personal penultimism after a lifetime of English teaching and concern about the relation of literature (in Dr Johnson's sense of the books one reads) to literacy, I sought, from many scores of books designed to capture children's interest in reading, a notion of what reading to learn might now mean. These are the merest prolegomena to the kinds of research that reading might need in the literacies of the future.

Information: A Cultural Construct

Information is what we pick up as we move about in the world. It becomes part of our thinking, or not, according to the links we make, to what we already remember and believe we know. No one who reads a newspaper or watches television needs a definition of information. For the purposes of thinking about information gleaned from books, I am apt to quote Gregory Bateson — repeatedly, I now realize: 'information is the difference that makes a difference' (Bateson, 1979).

Our current social world overwhelms us with information, so much so that I also repeat my conviction that part of being literate now is to know what we needn't read. I have difficulty with such notions as the 'retrieval' of information, as if it were an entity that could roll under a bed out of reach. The metaphor is apt, however, when we think of the fact that the information in a computer is hidden beyond sight: we need a mechanical operation to get it back and on to the screen. Books are more open: we see the works and the contents together. The convention that links a book to a reader is that the writer has to take responsibility for what appears on the page. At the word processor, I have no idea who says, 'Welcome to Macintosh'. Nevertheless, what links books and screens is the habit of making meaning from signs in a distinguishable context. Information is a cultural construct. Information texts are social acts.

Behind our social awareness of literacy is a new condition of ignorance. We cannot know everything. Children may gain the means of access to all knowledge, but they too will have to settle for much less. They will be lucky, and employable, if they develop a good understanding of operations for finding out, or a particular specialism or expertise which others want to make use of. But it looks as if new information-based literacies will divide the text-makers, who put on disks what is authorized as knowledge, from the teachers who let the machine do the teaching. Both are already higher in the employment and payment pecking-order than those who have no such skills. The literacy divisions created by information 'handling' may even be extended.

Information Texts and Literacy Myths

The reading of information books is often less straightforward for children whose early reading has been confined to one kind of introductory text than for those whose experience of books has been wider. When 7-year-olds experience difficulty with information books, it is certainly more closely linked to reading inexperience than to ignorance about the world. Observation shows that younger children will persevere in reading quite complex texts if they already know something about the topic and want to find out more about the subject that interests them. One source of my conviction is W.H. Auden's account of the imaginary world of his childhood, a lead mine, and the books he read about 'real' mines (Auden, 1970). I am persuaded that many children read 'fact' books to furnish their inner worlds. Yet, references to imagination are rare in books about the literacies of learning. The best pedagogic analysis of reading difficulty and demonstrations of how to overcome everyday stumbling blocks are in the articles by Raleigh and Moy about 'comprehension' (Raleigh and Moy, n.d.).

In the absence of directions about how to use books of information, children create their own myths: that they are expected to remember everything on a page after they have read it; or even that some people just know and never need to find out. They may insist that if something is in a book it must be true, a notion that needs more than one book to cure. Sometimes they actually suppress what they know from experience if they think it doesn't fit with the writer's view of things. At other times they are encouraged to discount the learning which has come from a story. When I was reading P D James' *Original Sin* I rejoiced to see how easily she slipped into her tale much of what she'd learned of the history of the Thames in such a way that the details stuck with the reader as part of the plot. This happens a great deal in books of stories, but is totally discounted by those who make a fuss about narrative in books of fact. By the time they are nine or ten, children understand that what they know, in the everyday sense, can be found in books in a different form. Thus they pore over books about 'the body' to see what they can learn about their insides. What they see are drawings of what look like gas cylinders linked by railway lines all marked with signposts, yet, although they cannot regard themselves through their skin, they are able to make some kind of meaningful sense of what they are looking at. Then they say that what they see is 'real', even though it is no one's body but a representation of a generalized example. When they begin to understand the nature of representations, children's learning changes. We have too few examples of how this comes about and the difference it makes.

The notion of books simply 'adding to' one's knowledge is quite inadequate. James Britton's metaphor, that understanding comes to pass like a photograph image emerging in a developing dish, is the memorable one here. Understanding is always an untidy business, no matter how orderly the setting out of the material in a book or on a screen, or how confident the reading. It is certainly possible to increase the efficiency of the learners' reading strategies, to teach certain short cuts. However, it is not the digging out of embedded information — the mere 'retrieval' — that counts as successful learning: what is important, and a much more complex matter, is how the new information affects the already known.

This leads to the vexed question of 'study skills'. Some specialist teachers instruct pupils to recognize different registers, genres and other distinctive types of writing in 'expository' texts (Littlefair, 1991; Neate, 1992). There is no doubt that directing learners' attention to the condition of the text they are reading makes understanding easier. But here I register my doubts about some of the remedies proposed for what are seen to be readers' difficulties, many of which come from too few encounters with continuous texts and too little direct help in reading them. Besides, what are often seen as readers' difficulties are writers' inadequacies in both style and substance.

The Textual Condition

Information books, as something to be read and regarded, are texts — that is, phenomenal events. The books' textual condition is one of perpetual change, of going out of date. This makes them unstable, a fact not generally recognized. 'Every text', says McGann, 'enters the world under determinate socio-historical conditions, and while these conditions may and should be variously defined and imagined, they establish the horizon within which the life history of different texts can play themselves out' (1991, p. 9). Information texts may or may not acknowledge the transience of their authority, but young readers who are just discovering book learning are apt to retain the information of the time when it became available unless subsequent learning modifies or changes it. (I still have to pause before I give the countries of Africa the names by which they are now known, so effective was my first geography teacher, and the textbook was new.)

Modern information books represent the state of the art in publishing for schools, and are where most of the money goes. The acknowledged leaders in this field at present are the publishers Dorling Kindersley. The directors claim to have 'brought information alive in such a compelling manner that it *rivals the excitement of film and television*'. They believe that they are changing current views of literacy. Since 1988, Dorling Kindersley have produced exploded photographs without shadows on brilliant white paper to 'show what things really look like'. They call their design technology 'Lexigraphics' which they say is a 'powerful and explicit medium which brings a new vitality to the still and silent printed page'. The editors' task is to ensure that each volume 'exploits the readers' innate curiosity . . . which makes us seek to learn and to understand'. Their philosopher is Marshall McLuhan: 'anyone who tries to make a distinction between education and entertainment doesn't know the first thing about either' (Dorling Kindersley, 1992, p. 3). *Eyewitness Guides*, the main series, are greatly admired and globally successful. Children like the books, find them easy to read and recognize them as interesting. The volumes impress by their range of subject matter, but when you see them all together in the publishers' own bookshop, the unity of design format conveys the notion that they are one topic in many volumes; in fact, 'the world on paper' (Olson, 1994).

In the style of television programmes, the writer is one amongst others in the list of credits. The designer of the pages has probably most say; the editor is often the leader of the team. Other aspects of the condition of a text include the editorial policy of the publisher, its bias in terms of race, gender issues and the degree of formality in the 'voice'. The information in some books is as impersonal as the words on a noticeboard. In others there is a degree of moral didacticism which is not immediately apparent; in the matter of the rainforests, whales and other endangered species, for example. The voices of some authorities exclude the readers' experience. Subject experts who want to engage the imagination of potential apprentices opt for more prose than pictures, but their books are rarely read by those who have the power and the money to choose books for school use and whose tastes are defined by the quality of the illustrations. The assumption about books for older readers is that the subject content should be written in a 'pre-disciplinary' form of the topic discourse, always in the third person. This is seen as part of pupils' learning to write 'academic prose' (Medway, 1980).

The textual condition of information books should be included in our concerns about how children learn to read and, especially, to write, not least because it is fairly clear that many publishers are now convinced that these books should aspire to the nature of television productions. A helpful structural analysis of information books comes from Christina Pappas (1986). She shows how, despite the variety of formats, many texts have a common pattern in the assemblage of 'obligatory and optional elements'. She is persuaded that children can be helped by having the common features of their information books pointed out to them. This might also let them see the same information presented in different ways, and to understand that no single text has universal authority.

Paradoxically, the very flexibility of the book is what current topic books best display. Meanwhile we have to investigate more imaginatively what many book producers, including artists and writers are apt to ignore: the relation between the word and the world is 'not a given, but a problem' (Scholes, 1985, p. 75). Where literacy is concerned it is *the* problem, in terms of its engagement with both.

Acts of Reading

Interested reading outside school is almost always an individual occupation, although whatever interests us usually finds its way into our conversations. Talking with others is what we do to make sense of our experience. *The Most Amazing Pop-up Science Book* opens to reveal, in working order, a telescope, record player with Edison's voice, camera obscura, sundial, compass, microscope and periscope 'in association with the Science Museum, London' (Young, 1994). This kind of exotic bookmaking is not entirely suitable for classroom use; better for individual exploring. But it would be difficult to imagine a reader who kept the workings a secret or who could manage to make the best of it all alone. Everyday talk promotes learning.

Here is a group of boys clustered round a copy of Stephen Biesty's *Incredible Cross-Sections*, a Dorling Kindersley best-seller. The pages show the intricacies of the inside of a submarine, a tank, an opera house, a modern telescope, an ocean liner, and a number of other complicated constructions, all in great detail. The readers stab the pages with their fingers, pointing to what they recognize, what they discover. To the bystander they seem to be arguing, but most of their utterances are wonderings of the 'how does it work?' kind. They persist until they sort out how to see the stars by the operations of the mirrors and agree that more written text would help them to interpret all the details.

Are they learning by reading, given that their activities seem neither organized nor sequential? I think so. The discussion makes the looking come to order. They help each other to contextualize what the pictures and the text convey. When the boys change to a book about football, something different happens. Again they stab the pages and talk loudly, scarcely listening to one another. This time they are not looking so intently; they assume they know what the book is telling them. Their excitement is a celebration of what they already know. They want to find the author's version of it to see if they are agreed, especially about the skill and worth of players (Medway, 1980). These are little more than superficial observations, but they suggest that reading, in contexts of social learning, needs better descriptions. This is certainly true of girls' interactions with topic books. Because they are not encouraged to extend their interest to subjects traditionally associated with boys, we have very little evidence about how girls read science texts, for example.

Teachers are interested in describing acts of reading in terms of how pupils make use of what they discover, but more case studies are needed. Concepts of print are emphasized in early learning, but these are different from the kind of reading children do without lessons when they engage with Raymond Brigg's *Father Christmas*, or the comics they know as theirs. Diagrams, maps and drawings are not read as sentences. Reading the media is, rightly, about the interpretation of content, but we still need to know something of where and how children's eyes light on moving images and where they go. In their *Eyewitness Guides* series, Dorling Kindersley have revoked linear reading and ordered up instead *spatial* reading. Newspapers also count on this kind of perception; space is what they sell. When they come to read information books with all their display features, children have learned enough about spatial reading from advertising to make them proficient in reading the scene. In relation to texts this has been called scanning and taught as a study skill.

The designs of information book pages invite young readers to engage also in *radial* reading. This is a kind of deliberate pausing to survey the composition of the textual condition and to draw other things into it. I have watched many groups of teachers investigating a collection of information books. The most common practice is not to begin reading at the beginning, but to hold the book in the right hand and use the thumb of the left hand to let the pages flip over, so that the textual encounter starts at the back. (This is observation, not criticism.) The paradigmatic instance of radial reading offered by McGann (1991) is when someone breaks off reading in order to look something up in another book, a word in a dictionary, say, then returns to the first text. The antithesis of radial reading is to be 'lost in a book', defying any interruption. These are matters of style and habit. Once considered, are they significant? I think so. To be literate is to read critically. We know that some communicators slant the meanings of their messages so that to read, say, a political text should always include a form of interrogation of it by the reader. No text is wholly innocent or neutral.

Now, if we go back to those who have analysed the texts of children's picture books in the context of children's literature (Lewis, 1990) we discover subtleties of design and the wonders of colour printing. Given the experiences children have of these things, designers who now make information books for them can count on a number of reading competences well beyond the singularity of linear print. Critics of picture books have ideas about what looking and seeing amounts to. But as this kind of examination is rarely given to information books by a critical community (there are, of course, appreciated singular exceptions), we assume that the environmental print and design that children encounter daily are the obvious forerunners of their understanding of pictures for learning. It would seem that, in the middle years of childhood, we could make some research forays into the nature of learning promoted by the texts that depend on some of these aspects of reading.

Different Starting Places

Children want to learn, and to learn to read is the opening of new ways of doing it. They find facts in fiction; think of all the boys who wanted to learn to sail as the result of reading *Swallows and Amazons*. That, after all, was what Arthur Ransome wanted to write about. We have to reconsider the fact-fiction divide and ask ourselves why some commentators are so persuaded that narrative is an inappropriate discourse for book learning. Part of the trouble with information books is that writers seem to try to stand in for the teacher. They ask the readers questions which are never answered. Some designers look no further than the production of pages as set pieces. The books are then assumed to promote the readers' own discovery. Texts which encourage further study are those that intrigue the learner with instances of experience which the readers can consider before they are overwhelmed with statements to remember. One of the salutary discoveries made by Margaret Mallett is that when children are shown pictures of squirrels, the one that interests them most shows a squirrel suffering from mange (Mallett, 1992).

In addition, very few books invite reflection-beyond-looking uninterrupted by the writer's determination to point things out, probably because the makers of the book are unwilling to admit that there is more to know, or that adults are also puzzled sometimes. Children need adults to accept the *proximal* nature of their finding out, but also to see things from that stance. We have agreed the insight of Vygotsky's (1978) notion of the 'zone of proximal development', but mostly from the side of the adult. From the learner's side the knowing is still in the making. I have found most satisfaction in books written by experts who have a clear sense of an intelligent curiosity on the part of young enthusiasts and who *write* for them in ways which dignify their curiosity. Michael Chinery's book on spiders was, for me, a reading experience I did not know was possible. But to discover this, readers have to agree to engage with a lengthy text, Latin words, a taste for learning something in depth — not simply scanned, and a commentary which includes wondering if Miss Muffett was a real person. She was. The material could easily be transferred to a screen, but the voice in the text would need to come too (Chinery, 1993). Thoughts of this kind are part of my pleasure in Walker Books' current series called *Read and Wonder*. These books break down the division between fiction and non-fiction. They extend the conventions of textual conditions so as to show how curiosity can be linked to finding out in a way more related to the *coming* to know of children's early learning, whether the text is prose, poetry or pictures, or, in this case, all three together. When they were reviewed in the *Times Educational Supplement* the reviewer insisted that young children could not learn from books like

Think of an Eel. Moreover, the books, as material objects are aesthetically satisfying in their diversity. But it's the wonder I want to start from, and to keep.

References

AUDEN, W.H. (1970) 'Freedom and necessity in poetry: My lead mine', in TISELIUS, A. and NILSSON, S. (eds) *The Place of Value in a World of Facts*, Nobel Symposium 14, Stockholm: Almqvist and Wiksell.

BATESON, G. (1979) *Mind and Nature: A Necessary Unity*, London: Wildwood House.

BIESTY, S. (1992) *Incredible Cross-Sections* (written by Richard Platt), London: Dorling Kindersley.

CARPENTER, H. and PRITCHARD, M. (1984) *The Oxford Companion to Children's Literature*, Oxford: Oxford University Press.

CARRUTHERS, M. (1990) *The Book of Memory: A Study of Memory in Medieval Culture*, Cambridge: Cambridge University Press.

CHINERY, M. (1993) *Spiders* (illustrated by Sophie Allington), London: Whittet.

CLANCHY, M. (1993) *From Memory to Written Record: England 1066–1307* (second edition), Oxford, Blackwell.

COMENIUS, J.A. (1659) *Orbis Sensualium Pictus* (third edition, introduction, by James Bowen), Sydney: Sydney University Press.

CRAGO, M.H. (1983) *Prelude to Literacy*, Carbondale: Southern Illinois Univ. Press.

DARTON, F.J.H. (1932) *Children's Books in England* (third edition edited by Brian Alderson, 1982), Cambridge: Cambridge University Press.

DORLING KINDERSLEY PUBLISHERS (1992) *Eyewitness: A Universal Language of Learning*, London: Publishers' Pamphlet.

FOX, C. (1993) *At the Very Edge of the Forest*, London: Cassell.

HMSO (1967) *Children in their Primary Schools* (the Plowden Report), London: HMSO.

HOLLINDALE, P. (1988) *Ideology and the Children's Book*, Stroud: The Thimble Press.

HOLLINDALE, P. (1996 in press) 'Drama' *The Encyclopedia of Children's Literature*, London: Routledge.

LEWIS, D. (1990) 'The constructedness of texts; Picture books and the metafictive', *Signal*, 62, May, pp. 131–46.

LESNIK-OBERSTEIN, K. (1994) *Children's Literature: Criticism and the Fictive Child*, Oxford: The Clarendon Press.

LITTLEFAIR, A. (1991) *Reading All Types of Writing*, Milton Keynes: Open University Press.

MACAULAY, D. (1990) *How Things Work*, London: Dorling Kindersley.

MALLETT, M. (1992) *Making Facts Matter: Reading Non-fiction 5–11*, London: Paul Chapman.

McGANN, J.J. (1991) *The Textual Condition*, New Jersey: Princeton University Press.

MEDWAY, P. (1980) *Finding a Language: Autonomy and Learning in School*, London: Readers' and Writers' Co-operative.

NEATE, B. (1992) *Finding out about Finding Out*, London: Hodder & Stoughton.

OLSON, D. (1994) *The World on Paper*, Cambridge: Cambridge University Press.

OPIE, I. and OPIE, P. (1959) *The Lore and Language of School Children*, Oxford: Oxford University Press.

PAPPAS, C. (1986) 'Explaining the global structure of children's information books.' Paper presented to the Annual Meeting of the National Reading Conference, Austin, Texas.

RALEIGH, M. and MOY, B. (n.d.) 'Comprehension — Bringing it back alive' in SIMONS, M. and PLACKETT, E. (eds) *The English Curriculum: Reading I Comprehension*, London: The English Centre.

ROSE, J. (1984) *The Case of Peter Pan, or The Impossibility of Children's Fiction*, London: Macmillan.

SCHOLES, R. (1985) *Textual Power: Literary Theory and the Teaching of English*, New Haven: Yale University Press.

SCOLLON, R. and SCOLLON, S. (1981) 'The literate two year old: The fictionalisation of self', in SCOLLON, R. and SCOLLON, S. (eds) *Narrative, Literacy, and Face in Inter-ethnic Communication*, Norwood, NJ, Ablex Publishing Corp. (from the series in O'FREEDLE, R. (ed.) *Advances in Discourse Processes*, Vol. VII.

VYGOTSKY, L.S. (1978) *Mind in Society*, MA: Harvard Educational Press.

WILLIAMS, R. (1983) *I*, Harmondsworth: Penguin Books.

WOLF, S.A. and BRICE HEATH, S. (1992) *The Braid of Literature: Children's Worlds of Reading*, Cambridge MA: Harvard University Press.

YOUNG, J. (1994) *The Most Amazing Pop-Up Science Book: A Three-Dimensional Exploration*, London: Watts.

Part IV: Questioning Dominant Canons and Practices

Introduction

So far, literature as imaginative fiction and poetry has not been central in most of the papers. We began with Heath's argument for the integratedness of the Arts and the Sciences in new projects of learning that break down the old subject divisions. Stories and poems are seen in several papers (Burton, Alan and Viv Kenyon, Esterhuysen) as literacies that have a place in mathematics and science where they have not traditionally belonged. Here, Carol Fox sees literature, either the classics or modern international/multicultural texts, as a canon of a special kind. Literature, she argues, embraces knowledge and non-fiction discourses (Meek, in this volume), but more importantly it exposes literacy practices themselves, particularly when it comes from outside the dominant or elite culture. In this sense it is a potentially subversive frame of knowledge.

Clay, in discussing canonical science, continues the multicultural themes of Part Four, arguing that not only has one frame of knowledge been traditionally valued, but that the exclusivity and value-free assumptions of modern science curricula threaten rights to democracy and citizenship. New sciences to ensure 'the survival of the planet' will need to re-evaluate and redeploy those hitherto silenced science practices of marginalized and non-dominant groups.

An account of the mathematics practices of a non-Western culture in the past, given by George Gheverghese Joseph, reverses the cultural canon of mathematics from West to East. Canonical mathematics, he reminds us, flourished in India and the East when the western tradition had barely begun. Gheverghese Joseph also returns us to the themes of Part One, for his rich account of the history of Indian mathematics reveals none of that artificial division between Art and Science critiqued by Heath in the opening paper of this book.

14 Dominant and Subversive Literacy Practices: The Case for Literature

Carol Fox

Very few teachers of English would want to end the reading of literature as part of the English curriculum. Among the many who value it are those who resist attempts to impose standard varieties upon speakers of non-standard forms and lists of canonical or classic texts. Such teachers of English, of whom Carol Fox counts herself one, nevertheless become uneasy when particular texts are described as elitist and irrelevant. In her paper she looks at the invented stories of five children who had been read to, before they started school, a great deal; the aspirations of a group of parents for their children's reading; the reading of a group of South African students, equivalent to those in Hewlett's paper, who had read little fiction and poetry in the language they required for their studies, English; and a group of her own undergraduates who were by no means members of the literacy club that is well versed in the classics. Her reflections on these four groups pick up several themes of this book. Her young children show that fiction is a vehicle for knowledge, and that children use stories as frames to think with, an idea which appears in the papers of Alan and Viv Kenyon, Meek and Nunes. The parents see stories and pleasure in them as fundamental to their children's learning — not just learning to read. The South African students feel deprived of an important way of experiencing something of other people's lives and cultures. The undergraduates find that the authors of the texts they read, whether canonical or post-colonial, mirror for them their own literacy processes. Literature she argues is a powerful form which is capable of subverting any attempts to make it the tool of authority.

In this article I shall refer to four groups of readers involved in my teaching and research in recent years. I shall argue that the notion of 'literacy practices' rather than that of 'literacy' is helpful in unravelling some of the contradictions implicit in being a teacher of reading/literacy/English in the context of competing models of what English is. Some of the issues I shall raise have had a good airing recently in the UK, in the struggle of English teachers against the writers of the National Curriculum[1] in which literacy is regarded as a unitary, single skill defined by what a reader can or cannot read: thus, for young readers literacy is assumed to emerge from the mastery of a set of phonic blends, progression through a structured skills programme, the acquisition of standard syntactic structures in speech and writing, and the experience of reading tried-and-tested 'classic' texts for children. English teachers have perceived that much would be at risk should this view of literacy prevail, not least the cultural and personal identities of large groups of children — those who do not speak standard English varieties at home, those whose first language is not English, and those whose reading matter does not include canonical texts. An irony of this unresolved struggle is that English teachers themselves do not quarrel with most of the major goals of their opponents, and have said so throughout.

Most English teachers aim to teach their pupils to read and write, to spell and punctuate, to be familiar with standard spoken and written varieties; and most English teachers try to introduce canonical texts, including Shakespeare, to their pupils. What has been at issue, and continues to be, is that the curriculum writers seek a monolithic, once-and-for-all literacy which it is the duty of school to provide, whereas many English teachers operate with notions of literacy practices that situate learners in a variety of historical, cultural, social, and linguistic contexts. While both groups want Shakespeare to be part of children's experience, they differ widely in their stance towards how the plays should be approached and for what purposes. Crudely put, the opposition is between 'knowledge' that can be tested, and experience that can include, develop, and extend the literacy practices of the cultures that children bring to school.

The literacy practices of the four groups interact with dominant literacies in different ways. But I shall use each case to argue that we need to go on reading literature with children and adults as part of a set of literacy practices that exposes and makes transparent the interplay of dominant and non-dominant languages, voices, and texts.

Pre-school Children

Five children aged 3½–5 were the subjects of a long-term piece of research I conducted throughout the 1980s. At the start of my study they were not independent readers and writers; they still faced the task of learning to read at school. They were English and white, one or both of their parents had received higher education, and in their early years they had had a very rich exposure to stories read aloud from books. Between them, in an informal setting at home and as part of their play, they recorded with their parents a total of 200 oral-monologue fantasy narratives. The aim of my study was to discover the effects of their early literacy practices on their oral storytelling before they learned to read and write.

The findings are well documented and can be briefly summarized. The children's experiences with books had influenced their vocabularies, the quality of their syntax, their ability to play with rhyme, rhythm, and prosody, and their awareness of such aspects of narrative discourse as point of view, chronology, and narrating. More importantly, they had developed a very strong sense of the metaphorical possibilities of the interplay between their own life stories and other stories, together with the ability to transform both real and fictional experience into new and original structures.

All five children learned to read and write very satisfactorily, though they did not always find that school literacy practices followed on from those at home. But more intellectually empowering than merely being 'ready for reading' was the fact that their early literacy practices had given them a clear sense of the power relationships between adults and children, indeed, between all the characters and groups of characters in their stories; and that, while acquiring the structures of written language and narrative, they had gained a critical, incipiently subversive, sense of the way experience can be represented.

The stories contained the beginnings of many non-narrative discourses, both academic and from the world out there — news broadcasts and weather forecasts, for example, together with early attempts at computation, experiments with numbers, descriptions of size, height, shape and so on, conceptions about the physical world, rainbows, birth and death, terrains and landscapes, ideas about the past in relation to the present and the future, and about values, moral problems, and the solutions to them.

My study has sometimes been regarded as justifying the prescription of similar early experience for groups of children who were not so apparently 'fortunate', and who were seen to be 'lacking' in literacy practices that would prepare them for literacy acquisition at school. However, the empowering, critical, and subversive aspects of the five children's story experience would also be available to children who came from a rich *oral* storytelling culture. This has been well documented by Heath (1983) in her study of Trackton, a black community whose children's language acquisition was mediated through stories and verbal play. The problem for these children was not that their early literacy practices were a poor preparation for school, but that their teachers had no knowledge of what they were, let alone how to build on them. In my visit to South Africa in 1994, I noted again and again how rich were the traditions of oral storytelling in the African cultures I encountered, their potentiality as major resources for literacy practices that would subvert the legacies of apartheid. Stories do not merely entertain us; they give us lessons in how they can be read, and what reading is. In the UK, while there is now some awareness of 'environmental print' as a classroom resource, the major literacy practices of many people are still left behind at the classroom door, in particular literacies related to TV, computer games, and comics/ newspapers/magazines.

If narratives, poems, rhymes, and other forms of verbal play, whether oral or written, can become early literacy practices that have metalinguistic and metacognitive outcomes for young readers across diverse cultures, then my storytelling study raises questions about their place in the other core literacies of the school curriculum. For example, Ahlberg's *The Jolly Postman* can be experienced as a simple story of a postman delivering letters, as a journey through a lot of other stories children may have heard or read, and as an exposure of a whole range of literacy practices/texts that surround *all* children, in their home lives. It brings before the reader literacy practices often marginalized by the school. Indeed, it could form the basis of a deconstruction of the power relationships implicit in each of the letters Ahlberg places in the envelopes on the pages of the book. Here is one of literature's great themes — reading itself. When Hamlet writes a speech for the players and advises them on the delivery of it, he is not merely giving tips to actors, but talking about the different literacy practices — interpretations — of audiences. He also suggests that a drama can 'catch the conscience of the King', that something transformative can happen as a result of seeing (or by implication, reading) a play. My children's invented stories carry within them a great variety of understandings, discourses and knowledge, and raise the question of the place of narrative and related imaginative forms in areas of the curriculum where they are commonly regarded as irrelevant.

Finally my young children's storytelling was perceived by them as play, with all the possibilities that play offered them to explore what was unsafe, forbidden, subversive, rude, dangerous, violent, and generally over-the-top. The spin-offs of that play for language, literacy, and thought described in my book suggest that listening to and telling stories are literacy practices ideally suited to preparing children for learning to read and write. It was striking, therefore, that none of the five children was given opportunities to invent oral stories in school, and that none of the texts offered to them for learning to read resembled those they had heard before school.

The Parents of Local Infant Pupils

In recent years there have been widespread moves towards parental involvement in children's literacy acquisition. This can mean, for example, visiting the homes of pre-school children in order to initiate a set of preparatory literacy practices, or inviting parents into the classroom to help with reading, or simply sending home children's reading books with a passage for the child and parents to share. Accounts of parent involvement usually show how reading improves as a result of parents knowing more about how reading is done at school. Seldom do they show teachers changing their practices as a result of what they have learned about literacy practices at home. Schools are most likely to adopt a policy of involving parents where a group of children is seen to be 'at risk' in acquiring literacy.

With thoughts of this sort in mind, I interviewed nineteen parents (mainly mothers) of infant children at a local primary school. The school is currently initiating parental involvement in the children's classroom reading, and I am trying to give some support by comparing the approaches of three local schools. The parents I spoke to attended two evening sessions set aside for consultations with the teachers about individual children's progress. As they waited to see the teachers, I invited them to chat with me about reading. My main concern was to ask them what they saw reading as for, why they wanted their children to learn it, and what literacy meant to them. I made it clear to them that I had no interest in identifying by name either them or their children, nor their children's teachers. The parents seemed eager to talk, and I made notes of what they said.

Nearly all the parents saw reading as something that would be transformative in their children's future, though this did not come over to me as a functional representation of what literacy is. They said things like:

reading is for their whole lives

they need it — it's the most important thing they do

to get on for their whole lives

so they can understand everything else they do

to learn

to get a start in life

for progress in school

In this view, education itself depended on learning to read, though most of the parents stressed that reading was also for pleasure:

for pleasure now — later for education

for younger children it's for stories, for older children it's for facts

their enjoyment is what they're reading for

One mother made a direct link between reading for pleasure and reading for knowledge:

if you like reading there's no end to learning

Two parents were more specific about what they expected reading to do cognitively:

reading broadens their imaginations

for opening up new worlds

One mother saw reading as connected with her child's future behaviour and social development. She started by saying that 'if you understand books you can see different ways people use the English language', and went on to explain that her child spoke well. She talked about TV programmes she had seen in which 9-year-olds swore and took drugs, and then talked of her own experience of being bullied at school. She ended by asserting that she did not want her daughter to be 'a Mum at 15'. For her, reading was directly connected to the avoidance of behaviour that would render her daughter a victim — early pregnancy or drug dependency. None of the parents saw reading as transformative in a narrow functional sense; nobody mentioned passing examinations, getting a good job, or joining a college or profession. Given that for some time now reading failure has been directly linked in the tabloid press and elsewhere to unemployability, I was surprised at how much more broadly transformative these parents saw the value of reading.

All the parents, even those who were at work and would have to make adjustments, responded positively to the invitation to come into the classroom regularly and help with their children's reading. It seemed to me that they needed no help in knowing the importance of literacy or in realizing its potential for empowering their children. What they wanted to know about, so that they could become effective partners with their children's teachers, was how it went in school.

I was surprised to find that the parents' views on how children learn to read were grounded in their own experience of helping their children at home, and expressed in terms of practical common sense. The crude and scandalized version of the 'phonics versus real books' debate in the popular press seems to have passed them by. One mother who was very enthusiastic about reading asserted that 'everybody knows you learn by putting sounds together', adding that teachers 'should not give children the word' but should 'make them try'. She talked at great length of her own enjoyment of novels, and her daughter's love of books. Another mother said she thought children learned to read by using memory at the beginning and then pointing to words: when her children come to recognize certain words, she encourages them to sound them out. A third mother suggested that children learn to read first by pictures, then by words, and it develops over time. She did not break words down in reading with her child, but thought you would need to for learning spelling. Another mother was very critical of a well-known reading scheme that one of her children had used at another school, on the ground that the words were too simple — 'and that is not what reading is all about'. She went on to say that the books 'had no storyline' and that 'children expect something and then get let down'. It seemed to me that what these working-class parents articulated about reading and learning to read opened up the possibility of a real, two-way relationship with their children's teachers.

All the parents professed to read with and to their children at home. They probably differed from the school's teachers and from the parents of the five children in my storytelling study in their knowledge of children's literature. They did not give me the names of any children's authors, other than Roald Dahl, who would be typically represented by the books in their children's classrooms. They spoke of fairy tales, particularly *Aladdin* and *Beauty And the Beast*, which their children had recently seen as Disney films. However, their insistence on *stories* as taken-for-granted and obvious first reading materials convinced me that there were few grounds for regarding their children as a group somehow less well prepared for future reading and writing. On the contrary, I felt that some teachers of literacy could learn a great deal about what reading is and how it is acquired from these parents.

Students at the University of the Witwatersrand, Johannesburg

The third group of readers contrast with the first two in that, although all are highly literate in more than one language, and all are successful in educational terms (having gained entry to one of South Africa's most prestigious universities), the literacies they have acquired do not include much experience of fiction.

The students were in their first year at university, studying a wide range of degree courses. My class of thirty-two men and women had acquired English as a second, third, or even fourth language. In their ESL (English as a Second Language) course, for which I was a visiting teacher, they were expected to develop their skills in English for academic purposes. The ability to receive and produce academic texts was seen as a set of crucial and empowering literacy practices that they need to acquire for the successful completion of a university course. Thus their one year ESL course was essentially a remedial supplement to their main degree study.

White students rarely or never appeared on ESL courses, a fact perceived and often resented by the students. As a virtually monolingual lecturer myself, I felt uncomfortable about assisting in a form of remediation for students whose linguistic competences far exceeded my own. And I should add that my colleagues at Wits, who ran the ESL course were only too aware of the problems, ironies, and even inherent racism of the deficit situation these students were defined as being in. Deficit was an inevitable result of apartheid: the students' backgrounds were often, though not always, underprivileged both educationally and economically, and their problems were compounded by the necessity to acquire English as the language of education in the new South Africa, a language towards which most felt a deep ambivalence. It proved to be impossible to exempt from the course even a student who held a first degree in science from a British university, since her performance in ESL tests showed that there was room for improvement. I was left wondering how well I myself would do on those tests.

I talked frequently to my students about books and reading, and increasingly felt that they were hindered by the fact that learning English had always been tied to educational and instructional purposes, and that it had never had a role in their personal, expressive, and imaginative uses of language. Many students openly declared that they 'hated' reading, and read only to fulfil the requirements of their courses. This attitude was reinforced by the enormous difficulties in obtaining books. Books are very expensive in South Africa, even for well-heeled academics, and only a handful of students owned more than five of any kind. Nobody owned more than ten. A random check revealed that thirty-two students had currently borrowed fifty-one books from the library, even though they were allowed four books each. Their difficulties with libraries ranged from never finding the books they wanted, to unfamiliarity with the library computer system and the risk of incurring fines for overdue books. Considerable hostility was expressed towards the library as an institution.

Although some students mentioned enjoying the odd set text studied for matriculation, reading fiction for pleasure and knowledge was an alien activity to most of them; something there was no time for and which would only divert from the urgent need to acquire the specific literacies required by the university syllabus. I recalled how easily the beginnings of school discourses had been incorporated into my five pre-school children's oral stories; but how it remains the case that educational disciplines tend to marginalize fiction as though it had nothing to do with higher forms of learning and knowledge.

A few students were aware of the narrowness of their reading diets, and felt the limitations of literacies that were so functionally based. Salmon was such a student. He wrote:

> We were politically minded and anything that did not have anything to do with politics was not of one's concern. We were living (and still are) in or among the society that was intolerable, we could not understand why should anyone disagree with us. Brutality and harassment was the order of the day . . . The moral of the statement above is that we are not concern or interested in knowing the feeling of other people and the diversity of the world we live in. There is a saying that goes, 'It is the nature of man to destroy anything he does not understand.' The point of fact is that most students at this college are concerned with one issue, that of passing, and not obtaining knowledge. That is why you find that they are concerned to read the books that have something to do with the course, no newspapers or fiction, or non-fiction material.

Despite its surface errors, this is a highly articulate statement of a real problem. Salmon operates with a clear distinction between what he calls 'knowledge' and passing examinations, and further perceives that there are literacies denied to him which might bring him closer to the knowledge he wants. His understanding that he has somehow missed out on experiencing the diversity of the world and the feelings of other people, relates to the views of the parents in the last section, that literacy was for 'broadening their imaginations' and 'opening new worlds'. There is a strong feeling here that literacies can be fundamentally transforming. I interpret what Salmon wrote as meaning that, in the process of political struggle, a full education had been sacrificed to a piecemeal one, restricted to passing the tests that acted as gatekeepers to the powerful communities in society. The price he has paid for the struggle is to be deprived of a literacy that would feed his imagination.

Those ESL students at Wits who were interested in more than narrowly functional reading matter did not see South African literature as somehow more relevant or meaningful to them, but told me they were interested in finding out about 'other people' through their reading. I should not have been surprised, therefore, by the actors' workshop production of *Julius Caesar* I witnessed one afternoon at a local (black) high school in Johannesburg. Shakespeare's text was strictly adhered to, and there were minimal costumes and no props, yet the pupils, unsupervised by their teachers, watched attentively for an entire afternoon. On reflection I saw this experience less as the imposition of an alien, colonial, and dominant literary on a colonized people, and more as a potentially liberating and 'world-opening' experience. In a fascinating article called *The Empire Writes Back*, Pico Iyer (1993) refers to the way in which, in post-colonial literatures in English, writers whose roots lie in colonized countries are able to take hold of the English literacy heritage and use it to reclaim the cultures that have been marginalized — 'to take the instrument of imperialism and turn it upon itself'. Looked at like this, a literacy that belongs to a dominant and culturally imperialist elite can become an instrument for exposing and subverting the literacy practices of that elite. For literature is a special case. *Macbeth* is a play that a government wishes to impose on the curriculum of every 14-year-old in England. It is also a play that has been performed impromptu in countless settings the world over as both a representation of, and an attack on, regimes of tyranny and oppression.

Undergraduate Students at the University of Brighton

The students I am writing about in this section are intending primary school teachers. They vary greatly in age and background, are largely white, and usually have no special examination qualifications in English. Adult literature is included in their English course in the belief that a powerful way for them to understand what it is to teach literacy is to experience, at their own level, texts that extend their knowledge and reading strategies while being pleasurable enough to reinforce the habit of voluntary reading.

Many (though not all) of these students come to us with fairly negative attitudes to reading. They often feel that somehow their reading was found wanting, that 'classic' texts are intimidating and 'not for us', and that reading for 'pleasure' is incompatible with working on examination set texts or with any kind of struggle for a text's meaning. Some are hooked on popular fiction — a literacy practice which is not frowned upon or discouraged, and which can sometimes be made good use of. Quite a few students perceive vaguely that they have missed out on literature, and they want some sort of transformation to result from their reading, one that will make them 'well read' or 'educated'.

By beginning the study of literature in a place accessible to all, through the study of fairy tales, myths, and legends, we find it possible to carve a pathway through to most other kinds of literature, from Shakespeare and poetry to 'postmodern' and feminist fiction, and texts from outside Britain. The emphasis is on making meanings by connectedness, looking at the processes of our own construction of meaning from print, always including children's books and discussing the way they relate to adult forms. We use media interviews and programmes about writers, as well as feature films and animated versions of stories, to help students find their way into texts. Having a wide range of texts to choose from, understanding that they are allowed to abandon texts that they perceive to be unmanagable, and being encouraged to respond freely to the books in their own reading journals, the students discover that by creating with others their own networks of meaning they rapidly enter literary worlds from which they felt excluded in the past.

Whether students are reading classic texts by George Eliot or Henry James, or modern works by Toni Morrison or J M Coetzee, they often experience the strangeness of a new and unfamiliar culture as a struggle to read and understand. Their efforts to make sense of unfamiliar chronologies, new forms of English, and cultural assumptions they have never before encountered focus their attention on the process of reading itself, one that is highly relevant to those who will teach reading to children. Initially, many students are reluctant to start one book before they have finished another, to borrow more than one book at a time, to skim or skip passages they find tedious, and to accept uncertainty at the beginning of a new work. In talking about these issues, it becomes clear that lying behind them are 'school' literacy practices, which suppressed the students' own initiatives and strategies. After suggesting that the students experiment with different ways of reading, I have found comments in their journals that imply that reading has become easier because now they are 'allowed' to read in a variety of ways. Such comments tell me that for many of them ways of reading have been construed as requiring legitimation by somebody else.

We also discover that reading itself, the conflicting voices of different literacies, the attempts of authors to give linguistic forms to experiences that have not been included in literature in the past, all these often become an author's subject or part of it. The students' own struggles very often mirror those of the characters they read about, so that the relationship between different literacies becomes exposed and transparent; and dominant literacies and the assumptions about power they carry with them are up for question and examination. George Eliot's novel *The Mill on the Floss*, for example, is read by many of my students as a feminist text: they regard Maggie Tulliver as the victim of male power structures both within her family and in society at large. Thus, these structures prevent Mr Tulliver from seeing that it is his daughter who has the aptitude and hunger for Latin and Greek, so that what is denied to her is thrown away on his son Tom. Maggie's growing literacy can bring her no material empowerment; indeed the risk that she may have to use that literacy in becoming a governess is regarded as a great misfortune and enormously disempowering.

Post-colonial texts pose questions of literacy in acute and demanding form. When students read Toni Morrison's *Beloved*, they often struggle with its non-chronological structure, the unfamiliar rhythms and cadences of the language, and the complexity of its rich metaphors. As they try to make sense of this 'difficult' text, they become aware of Morrison's need to forge a written language for what was not recorded by those who were its victims — slavery. They see the meaningful irony of Morrison's taking highly wrought poetic or 'literary' language, the instrument of dominant literacy in the past, and turning it back upon itself so that it can represent the unrecorded experience of the powerless. In Richard Wright's autobiography *Black Boy*, Richard's whole journey from South to North, from victim to master of his own life, is expressed in terms of his struggle for reading and writing. Although it was stories regarded as dangerous in his Bible culture that he found liberating, nevertheless it is the Bible literacy of his roots that gives his prose its own colour and feeling. Richard's journey towards the literacies of power has its inception in the experience of hearing *Bluebeard* read aloud.

In Graham Swift's *Waterland*, students see several literacies set alongside one another. Tom Crick's narrative of his own life is interwoven with the discourse of the 'O'level history curriculum. In education the personal narrative has no status and Tom is sacked. Students can be daunted by the different languages of *Waterland*,

and initially puzzled by the appearance of technical passages on land drainage or the life history of the eel; yet they come to understand how these discourses are part of the metaphorical structure of the novel, and that we make knowledge and the literacies which carry it meaningful in terms of our own histories and languages.

Waterland raises many questions about the relationship between personal narratives, fiction, and the literacies of academic education, questions that are also raised by my five pre-school children's oral stories. The parents from the local primary school seemed very aware that learning literacy for knowledge alone would be insufficiently transformative for their children: they wanted their children to *like* reading, to love books. Salmon, the South African student, saw that just in terms of education, his political struggle had been for something much bigger than merely the academic literacy needed for his degree course.

Far from being the dominant literacy practice that the writers of the National Curriculum for English aspired to, literature is capable of subverting all attempts to make it the instrument of a powerful group. Literature is the most powerful means of seeing and understanding many ways of reading, many literacy practices.

Note

1   Several versions of the National Curriculum for English have been produced since 1989. Each has attempted, either through lists of 'exemplary' books, or through named set texts on which pupils are to be formally tested, to impose literature as a 'cultural heritage' on schools and pupils.

References

AHLBERG, J. and A. (1986) *The Jolly Postman*, London: Heinemann.

FOX, C. (1989) 'Children thinking through story', *English in Education*, 23(2), NATE.

FOX, C. (1993) *At the Very Edge of the Forest*, Cassell: London.

FOX, C. (1995) 'The person behind the mask: Student teachers' readings of multicultural literature' in GOODY, J. (ed.) *Opening New Worlds*, Sheffield: NATE.

HANNON, P. (1995) *Literacy, Home and School*, London: Falmer Press.

HEATH, S.B. (1983) *Ways with Words*, Cambridge: Cambridge University Press.

IYER, P. (1993) *The Emprire Writes Back* in Bua (South Africa, 1994) Copyright Time Inc.

MEEK, M. (1988) *How Texts Teach What Teachers Learn*, Stroud: Symbol Press.

MORRISON, T. (1987) *Beloved*, London: Chatto and Windus.

STREET, B. (1992) *Cross, Cultural Perspectives on Literacy* in DOMBEY, H. and ROBINSON, M. (eds) *Literacy for the 21st Century*, University of Brighton: Literacy Centre.

SWIFT, G. (1983) *Waterland*, London: Heinemann.

WRIGHT, R. (1946) *Black Boy* (1970 edition), London: Jonathon Cape.

15   Scientific Literacy: Whose Science? Whose Literacy?

John Clay

John Clay critiques the dominant Eurocentric models of scientific literacy that have been adopted for school science courses internationally. He argues that the dominant view of science in the West, and therefore of school science, is erroneous in claiming it to be objective, culture-free and value-free; and that it thereby disenfranchises learners who are disaffected by the social and ethical implications of many scientific applications. Clay is arguing for more inclusive forms of scientific literacy which accept that there cannot be a single, universal, ahistorical, and acultural science.

Introduction

In this paper I intend to examine how far the literature relating to scientific literacy converges in its meaning and understanding of the term. Science educationalists in Britain and elsewhere have attempted to identify the abilities that characterize a person who is 'scientifically literate', but it would appear that all the studies undertaken tend towards a normative view of scientific literacy that is highly Eurocentric. The dominant discourse about scientific literacy disregards forms of scientific literacy that are essentially functional, which operate in groups bound by a common set of values and/or occupations. Traditional forms of knowledge — utilized by such groups as members of families in a travelling circus, or nomadic people, which enable them to adapt to and shape their environment in a methodical way that is grounded in practice—are not considered as forms of scientific and technological literacy. In this paper I intend to show that the models of scientific literacy intended for schools are in conflict not only with the functional scientific literacies mentioned above but also with the concerns of many young people. This paper attempts to offer alternative frameworks in defining scientific literacy, in order to equip future citizens in playing an active part in improving the quality and diversity of all forms of life on this planet.

Models of Scientific Literacy Operating in Britain and Elsewhere

The English and Welsh Model

The National Curriculum Council (NCC) for England and Wales has statutory responsibility for the curriculum in all maintained schools. The NCC's model of scientific literacy consists of two types of understanding, namely, conceptual and procedural. It defines *conceptual understanding* as scientific knowledge drawn together into a series of overarching ideas or concepts (listed and described in Attainment Targets (ATs) 2–4 and in accompanying programmes of study). *Procedural understanding* (Attainment Target 1) is portrayed as an overall strategy for the discipline, in which a strictly defined set of scientific skills in combination with the concepts listed in ATs 2–4 make up the taught discipline. These four ATs are intended to encapsulate both the process and product which together form the totality of science for the compulsory years of schooling. It states that this package of experiences and understandings would promote scientific literacy in children/pupils[1] and equip them to find answers to problems set in everyday and scientific contexts (NCC, 1993).

There is in reality a yawning gap between rhetoric and practice. For example, the NCC in maintaining support for a model of the curriculum that separates science from technology cannot hope to address adequately the potentialities or the consequences of that technology arising directly from the applications of science. This model of scientific literacy portrays science, as a way of 'knowing' and 'doing', in very narrow terms, and would appear to be promoting science education for preparing future citizens merely as consumers and global tourists. It is because this model of scientific literacy takes no account of the values dimension. This contrasts sharply with the model of scientific literacy proposed by the American Association for the Advancement of Science (AAAS).

An American Model[2]

In 1993, the AAAS outlined in its publication *Project 2061: Science for All Americans*, a vision of school science. In an accompanying volume, *Benchmarks for Scientific Literacy*, it offered a model of scientific literacy which acknowledges that the study of science is more than ensuring narrow utilitarian outcomes. The report maintains that science, as a way of knowing, should be made explicit in the curriculum, and should include three distinct strands; (a) the scientific world view; (b) scientific inquiry, and; (c) the scientific enterprise. Project 2061 promotes a cross-curricular approach — whereby science, mathematics, and technology are closely linked and interwoven to form a broadly based science curriculum. The report devotes a considerable amount of attention to the way the three disciplines are interdependent.

The International Model

Scientific and technological literacy for all are seen as important goals world-wide. In 1993, UNESCO and the International Council of Associations for Science Education (ICASE) launched a global initiative, Project 2000+, which set out to mobilize governments and non-governmental bodies in every country to initiate programmes for the development of scientific and technological literacy for all. The rationale for Project 2000+ was based on the declaration of the World Conference on Education for All (1990) calling for the basic learning needs of every person to be met. These needs included literacy and basic knowledge to enable human beings to participate fully in improving the quality of their lives, and to make informed decisions through a process of lifelong learning. The problems facing societies across the world were seen as issues of population, health, nutrition, environment, and sustainable development at local, national and international levels. The way to deal with these problems was viewed as a matter of increasing the scientific and technological literacy 'on the part of the populace for both understanding and the decision-making involved to stimulate the necessary action' (Holbrook, 1994, p. 10). Regrettably, Holbrook cites the criteria developed by the National Science Teachers Association of America (NSTA) for defining a scientific and technologically literate person as a model for adoption internationally. The list includes seventeen attributes of which only two deal explicitly with the social, political and ethical dimensions related to science, and furthermore makes the assumption that the world we inhabit exists solely for the benefit of humans.

The three models of scientific literacy summarized are based on the premise that the 'scientific method' is universal, objective, and unproblematic. Despite some differences in terms of emphases and approaches all three models continue to promote a vision of a scientifically literate person that would appear to be acultural, Western, Eurocentric, and human-centred. This dominant view of scientific literacy has been exported to many different nations and cultures. Ogawa (1989) has expressed strong reservations about this form of neo-colonialism whilst acknowledging the powerful contribution that Western science has made to our modern civilization. However:

> ... this dominance raises important questions. I am concerned that most non-Westerners face the prospect of losing their identity during the modernization process. Here, I must come back to the question of what the objectives of 'science' as a school subject should be. I think that every culture has its own expectations of this school subject, just as it has it own science ... we cannot simply associate a set of general or universal goals with this kind of subject ... the goals need to be examined and defined by each particular society and tailored by that society to fit its own needs. (p. 19)

The adoption of any one model of scientific and technological literacy, without a critical interrogation of its epistemological basis and the consequences of its applications, is to indulge in a form of 'naive consciousness' (Freire, 1972).

Epistemology of Science

There now exists a wealth of research and scholarship that questions the dominant epistemology of science, not only because of its claim to objectivity and neutrality but also for its intrinsic Eurocentrism. A group of Indian scientists have attacked 'modern science' for its violence against our planet and all its living inhabitants. In *Science, Hegemony and Violence: A Requiem for Modernity* (Nandy, 1988), they offer several powerful critiques of science, and question the cultural heritage of 'modern science'.

The version of scientific progress that has been accepted unquestioningly as the history of science arbitrarily begins with Francis Bacon (seventeenth century). Thus, the British Broadcasting Corporation through its World Service broadcast a major series called *They Made Our World* in twenty-six episodes which dealt with scientists, engineers, inventors and other thinkers considered to have shaped the world we live in. Reiss characterizes the breadth of the producer's criteria for selection:

> Of the 28 people listed, none is a woman and none comes from outside Western Europe and the USA ... who a great scientist is partly depends on one's point of view. There are no absolute or universal criteria by which scientific excellence can infallibly be judged. (1993, p. 19)

The overall thrust of Reiss' argument is that powerful and influential organizations such as the BBC are guilty not only of sins of omission but also of perpetuating false myths. School science textbooks acknowledge to varying degrees the contribution that French, German and other European males have made to science, but they scarcely mention the organized and systematic science that has been practised in the Arab, Persian, Indian and Chinese worlds. The scientific culture that is transmitted is wholly Eurocentric and said to begin with the Renaissance or Age of Enlightenment. The centuries preceding have often been lumped together as the 'Dark Ages'. The kingdom of Zimbabwe in Africa, the Aztec and Maya cultures of the Americas and the advanced societies of the Near, Middle and Far East were simply not considered as possessing scientific cultures of their own or even as contributing to present day scientific understandings.

The contributions made by women scientists are slowly being admitted to the cultural heritage but this is little more than tokenistic. The most powerful and persuasive critiques of 'modern science' have come from feminists. There is a plurality of feminist perspectives and these have opened up spaces for alternative visions. In her collection of essays, *Reflections on Gender and Science*, Keller writes:

> Feminism ... encourages the use of expertise that has traditionally belonged to women — not simply as a women's perspective but as a critical instrument for examining the roots of those dichotomies (subjectivity vs objectivity; feeling vs reason) that isolate this perspective and deny its

legitimacy. It seeks to enlarge our understanding of the history, philosophy, and sociology of science through the inclusion not only of women
and their actual experiences but also of those domains of human experience that have been relegated to women: namely, the personal, the emotional, and the sexual. (1985, p. 9)

Vandana Shiva (1988), an Indian physicist and environmentalist, targets specifically the Western claims to a monopoly of knowledge that is consequent upon
a reductionist science. She argues that this has resulted in:

. . . fourfold violence — violence against the subject of knowledge, the
object of knowledge, the beneficiary of knowledge, and against knowledge
itself . . . [stating] violence is inflicted on the subject socially through the
sharp divide between the expert and the non-expert — a divide which
converts the vast majority of non-experts into non-knowers even in those
areas of life in which the responsibility of practice and action rests with
them. But even the expert is not spared: fragmentation of knowledge
converts the expert into a non-knower in fields of knowledge other than
his or her specialization . . . The object of knowledge is violated when
modern science, in a mindless effort to transform nature without a thought
for the consequences, destroys the innate integrity of nature and thereby
robs it of its regenerative capacity. The multidimensional ecological crisis
all over the world is an eloquent testimony to the violence that reductionist
science perpetrates on nature. (p. 233)

Despite these onslaughts against the positivist traditions of reductionist science, the
school science curricula remain impervious to these criticisms.

Science in Schools

The dominant version of science and how this affects what and how science is
taught and learnt within the education system has been extensively critiqued by
Cawthorn and Rowell (1978) and Reiss (1993). Science as objective and value-free
knowledge has become an established orthodoxy. It is questionable whether the aim
of science for all is compatible with the aim of science for future scientists. For
example, the National Curriculum in England and Wales makes the study of
science compulsory from the ages 5–16. This apparently 'equal entitlement' is in
practice far from equal because at the age of 14, students are guided to pursue one
of three options. Those who are considered able study the three sciences, biology,
chemistry, and physics as specialist subjects; whilst the vast majority are prepared
for the 'balanced science' route. This route leads to two outcomes; in the first of
these the full curriculum content as laid down by statute is studied leading to a
double award at 16; the second route is for those who are seen as incapable of
studying the full statutory curriculum, and the reduced programme only merits a

single award at 16. In practice, the three differentiated routes lead to outcomes that limit the choice of further study in the sciences.

The case for a broad and balanced approach to science from 5–16 has been vigorously argued for by a broad constituency of the scientific community which includes the Royal Society and the world's largest professional body of science teachers, the Association for Science Education. Although this consensus has existed throughout the past twenty years, it has not been realized in practice. The fact that the three levels of difficulty which effectively predict different scientific futures for the students involved in them have persisted exposes the weakness in the scientific literacy that is proposed for everybody. The three differentiated routes are not merely an implicit acknowledgment that the proposed scientific literacy for all is a sham but are themselves subject to the very cultural and gender factors I referred to earlier in the paper. Students' choices of route would be further complicated by other factors in the social context such as developing puberty, the biases of science teachers themselves, and the way society still constructs a science career as difficult, abstract, and male.

Alternative Scientific Literacies

Science taught in English and Welsh schools has undergone many changes since the introduction of the National Curriculum in 1989. Along with English and mathematics, science is a core subject from the age of 5–16, but will this new-found status as an essential subject automatically create the desired scientifically literate society of the future? Chapman, in a provocative paper, argued:

> Whether the educational priorities of what, for most young people, will be a post-industrial society really require such an emphasis on science as exists in the National Curriculum is, to put it at its mildest, debatable. (1991, p. 258)

He underlined the dubious nature of the claims made for compulsory science education. I readily concur with the sentiments that he expresses but disagree with his analysis that:

> The survival of the planet, and the reduction of the obscene disparities of wealth both between and within nations, which characterize today's world and its economic system, are issues demanding education in economics, politics and sociology not science and technology. (*op cit.*, p. 271)

The problem is that the dominant discourses in economics, politics and sociology are themselves grounded in the positivist principles that have successfully excluded all alternatives. As Nandy (1988) has argued, the culture of modern science is incompatible with democratic governance since it undermines the democratic rights of citizens by turning them into the subjects of modern science and technology. He maintains that:

> In India at least, the culture of modern science has built an inverse rela-
> tionship with the culture of open politics and has begun to produce new
> forms of secrecy, centralization, disinformation and authoritarian organ-
> izational structures. (p. 10)

The physicist Fritjof Capra (1983) has criticized Marxist as well as non-Marxist
economic models and theories as being deeply rooted in the Cartesian paradigm,
pursuing uninterrupted, indiscriminate and undifferentiated growth, and therefore
inappropriate to deal with the problems we will increasingly face in the next century. He maintains that:

> It is a reflection of linear thinking; of the erroneous belief that if some-
> thing is good for the individual or group, then more of the same will
> necessarily be better. (p. 224)

In its very structure our view of the world is so deeply imbued with the dominant
science method that to encompass the multiplicity of other equally valid views held
in societies beyond our own, we need to encompass different scientific literacies.
We need scientific literacies that are more inclusive and yet do not inhibit the
education of future scientists, capable of asking fundamental questions that will
continue to require tentative answers. What I am arguing for is not a reordering of
the current science curriculum but a fresh look at what forms of in-school and out-
of-school science we are likely to require in the next century (see Jenkins, this
volume). Science in the future will need to be more democratic and accountable to
society at large and take account of the social and cultural consequences of its
applications.

A group of student teachers who were halfway through a four year degree
programme wrote an essay entitled; 'Present your view of what constitutes scientific literacy: What would the understanding and capabilities of a scientifically
literate young person be?' Of the forty-two essays submitted, only ten seriously
questioned the dominant discourse of scientific literacy. The attempts made by the
rest could be broadly grouped as tending wholly or substantially towards the view
as caricatured by Reiss (1993). The data collected from this exercise requires deeper
analysis and interpretation and could provide further insights into the way our
teaching programme in science education is constructed. Nevertheless, a tentative
conclusion that I wish to draw from this exercise is that, despite our attempts as a
team of science educators to provide a reflective and critical approach, the dominant
models of scientific literacy remain hegemonic.

Science and Citizenship

Education for citizenship requires emphases that take us beyond narrow national-
isms fostered to maintain inequalities, both locally and globally. Citizenship education in its myriad forms have historically concentrated on civics and political

structures (T.H. Marshall, 1994). A more recent notion of *social citizenship* has been developing in all the countries in the European Community including the United Kingdom as part of the post-World War II settlement. This is in contrast to the United States of America where historically the emphasis has been on the citizen in relation to constitutional rights. Despite their different emphases, all three kinds of citizenship education have employed scientific procedures, practices and expertise in defining or interpreting rights and responsibilities within the overall civil, political and social framework. However, over the past two decades demands for *environmental citizenship* are becoming more urgent and are in a piecemeal way being adopted, albeit reluctantly, by the political establishment. This new concep-tion of citizenship has partly emerged as a result of modern scientific and techno-logical developments and their side-effects. This example suggests that we should be vitally concerned with new scientific literacies beginning in schools, and to this end the distinguished physicist Albert Baez has commented that:

> To speak about what ought to happen demands making value judgements and choosing objectives so let me describe what I think is the long-term aim of science education. I believe that science and technology, and hence science education, should help mankind [sic] improve the quality of life on this planet. By life I mean all living things, plants and animals, and par-ticularly people; men and women in all walks of life and in all parts of the world, developed and developing. (1993, pp. 282–3)

It is interesting to note that the author wrote about these issues as long ago as 1980, and that although he argues for a model of science education to promote greater equality of humankind, his proposals would still be considered far too anthropocent-ric by environmentalists who would advocate forms of science that recognized the interrelatedness of the whole natural world. It is worth noting that the science curriculum for elementary education in Japan makes an explicit reference to nur-turing a rich desire to love nature through systematic study (Ogawa, 1993). Ogawa maintains that the elementary school science in Japan is rooted in the indigenous culture and has remained 'Japanized' as a result. In Japan, elementary school sci-ence has been a feature of the education system since 1891. In Britain, on the other hand, formal science in the primary curriculum has been of more recent import. In the past the emphasis was on the much derided nature study. Since 1989, statutory primary science in schools has increasingly come to resemble a cut-down version of secondary science, with all its attendant shortcomings. The National Curric-ulum's model of scientific literacy has in practice taken us further away from the interrelatedness of the Japanese model.

Conclusion

A scientifically literate citizen of the twenty-first century will require new sets of skills that are transferable and not located within any one school subject. A multidisciplinary approach to knowledge construction would provide a starting point. The existence of subject hierarchies, and furthermore, the content within those subjects that constitutes 'valid knowledge', is itself circumscribed by patriarchy and its dominant cultural values. In an open society where we are all considered to be learners, we will need to acquire the complex skills necessary to perceive ways in which knowledge is constructed and ordered. We will then be able to analyse whether this knowledge contributes towards the legitimation of inequalities and oppressions. We need to question the value of a school curriculum that is based on the assumption that the ways of knowing can be compartmentalized into five, seven or ten subjects and within that framework, that some subjects are intrinsically 'superior' to others. The social purposes of education need to regain primacy of purpose, and scientific literacies should contribute to that end. It will not be an easy task because what is proposed is not merely a reorientation but a reconstruction of science education.

In conclusion, the following extract from Paulo Friere's writing powerfully expresses the arguments I have tentatively put forward towards alternative visions of scientific literacy.

> Those who use cultural action as a strategy for maintaining their domination over the people have no choice but to indoctrinate the people in a mythified version of reality. In doing so, the Right subordinates science and technology to its own ideology, using them to disseminate information and prescriptions in an effort to adjust the people to the reality which the 'communications' media define as proper. By contrast, for those who undertake cultural action for freedom, science is the indispensable instrument for denouncing the myths created by the Right, and philosophy is the matrix of the proclamation of a new reality. Science and philosophy together provide the principles of action for 'conscientization'. Cultural action for freedom is always a utopian enterprise. That is why it needs philosophy, without which, instead of denouncing reality and announcing its future, it would fall into the 'mystification of ideological knowledge. (Siraj-Blatchford, 1995, p. 1)

Notes

1   The term 'children' is used in the Key Stages 1 and 2 document intended for the primary phase of schooling, but 'pupil' is used for Key Stages 3 and 4, the secondary phase.
2   The use of the term American to describe what is in essence a USA model typifies the arrogance of the AAAS in presuming to speak for the rest of North America, let alone the whole continent of South America.

References

AMERICAN ASSOCIATION FOR THE ADVANCEMENT OF SCIENCE (1989) *Project 2061: Science for All Americans*, New York: Oxford University Press.

AMERICAN ASSOCIATION FOR THE ADVANCEMENT OF SCIENCE (1993) *Benchmarks for Scientific Literacy*, New York: Oxford University Press.

BAEZ, A.V. (1993) 'Curiosity, creativity, competence and compassion — Guidelines for science education in the year 2000', in WHITELEGG, E., THOMAS, J. and TRESMAN, S. (eds) *Challenges and Opportunities for Science Education*, London: Paul Chapman Publishing.

CAPRA, F. (1983) *The Turning Point: Science, Society and the Rising Culture*, London: Flamingo.

CAWTHORN, E.R. and ROWELL, J.A. (1978) 'Epistemology and science education', *Studies in Science Education*, 5, pp. 31–59.

CHAPMAN, B. (1991) 'The overselling of science education in the eighties', in WHITELEGG, E., THOMAS, J. and TRESMAN, S. (eds) (1993) *Challenges and Opportunities for Science Education*, London: Paul Chapman Publishing, p. 258.

CLAY, J.A. 'The disciplines of science and technology in the school curriculum and their contribution towards democratic education in a multicultural society', in GILL, K. (ed.) *New Visions of the Post-Industrial Society*, London: Springer-Verlag.

CLISP (1984) *Children's Learning in Science Project*, Leeds University: Centre for Studies in Science and Mathematics Education.

DES (1985) *Science 5–16: A Statement of Policy*, London: HMSO.

DES (1987) *National Curriculum: Task Group on Assessment and Testing*, London: HMSO.

DfE (1995) *Science in the National Curriculum*, London: HMSO.

FREIRE, P. (1970) *Cultural Action for Freedom*, Harmondsworth, Middlesex: Penguin Education.

FREIRE, P. (1972) *Pedagogy of the Oppressed*, Harmondsworth, Middlesex: Penguin Education.

FREIRE, P. (1976) *Education: The Practice of Freedom*, London: Writers and Readers Publishing Cooperative.

HOLBROOK, J. (1994) 'Scientific and technological literacy for all — The role of educators', *Science Education International*, 5(3), September.

KELLER, E.F. (1985) *Reflections on Gender and Science*, New Haven, CT: Yale University Press.

MARSHALL, T.H. (1994) 'Citizenship and social class' quoted by FRASER, N. and GORDON, L. in STEENBERGER, VAN B. (ed.) *The Condition of Citizenship*, London: Sage.

NANDY, A. (ed.) (1988) *Science, Hegemony and Violence: A Requiem for Modernity*, Oxford: Oxford University Press.

NATIONAL CURRICULUM COUNCIL (1993) *Teaching Science in Key Stages 3 and 4*, York: NCC.

OGAWA, M. (1989) 'Beyond the tacit framework of "science" and "science education" among science educators', in WHITELEGG, E., THOMAS, J. and TRESMAN, S. (eds) (1993) *Challenges and Opportunities for Science Education*, London: Paul Chapman Publishing.

REISS, M.J. (1993) *Science Education for a Pluralist Society*, Buckingham: Open University Press.

RICHARDSON, R. (1990) *Daring to be a Teacher*, Stoke-on-Trent: Trentham Books.

SIRAJ-BLATCHFORD, J. (1995) *Praxis Makes Perfect: Critical Educational Research for Social Justice*, Ticknall, Derbyshire: Education Now Books.

SHIVA, V. (1988) 'Reductionist science as epistemological violence', in NANDY, A. (ed.) *Science, Hegemony and Violence: A Requiem for Modernity*, Oxford: Oxford University Press.

STEENBERGER, VAN B. (ed.) (1994) *The Condition of Citizenship*, London: Sage.

UNESCO (1993) *International Forum on Scientific and Technological Literacy for All: Final Report*, Paris: UNESCO.

16   Calculating People — Origins of Numeracy in India and the West

George Gheverghese Joseph

At the symposium George Gheverghese Joseph welcomed the opportunity to share ideas from colleagues outside mathematics. He said; '[he] had not understood everything, yet has found it very challenging to be part of a group from very different backgrounds trying to find links'. Perhaps in his concern with his lack of understanding he was echoing part of the two culture debate of C P Snow. Yet he was also concerned with the exclusive ideological and political nature of numeracy that left some groups outside mathematics. He pointed out the fuzzy nature of the term numeracy, *its use to describe counting or quantitative techniques in economics and sought to reflect on these problems by comparing European and Indian mathematical traditions.*

His study of these then enables us to see how cultural differences affect our perceptions of the uses of numeracy and illuminate different attitudes to numeracy and the acquisition of numeracy practices. His description of the development of numerical notation in India and its links with letters of the alphabet reflected in the character of mathematical literature and reasoning in India points up the close relationship between literacy and numeracy. This development of numeracy was driven by intellectual and recreational activities and not by commercial needs. Europe in contrast was very late in embracing and using numbers, developing an anti-numerical position due to social and cultural pressures. The development of a written mathematical notation here was also much later than in India. Yet as the social and economic needs of Europe changed so did their uses of mathematics and, through colonialism, Europe imposed a world-wide dominance of Western mathematics and the submersion and, ultimately, the loss of indigenous numeracy practices and attitudes. Gheverghese Joseph's paper links to Heath's opening contribution and his use of historical evidence links in to the paper by Meek. We close with this paper because it unites so many of our central ideas such as numeracies and language, the arts and sciences, cultural pluralism, ideology and power.

In all activities, worldly or spiritual, **ganita** [calculation] is of the essence. In the art of love, in the performance of music, in dancing and drama, in the art of cooking, in the practice of medicine and architecture, in poetic composition, in [formulating] the rules of logic and grammar, in these and many other pursuits, **ganita** has an important place. In relation to the movement of the sun and other heavenly bodies, concerning eclipses and conjunction of planets, in finding out the **triprasna** [direction, position and time] of the moon — indeed in all these [**ganita**] is required. The number, the diameter and perimeter of islands, oceans and mountains, of the inhabitants who reside there, the lengths of their lives, their eight attributes, all these are worked out through **ganita** . . . (from the Preface to *Ganita Sara Samgraha* of Mahavira, fl. AD 850)

Introduction

The word 'numeracy' as a recent addition to the English language, is not yet weathered to smoothness through frequent use. The Oxford Dictionary definition is lean: 'ability with or knowledge of numbers'. The word, intended to parallel 'literacy', was coined in the late 1950s. C P Snow had articulated a concern that the humanities and the sciences were diverging into two cultures consisting of innumerate artists and illiterate scientists. He argued that 'illiterate' did not mean 'unable to read' nor did 'innumerate' mean 'unable to add', but the terms referred to a degree of deficiency that hindered communication between the two groups.

The 'two culture' debate is instructive in defining 'numeracy'. It cautions us against searching for a threshold, which, when crossed, would transform an innumerate society into a numerate one and makes us wary of searching for a bundle of hierarchical skills that would constitute numeracy.

A historical and cross-cultural perspective on numeracy is useful for various reasons. It shows how cultural differences affect one's perception of the *uses* of numeracy. It helps us to examine the acquisition of numeracy skills. It illuminates different attitudes to numeracy. It could also reveal the existence of historical cultures with a noticeable predilection for numbers and a positive delight in calculation.[1]

The Indian Numerical Tradition

Fascination with large numbers has been an abiding characteristic of Indian civilization.[2] In *Rumayana*, the great Hindu epic of about two thousand five hundred years old, there is a description of two armies facing each other. The one led by Ravanna contained:

$$10^{12} + 10^5 + 36(10^4) \text{ men.}$$

Facing them was the rival army of Rama who commanded:

$$10^{10} + 10^{14} + 10^{20} + 10^{24} + 10^{30} + 10^{34} + 10^{40} + 10^{44} + 10^{52} + 10^{57} + 10^{62} + 5 \text{ men!}$$

What is interesting is that so long ago, there were names for powers of ten up to 62.[3] This practice of reckoning in 'tens' and the growing facility with large numbers eventually led to one of India's greatest contributions to mathematics — our number system.

The early recognition of such large numbers led to the adoption of a series of names for successive powers of ten. The importance of these number names in the evolution of the decimal place-value notation cannot be exaggerated.[4] The word-numeral system was the logical outcome of proceeding by multiples of ten. Thus, in an early word-numeral system dating back over two thousand five hundred years ago, 60799 is denoted by the Sanskrit words: **sastim** (60), **sahsara** (thousand), **sapta** (seven), **satani** (hundred), **navatim** (nine ten times), and **nava** (nine).[5]

To understand the persistence of word-numerals in Indian mathematics, it is necessary to recognize the importance of the oral mode of preserving and disseminating knowledge. An important characteristic of early written texts in India was the '**sutra**' style which presented information cryptically, leaving out details to be filled in by teachers and commentators. The **sutras** were short pithy sentences, usually in verse as a mnemonic aid.

As a replacement for the older word-numeral system, a new system known as **bhuta-samkhya** was devised to help versification. Numbers were indicated by well-known objects or ideas commonly associated with the numbers. Thus, *zero* was represented by **sunya** (void) or **ambara akasa** ('heavenly space' probably meaning ether) or . . . ; *one* by **rupa** (moon) or **bhumi** (earth) or . . . ; *two* by **netra** (eyes) or **paksha** (waxing and waning of the moon) or . . . ; *three* by **kala** (time: past, present and future) or **loka** (heaven, earth and hell) or . . . ; and so on. With multiple words available for each number, the choice of a term would be dictated by literary considerations. This form of notation continued for many years in both secular and religious writings because it was both mnemonic and aesthetic.

There were two major problems with the **bhuta-samkhya** system. First, to decode the words for their numerical values required familiarity with the philosophical and religious texts from which the correspondences were established, and was thus 'exclusionist'. Second, at times the same word stood for two or more different numbers, as some writers had their own preferences. For example, **paksa** has been used for 2 as well as 15, **dik** for 8 and 10 as well as 4.

A third system of numerical notation originated in the work of the astronomer-mathematician of India, Aryabhata (b. AD 476). In his **Aryabhatiya** there is an alphabetic scheme for representing numerals, based on distinguishing between classified (**varga**) and unclassified (**avarga**) consonants and vowels. The **vargas** fall into five phonetic groups: **ka-varga** (guttural), **ca-varga** (palatal), **ta-varga** (lingual), **ta-varga** (dental), and **pa-varga** (labial). Each group has five letters associated with it, where the letters run from k to m in the Sanskrit alphabet, representing numbers from one to twenty-five. There are seven **avargas** consisting of semi-vowels and sibilants representing numerical values 30, 40, 50, 60, 70, 80, 90. An eighth **avarga** is used to extend the number to the next place value. The ten vowels denote successive integral powers of 10 from 100 onwards.

This form of representation has the advantage of brevity and clarity but is limited in the formations of words that are pronounceable and meaningful, both requirements for easy memorization. For example, the representation of the number of revolutions of the moon in a **yuga** (57 753 336) is the unpronounceable and meaningless word 'cayagiyinusuchlr'!

From a refinement of Aryabhata's system of notation emerged the **katapayadi** system, popularised around the seventh century AD. Here, every number in the decimal place-value system can be represented by words, each letter of the word representing a digit. The Sanskrit letters k (क) to jh (झ) indicate one to nine, and so does t (ट) to dh (ध); p (प) to m (म) stand for one to five and y (य) to h (ह) for one to eight. A vowel not preceded by a consonant stands for zero but vowels following consonants have no special value. In the case of conjunct consonants, only the last consonant has a numerical value. Number-words are conventionally read from right to left so that the letter denoting the 'units' is given first and so on.

This system helped recall since memorable words can be made up using different chronograms. For example, if such a system is applied to English, the letter b, c, d, f, g, h, j, k, l, m would represent the numbers zero to nine. So would n, p, q, r, s, t, v, w, x, y. The last letter, z, denotes zero. The vowels, a, e, i, o, u are helpful in forming meaningful words but have no numerical values associated with them. Thus the word 'Madras' represents 9234 and 'love' is 86, reading our usual way from left to right.

The close relationship between literacy and numeracy implied by such varied systems of numerical notation, may be rooted in the emergence of Sanskrit from other Indo-European languages. A long tradition of oral communication had impressed itself on the nature and transmission of knowledge in Indian culture. As Sanskrit became a written language, three kinds of scientific Sanskrit developed: grammatical, logical and mathematical Sanskrit.

The potential for scientific use of the language was greatly enhanced by Panini's formulation of its grammar, about two thousand six hundred years ago. In a book entitled *Astadhyaya*, Panini offered what must be the first attempt at a structural analysis of a language. From just six thousand **sutras** (or rules expressed as aphorisms), he built virtually the whole structure of the Sanskrit language whose general 'shape' hardly changed for the next two thousand years and inspired the scientific study of prosody leading to combinatorics (Alsdorf, 1991).

Mathematics grew out of philosophy in ancient Greece but it evolved from linguistic development in India. The geometry of Euclid's *Elements* starts with definitions, axioms and postulates and then develops an imposing structure of closely interlinked theorems, each logically coherent and complete. Similarly, Panini began his study of Sanskrit by taking about seventeen hundred basic building blocks — vowels, consonants, nouns, pronouns and verbs, and so on — and grouped them into classes. With these roots and some appropriate suffixes and prefixes, he constructed compound words by a process parallel to the way in which a function in modern mathematics is specified. Consequently, the facility of the language came to the reflected in the character of mathematical literature and reasoning in India. It may even be argued that the algebraic character of ancient Indian mathematics is a by-product of the well-established tradition of representing numbers by words.

Yet *mathematical* Sanskrit remained the least artificial of the three kinds of scientific Sanskrit mentioned earlier, with the greatest artificiality found in the development of *grammatical* Sanskrit by Panini and Patanjali, followed five hundred years later by the *logical* Sanskrit of **Nyaya** that culminated a thousand years later in **Navya-Nyaya**. This has some important implications for a comparative study of the historical development of Indian and Western mathematics which can only be touched upon here. As Staal argues, the differences between the two traditions may help to solve an important puzzle:

> We have seen that India experienced at an early date a scientific revolution in the human sciences. Artificial expressions for ritual relationships and an artificial language for Sanskrit grammar were constructed. Indian linguistics attained a measure of universality after more than two millennia when Sanskrit scholars made it accessible and the outside world began to assimilate it. In the meantime, other Indian scientists adopted opposite strategies: logicians enveloped their discipline in heavily nominalized Sanskrit and mathematicians developed artificial notations outside Sanskrit which did not develop into a language. Some time later, European scientists began to construct artificial mathematical languages for use in the natural sciences, but they began to replace natural languages. From that nucleus exploded the scientific revolution which became universal. (1995, p. 112)

The Spread of Numeracy in India

A search for the social origins of numeracy must consider the everyday practices that make numerals and operations on them familiar to ordinary people. Indian mathematics education for all may have been set by a Jaina text, called **Sthananga Sutra** dating back to about 300 BC (Rajagopal, 1991). Of that the first two topics out of ten, **parikarma** (number representation and the four fundamental operations of arithmetic) and **vyavahara** (arithmetic problems, including the 'rule of three'), came to be referred to as **patiganita** (etymology: 'sand-calculation').

An important part of **patiganita** was number representation. Tradition, among the Nambudri Brahmins of Kerala, required that a male child soon after his initiation ceremony and a basic course on reading and writing Malayalam be introduced to a simplified system of word-numerals (**aksarsamkhya**) based on Aryabhata's system discussed earlier. With the help of **aksarsamkhya**, the student would memorize and recite simple rules of arithmetic, and remember a set of numerical formulae for astrological calculations. Only after this system of number representation was understood was the student introduced to the written numerals.

There are early British descriptions of indigenous village schools, such as those reported in Bengal and Bihar by William Adam in 1838 (Dharampal, 1983). There were four stages of elementary schooling. The first seldom exceeded ten days, during which time the young child was taught 'to form letters of the alphabet on the ground with a small stick or slip of bamboo', or on a sand-board. The second stage, from two and a half to four years, involved pupils learning to read from, and write on, palm leaves. The pupil was expected to memorize 'the Cowrie Table, the Numeration Table as far as 100, the Katha Table and the Ser Table', tables of weights and measures. To help them with this enormous task, different systems of word-numerals were taught. The third stage, of two to three years, was spent on improving literacy skills practised on plantain leaf as well as completing the basic course on **patiganita**. In the last stage, of up to two years, pupils read religious and other texts both at school and at home, had training in commercial and agricultural accounts, and composed letters and petitions. A few would continue their education in higher institutions where Sanskrit was the language of instruction and the teachers and students were predominantly Brahmins.

Apart from numeracy skills, **patiganita** consisted of all the mathematics needed for daily living. The **'vyavaharaganita'** included problems involving calculation of volumes of grains and heaps, estimating amounts in piles of bricks and timber, construction of roads and building, the calculation of the time of the day, interest and capital calculations, barter and exchange, and recreational problems. In modern terminology, this is practical mathematics, which includes commercial mathematics.

The European Numerical Tradition

The story of the rise of numeracy in the West has been well told by Cohen (1982), Murray (1986, pp. 141–80) and Swetz (1987). About four hundred years after Gerbert of Aurillac (later Pope Sylvester II) wrote a pamphlet on reckoning, and about two hundred years after Leonardo Fibonacci's influential **Liber Abaci** (1202) which introduced the Indo-Arabic numerals in a systematic fashion into Europe, 'there emerged [among] a significant proportion of society that familiarity with numbers which was a precondition of Renaissance mathematics' (Murray, 1986, p. 162).

At first this emergence of 'the arithmetical mentality' had less to do with the introduction of these new numerals, and more with the understanding of the place-value representation of numbers on the abacus. We have two indicators of earlier European attitudes to numbers. The first was the absence of numbers from books before the thirteenth century. Technical books describing such activities as painting and illuminating, carpentry, and architecture contained quantities such as 'a bit more' or 'a medium-sized piece'. Where measures were mentioned, they consisted of examples like 'forty fingernails' or 'twenty thumb-tips'. Dates of births and deaths and of other important events were notably absent from the *Lives of Saints* printed in many parts of Europe.

The second indicator of the 'pre-arithmetical mentality' of Europe was the absence of a proper understanding of numerical magnitudes. Numbers such as 'hundred' reportedly uttered by Germans in the sixth century AD, or 'thirty thousand', or 'hundred thousand', found in twelfth-century texts, denoted large magnitudes rather than actual values. Twelfth- and thirteenth-century contemporary records give the size of the English army at the Battle of Bannockburn varying between 100,000 and 300 000 men, which is over twenty times the highest found in other records (Murray, 1986, p. 180). This reminds one of the fantastic estimates of the army on both sides found in the Hindu epic, *Ramayana*, quoted earlier. But there were two major differences. In the Indian case, the large numbers were indicative of a battle fought not between men but gods. Also, the numbers mentioned, being part of a well-constructed system of word-numerals, were easily comprehended by those who listened to the epic of that time. Neither of these factors apply in the British case.

A possible explanation for this European shyness of numbers and scorn for numerical precision may be the strong antipathy to numbers existing in the intellectual climate of the time. Cicero's view of mathematical arts as an example of 'vicious' study was frequently quoted by medieval scholars. However, a strange ambivalence towards numeracy prevailed, with Church Fathers encouraging calculation for purposes of interpreting the numbers in the Bible and for reconciling the Roman solar and the Jewish lunar calendars. Simultaneously, however, they discouraged numeracy, as illustrated by the abbot, Stephen of Obazine, who in 1130 dissuaded his subordinates from stock-taking of provisions in his monastery at a time of famine, lest it should be regarded as distrusting God.

Another aspect of this anti-numerical strand in medieval Europe is pertinent: the dearth of institutions teaching practical arithmetic. While, by the end of the thirteenth century, arithmetic was a minor discipline in a few European universities, the teaching was often theoretical and lacked practical applications. A profession known as reckoning masters together with reckoning schools originated in Italy. These schools, for the 12–16-year-old sons of the middle classes were important in spreading the knowledge of Indo-Arabic numerals and the associated arithmetic. (For further details see Swetz, 1987, pp. 18–24.) From their ranks came notable Italian mathematicians, including Pacioli (1445–1514), Tartaglia (*ca.* 1500–1557) and Cardano (1501–1576). It was Pacioli who first broke away from the tradition of writing an arithmetic for a particular section of the community and addressed instead a wider public. His *Summa de Arithmetica, Geometria et Proportionalitia* (Venice, 1494) was an encyclopaedia that contained the mathematical knowledge of his time.

The period between Leonardo Fibonacci and Geronimo Cardona is important in the spread of the Indo-Arabic numerals in Western Europe, when Europe was learning and absorbing knowledge about these numerals, their use in commercial problems, and in algebra. Europe was also re-learning the knowledge that had been developed by Hellenic civilization, inherited from the Egyptian and the Mesopotamian civilizations. The Arab contribution to this learning process in Europe was immense. By recalculating planetary positions and lunar tables appropriate for the latitudes of their principal cities, the Arabs had adapted astronomical methods. All this required trigonometry and geometry and extensive arithmetic calculations. The Arabs had acquired and then transmitted that knowledge principally from the Indians. They were also the agents through whom Hellenic manuscripts were transmitted to Europe. The stage was set for the emergence of modern mathematics in Europe.

In studying the emergence of modern mathematics in Europe insufficient attention has been paid to the development of an artificial language of mathematics.

The first European mathematician of note to recognize its importance was Leibniz (1647–1716), who sought a universal language which would serve as an ideal vehicle for communication in philosophy and science. He regarded the progress made in mathematics as primarily due to the construction and development of special notations as part of an artificial language, and his contributions to new notations outstrip those of any other mathematician (Cajori, 1929, pp. 180–96). On the shoulders of the giants of the seventeenth century, notably Galileo, Kepler, Newton, Leibniz and a few others, was built the impressive structure of modern mathematics, created with the development of the highly flexible but artificial language of mathematics.

Conclusion

In the last twenty-five years there has been a growing interest in the origins of practical mathematics in Western culture. It has been recognized that practical mathematics is part of the social milieu from which interest in science grew, and that the nurturing of interests in matters scientific was encouraged by the numeracy of the public. Both the 'algorism' books in Latin and practical mathematics books in the vernacular played important roles in creating a numerate public, the former mainly in the education of the Churchmen and the latter in reaching a wider audience. These developments were part of a commercial revolution that occurred in Western Europe. In India, the situation was different.

The level of numeracy in traditional Indian society was high, partly because of the manner in which 'numeracy' was acquired and passed on, and partly because there were no institutional, religious or philosophical inhibitions to the acquisition and practice of numeracy.[6] Yet the absence of a commercial revolution in India meant that the social milieu which nurtured interest in science in Europe was missing. In particular, no artificial language evolved and while notations were fun and intellectually distracting, they did little to advance science which ultimately stagnated. And practical mathematics, the handmaiden of numeracy, continued to remain at the same level for about a thousand years, eventually to be submerged by the rise of Western mathematics. Even the remnants of indigenous numeracy that exist in subterranean occupations, such as astrology and traditional architecture, may soon become a historical memory.

Notes

1   The basic thrust of this paper grew out of three disparate strands: the strong 'maths-phobia' exhibited by many social science students faced with a compulsory course in quantitative methods, the reading of Vikram Seth's *Suitable Boy* (1993), and my childhood experience in South India. Seth's book contains some wonderful vignettes showing how problems and puzzles from elementary mathematics have formed part of ordinary day-to-day conversation in India, whether on the breakfast table or during an earlier era, what Vatsyayna, the author of *Kamasutra*, recommended as a prelude to love-making.

2 Not only large numbers but very small ones as well. Operations with zero attracted the interest of both Bhaskaracharya (b. 1114) and Srinivas Ramanujan. In an elementary class that Ramanujan attended, the teacher was demonstrating the concept of division. He pointed out that if three bananas were shared out equally between three children, each child would get one banana. And, the share would be one banana if four bananas were shared among four children, five bananas among five children and so on. And when the teacher generalized this idea of sharing out x bananas among x boys, Ramanujan asked whether, if x equalled zero, would each child then get one banana!

3 In Vikram Seth's *Suitable Boy* (p. 191) appears a conversation between Bhaskar, a mathematically precocious boy of 10, and Haresh, who are discussing the naming of powers of ten. They noted that some powers of ten have special names, like thousands, but some do not, like 10^4, 10^8, or 10^{10}. Bhaskar is amazed that some names are missing. The boy's anxiety could have been easily allayed, for in *Tattiriya Samhita* (dated around 1000 BC), appears the word **madhya** for 10^{10}. There are also words for 10^4 (**ayut**) and 10^8 (**nyarbuda**).

4 An early recognition of the meaning of the place-value notation is found in the following simile from *Vyasabhasya* (a commentary) on the *Yogasutra* (III.13), dating around the beginning of the Christian Era: 'Just as a stroke denotes 100 in the "hundreds" place, 10 in the "tens" place and 1 in the "units" place, even so one and the same woman is called mother, daughter and sister (by different persons).'

5 Such a system presupposes a precise vocabulary of number names in which the principles of addition, subtraction and multiplication are used. The number, one thousand nine hundred and ninety four would be expressed by words or word combination showing [(1 × 1000) + (9 × 100) + (9 × 10) + 4]. Compare this with the Roman representation, MCMLXXXXIV, in which only the principles of addition and subtraction are embalmed [i.e., (2000 − 100) + (50 + 10 + 10 + 10 + 10) + (5 − 1)].

6 What is often absent from a discussion of contrasting mathematical traditions is an awareness of more fundamental differences in cognitive structures and in methodological conceptions regarding the nature of mathematical objects. The conception of numbers was very different in India compared to the West, and especially Greek heritage. Following the Babylonian tradition, and unlike the Pythagoreans and Euclid, numbers were not regarded as made up of primordial atoms but as entities whose value depended on their efficacy for mathematical operations. It is this outlook that facilitated the creation of a place-value system containing fractions, negative numbers and zero. As early as the seventh century, Brahmagupta was considering zero and negative numbers on a par with other numbers by formulating explicit rules for arithmetical operations with such numbers. By emphasizing the primacy of operations in determining the existence of numbers, Indian (for that matter Chinese) mathematics steered clear of any problem caused by incommensurability, the bane but at the same time the fertile seed of Greek mathematics. For further discussion, see Joseph (1994).

References

ALSDORF, A. (1991) 'The *pratyayas*: Indian contribution to combinatorics', *Indian Journal of History of Science*, 26(1), pp. 17–61.

CAJORI, F. (1929) *A History of Mathematics*, New York: Macmillan.

COHEN, P.C. (1982) *A Calculating People*, Chicago: The University of Chicago Press.

DANTZIG, T. (1954) *Number: The Language of Science*, New York: Macmillan & Co.

DHARAMPAL (1983) *The Beautiful Tree*, New Delhi: Biblia Impex.

JOSEPH, G.G. (1992) *The Crest of the Peacock: Non-European Roots of Mathematics*, London: Penguin Books.

JOSEPH, G.G. (1993) 'The dance of numbers and the delights of calculation', in JULIE, C. et al. (eds) *P D M E Curriculum Reconstruction for Society in Transition*, Cape Town: Maskew Miller Longman, pp. 286–91.

JOSEPH, G.G. (1994) 'Different ways of knowing: Contrasting styles of argument in Indian and Greek mathematical traditions', in ERNEST, P. (ed.) *Mathematics, Education and Philosophy: An International Perspective*, London: Falmer Press, pp. 194–204.

JOSEPH, G.G. (1995) 'Cognitive encounters in India during the age of Imperialism', *Race and Class*, 36(3), pp. 39–57.

KUNJUNNI RAJA, K. (1963) 'Astronomy and mathematics in Kerala', *Adyar Library Bulletin*, 27, pp. 117–67.

MURRAY, A. (1986) *Reason and Society in the Middle Ages*, Oxford: Clarendon Press.

RAJAGOPAL, P. (1991) 'The Sthananga Sutra programme in Indian mathematics', *Arhat Vacana*, 3(2), pp. 1–8.

RANGACHARYA, M. (1912) *The Ganitasarasamgraha of Mahaviracharya*, Madras: Government Press.

SETH, V. (1993) *A Suitable Boy*, London: Phoenix House.

SHUKLA, K.S. (1976) *Aryabhatiya of Aryabhata*, New Dehli: Indian National Science Academy.

STAAL, F. (1995) 'The Sanskrit of science', *Journal of Indian Philosophy*, 23, pp. 73–127.

SWETZ, F. (1987) *Capitalism and Arithmetic*, Le Salle, Illinois: Open Court.

Notes on Contributors

Dave Baker is Senior Lecturer in Mathematical Education in the School of Education at the University of Brighton. He spent the early years of his life in South Africa and had to leave Apartheid South Africa for political reasons. He taught in secondary schools before becoming a teacher educator and has subsequently taught at the University of Melbourne, Australia. His research interests have developed from the use of computers in the teaching and learning of mathematics in primary schools to the implications of numeracies as social practices. He is co-author of *How Big is the Moon?* (1990, Oxford University Press, Australia); and *Literacy and Numeracy: Concepts and Definitions* (1995, International Encyclopaedia of Education, Pergamon, UK).

David Barton is interested in the role of literacy in people's day-to-day lives, in adult literacy, and in children's emergent literacy. He has been associated with three books which have been published recently: *Literacy, An Introduction to the Ecology of Written Language* (Oxford Blackwell, 1994); *Worlds of Literacy* (co-ed., Multilingual Matters); and *Sustaining Local Literacies* (ed., Multilingual Matters/ Education for Development). He is Senior Lecturer in Linguistics at Lancaster University.

Leone Burton is Professor of Education (Mathematics and Science) at the University of Birmingham, UK. She has published widely in the area of mathematics education being particularly known for her interests in enquiry-based methods of learning mathematics: see, for example, *Children Learning Mathematics: Patterns and Relationships* (Nash Pollock, 1994); *Thinking Things Through* (Basil Blackwell, 1984); and *Thinking Mathematically* (1982 with John Mason and Kaye Stacey, Addison Wesley). Publications in social justice include her edited collections *Who Counts? Assessing Mathematics in Europe* (Trentham, 1994); and *Gender and Mathematics: An International Perspective* (Cassell, 1990).

John Clay is a Senior Lecturer in Science Education at the University of Brighton. He worked in a similar capacity prior to his present post at the University of Greenwich. He has taught science in secondary and middle schools in Croydon and Merton. He is an active member of the Antiracist Teacher Education Network (ARTEN) and is concerned with Equal Opportunities in education. His current research interests are in the field of scientific literacies in teacher education and in intercultural education in Europe. He has co-authored the *following: Racism and Teacher Education: Moving Towards a Europe-wide Antiracist Response, Post-1992* (Free University,

Amsterdam, 1992); 'The citizen as "individual" and "nationalist" or "social" and "internationalist"? What is the role of education?', *Critical Social Policy* (1992); 'Euroracism, citizenship and democracy: The role of teacher education', *International Studies in Sociology of Education* (1993); and *Race, Gender and the Education of Teachers: Moving Beyond Permeation* (Open University Press, 1993).

Henrietta Dombey is Professor of Literacy in Primary Education in the School of Education at the University of Brighton. After several years of teaching primary children in Inner London schools, she moved into teacher education, where she has worked for some twenty years. During this time her students, her own children and the teachers and children with whom she has worked have taught her much about reading and how we learn to do it. A keen member of the National Association for the Teaching of English which she chaired from 1987 to 1989, she played an active part in the debate leading to the construction of the National Curriculum in English and has been similarly involved in the debate occasioned by its revision. She is also very much involved with the European early childhood organization IEDPE, l'Institut Européen pour le Développement des Potentialités de tous les Enfants, for whom she organized the literacy section of a large international conference in Barcelona in 1992. She has lately become interested in what children think reading is for and what they perceive it can do for them. Among her many publications are *Words and Worlds: Reading in the Early Years of school* (1992 NATE/NAAE); and *First Steps Together: Early Literacy in European Contexts* (1994, edited with Margaret Meek Spencer, Trentham Books, UK) and Editions Retz Paris.

Peter Esterhuysen is a former academic and literacy teacher turned media junkie. Five years ago he founded the Storyteller Group, a comic publishing company, with Neil Napper. Since then he has written more than twenty comic books and helped to create three popular comic series. His comics cover a range of stories and topics, from voter education to comic versions of classic texts; from AIDS education to the stories told by school students. Peter is interested in all forms of popular media: their relation to language, power and cognition; and African jazz. He has written a book on Kippie Moeketsi, a tragic figure who had a profound influence on South African jazz.

Carol Fox taught English in comprehensive schools in Inner London for many years. Subsequently she began research on the oral invented stories of young children who had very extensive experience of hearing books and stories read aloud. Her account of the 200 stories she collected from five pre-school children is given in the book *At the Very Edge of the Forest* (1993, Cassell). She has been teaching in the Faculty of Education in the University of Brighton since 1984. In 1994 she was a guest lecturer for three months at the University of Witwatersrand in Johannesburg. She is a member of NATE's multicultural committee, and the author of many articles in books and academic journals. She also reviews children's literature for the TES.

George Gheverghese Joseph is Reader in Economic and Social Statistics, University of Manchester. After working for six years as an education officer in Kenya, he returned to the UK to do his postgraduate work at Manchester and then joined the Department of Econometrics and Social Statistics. His teaching has ranged widely over a broad spectrum of subjects in applied mathematics and statistics including multivariate analysis, linear programming, demography and quantitative economics. He has travelled widely in developing countries and has held visiting appointments in Tanzania, Zimbabwe and Papua New Guinea and a Royal Society Visiting Fellowhip (twice) in India. His publications include three books: *Women at Work* (1983, Philip Allan); *The Crest of the Peacock: Non-European Roots of Mathematics* (1992, Penguin); and a joint publication, *Multicultural Mathematics* (1993, Oxford University Press). In recent years, his research and publications have been mainly in the cultural and historical aspects of mathematics with particular emphasis on the non-European contributions to the subject. He is at present working on the *Development of Infinite Series in Three Mathematical Traditions*. This has involved so far referring to primary sources (in Sanskrit and Malayalam) on the emergence of this topic in Indian mathematics between the fourteenth and sixteenth centuries in Kerala, predating the work of Gregory, Newton and Liebniz by more than two hundred years. A comparison of the motivations and methods of demonstration in the Indian, Chinese and European traditions is one of the primary objectives of this project.

Shirley Brice Heath is Professor in the Department of English at Stanford University, United States of America. Her ethnographic study of literacies in three communities in the Piedmont Carolinas, *Ways with Words* (Cambridge University Press, 1983), is a classic seminal text which informs many of the papers in this volume. It is a seminal text not only in terms of its subject matter but in terms of its methodological approaches. More recently Heath has been studying youth organizations in urban and rural areas of the USA. She has additionally carried out historical research on the literacy practices of a Lincolnshire (England) mother and her children in the eighteenth century. Among her many publications is a study of a young child's interactions with literature and stories, *The Braid of Literature* (Cambridge University Press, 1994). In 1994 she visited South Africa to begin ethnographic research there.

Lynn Hewlett is a Lecturer in the Department of Applied English Language Studies at the University of the Witwatersrand, South Africa. She has taught in further and adult education colleges in the UK and at tertiary level in South Africa. Her current research interests are in the areas of language and culture, curriculum development and language in education polices and practices. In 1996 she is to begin her doctoral study at the University of Colorado, USA.

Edgar W. Jenkins is Professor of Science Education Policy, Chairman of the School of Education and Deputy Director of the Centre for Policy Studies in Education at the University of Leeds, UK. He is the author or co-author of numerous articles and books, the latter including *From Armstrong to Nuffield: Studies in twentieth-*

century science education in England and Wales (London, Murray, 1979); *Techno-logical Revolution? The politics of school science and technology in England and Wales since 1945* (Falmer Press, 1985); and *Inarticulate Science? Perspectives on the public understanding of science and some implications for science education* (Driffield Studies in Education Ltd., 1993). He is the editor of the research review journal *Studies in Science Education* (Driffield Studies in Education Ltd.) and of the *International Journal of Technology and Design Education* (Dordrecht, Kluwer).

Alan and Viv Kenyon are primary school teachers who have worked in cross-cultural settings in primary education since the late 1960s. They both worked in rural teacher education colleges of the Eastern Cape in South Africa. Viv pioneered a small non-racial nursery school in the early 1970s. She is currently a Senior Lecturer at a teachers' college in Cape Town. Alan is leaving the University of Cape Town after seven years as Senior Lecturer in Primary Education to spend more time in primary science teacher development in township schools. Both have an abiding interest in promoting oral story telling and its vital link to school learning and literacies.

Margaret Meek is Emeritus Reader at the Institute of Education in the University of London where she supervises research students. She is the author of *Learning to Read* Bodley Head, London (1982), *On Being Literate* Bodley Head, London (1991) and *How Texts Teach What Readers Learn* Thimble Press, Stroud Gloc (1988). A new book 'Book Learning' is in preparation. Her main concerns are children's literacies, the theories and texts which further and enhance them, and the continuing education of teachers. She was awarded the Eleanor Farjeon Prize for services to children's literature. The National Literacy Trust, The Foundation for Language in Primary Education, and the International Institute for the Development of Potential in All Children engage her interests on their boards and committees.

Terezinha Nunes is Senior Lecturer at the Institute of Education, University of London. Her research work focuses on socio-cognitive processes in children's development with particular emphasis on literacy and numeracy. She formerly worked in her home country Brazil, where she investigated mathematics and literacy practices outside school.

Alan Peacock is a Senior Lecturer in Primary Science and Coordinator of International Affairs at the University of Exeter School of Education. He was a teacher for eleven years before working in teacher education, research and evaluation, first in England then in a range of other countries including Scotland, Kenya, Namibia and Botswana. He has a doctorate in curriculum development from the University of Ulster, and has published widely in the field of primary science, focusing on investigation skills, the inservice training of teachers, the evaluation of inservice training, and the analysis and use of text material. He is currently involved in a number of consultancies and research projects in this field in South Africa, Mozambique and Kenya.

Brian V. Street is Senior Lecturer in Social Anthropology at the University of Sussex and Visiting Professor of Education in the Graduate School of Education, University of Pennsylvania. He undertook anthropological fieldwork in Iran during the 1970s, and has since worked in the USA, Britain, and South Africa. He has had a long-standing interest in 'Representations' and his book *The Savage in Literature* (1975, RKP) was one of the early examples of research on Colonial Discourse in the context of what is currently termed 'reflexivity'. He has worked at the interface of linguistic and anthropological approaches, and recently addressed the use of the concept of 'culture' in these disciplines in 'Culture is a verb' (in Graddol, D. (ed.) *Language and Culture*, Multilingual Matters, 1993). He has written and lectured extensively on literacy practices from both a theoretical and an applied perspective. He is best known for *Literacy in Theory and Practice* (1985, CUP) and has recently published an edited volume *Cross-Cultural Approaches to Literacy* (1993, CUP). A collection of his articles *Social Literacies*, will be published shortly by Longmans.

Author Index

AAAS (American Association for the Advancement of Science), 43, 50, 185, 192
Agar, D., 94
Aitken, H.G.J., 49, 50
ALBSU, 57, 58, 59, 61
Alsdorf, A., 197, 202
Arber, S., 60, 61
Association for Science Education, 189
Auden, W.H., 163, 169
Auerbach, E., 59, 61

Bacon, F., 187
Bagshaw, M., 45, 50
Bahktin, M., 96
Baker, D., 1, 7, 71, 81, 85, 87
Ball, A., 95
Ball, D.L., 139, 144
Bamgbose, A., 139, 140
Barton, D., 6, 7, 60, 61
Bateson, G., 163, 169
Bay, M., 141, 145
Baynham, M., 67, 69
Berenschot-Moret-Basboom Consultants, 142, 144
Bernstein, B., 97
Beveridge, M., 82
Biesty, S., 166, 169
Bishop, A., 82
Bizell, P., 97, 98
Brookes, H., 98
Burnett, F.H., 66, 69
Burton, L., 5, 62, 71

Cajori, F., 201–2
Calinger, B.J., 43, 50
Camitta, M., 67, 69
Capra, F., 190, 193
Carpenter, H., 162, 169
Carraher, D., 73, 81
Carruthers, M., 162, 169
Cawthorn, E.R., 188, 193
Cazden, C., 96
Champagne, A.B., 43, 50

Chapman, B., 189, 193
Chinery, M., 168, 169
Clanchy, M., 159, 162, 169
Clark, M.M., 58, 142, 144
Clarke, J., 142, 144
Clay, J., 1, 8
Cleghorn, A., 140, 144
Cockcroft Report, 47, 50
Coetzee, J.M., 181
Cohen, P., 199, 202
Cole, M., 74, 78
Colle, R., 142, 144
Comenius, J.A., 162, 169
Cope, B., 95
Crago, M.H., 160, 169
Cummins, J.J., 141, 144

Dansereau, D.F., 141, 144
Dantzig, T., 202
Darton, F.J.H., 160, 169
Davey, A., 44, 45, 50, 51
Delpit, L., 95, 98
DfE, 63, 70
Dharampal, 198, 203
Dombey, H., 6, 7, 52, 62
Dorling Kindersley Publishers, 165, 166, 167
Dorsey-Gaines, C., 60, 61
Dwyer, F.M., 142, 144

Eliot, G., 182
Ely, D., 142, 144
Esterhuysen, P., 2, 7, 8, 9, 137

Fatt, J.P.T., 141, 144
Felter, K., 142, 144
Ferman-Nemser, S., 139, 144
Feynman, R., 25
Figlan, M., 25
Fox, C., 1, 8, 71, 160, 169
Freire, P., 186, 192, 193

Gardner, P., 49, 51
Gay, J., 74

Gee, J., 95
Genette, G., 64, 70
Gerlach, V., 142, 144
Gheverghese Joseph, G., 8, 71,
    202–3
Gilbert, S.W., 141, 144
Glass, S., 142, 144
Goodnow, J., 79
Greenwood, S., 44, 51
Gregory, E., 67, 70

Halliday, M.A.K., 24, 28
Hamilton, M., 60, 61
Hannon, P., 59, 61
Head, J., 74
Heath, S.B., 1, 7, 9, 65, 67, 70, 81, 160,
    170, 194
Heath, S.B., 60, 61
Hewlett, L., 4, 7, 62, 71, 98
HMSO, 161, 169
Hollingdale, P., 160, 169
Hyltenstam, K., 139, 140, 141, 144

ICASE (International Council of
    Associations for Science Education),
    186
Ivanic, R., 61
Iyer, P., 180

James, H., 181
James P.D., 164
Jenkins, E.W., 6, 7, 44, 45, 50, 51

Kalantzis, M., 95
Keller, E.F., 187, 193
Kennedy, M., 139, 144
Kenyon, A., 5, 7, 21, 28, 62, 137
Kenyon, V., 5, 7, 21, 62, 137
King, C., 69, 70
Klassen, C., 60, 61
Knopfmacher, N., 94
Kunjunni Raja, K., 203

Lave, J., 49, 51, 84, 87
Layton, D., 44, 45, 50, 51
Lerman, S., 82
Lesnik-Oberstein, K., 160, 169
Levi-Strauss, C., 27, 28
Lewis, D., 160, 167, 169
Light, P., 76
Lily, W., 161
Littlefair, A., 164, 169
Lovitts, B.E., 43, 50
Luria, A., 78

Mabizela, M., 96
Macaulay, D., 162, 169
Macdonald, C.A., 140, 144
MacGill, S., 45, 50, 51
Mallett, M., 168, 169
Marsh, C., 60, 61
Marshall, T.H., 191, 193
Martin, J.R., 24, 28
Mason, J., 76
Maybin, J., 60, 61
McGann, J.J., 165, 167
McLaughlin, M.W., 61
McLuhan, M., 165, 169
Medway, P., 166, 167
Meek, M., 8, 9, 64, 70, 159, 194
Mitchell, C., 82
Moll, I., 92
Moll, L., 60, 61
Moreno, C., 74
Morrison, T., 182
Murphy, C., 142, 144
Murray, A., 199, 200, 203

Nandy, A., 187, 189, 193
National Science Teachers Association of
    Science, 186
Neate, B., 164, 169
Nunes, T., 7, 73, 75, 76, 81

Ogawa, M., 186, 191, 193
Olson, D., 162, 165, 169
Opie, I., 160, 169
Opie, P., 160, 169

Padmore, S., 60, 61
Paley, V.G., 25, 28
Pappas, C., 166, 169
Peacock, A., 7, 137, 143, 144
Peires, M., 91
Pritchard, M., 162, 169
Project 2000+, 186
Project 2061: Science for All Americans,
    185

Rajagopal, P., 198, 203
Raleigh, M. and Moy, B., 164, 170
Rangacharaya, M., 203
Raubenheimer, D., 23, 28
Ravetz, J., 48, 51
Reder, S., 82
Reid, D.J., 141, 145
Reiss, M.J., 187, 190, 193
Rogoff, B., 49, 51
Rose, J., 160, 170

Roth, K.J., 141, 145
Rowell, J.A., 188, 193
Russell, A., 137, 143, 144

SAAAD, 96
Scheub, H., 26, 28
Schliemann, A., 73, 81
Scholes, R., 166, 170
Science Council of Canada, 43, 51
Scollon, R., 160, 170
Scollon, S., 160, 170
Scribner, S., 78
Semple, C., 87
Seth, V., 201, 203
Sewell, B., 47, 51
Shakespeare, W., 174, 176, 180, 181
Shukla, K., 203
Shulman, J., 138, 139, 145
Sivilla, I.N., 140, 145
Slominsky, L., 92
Solsken, J., 66, 70
SPACE, 142, 145
Staal, F., 198, 203
Staver, J.R., 141, 145
Stead, T., 87
Stevens, W., 5
Story Teller Group, 2
Street, B.V., 1, 5, 65, 70, 81, 85
Stroud, C., 139, 140, 141, 144
Swetz, F., 199–200, 203

Swift, G., 182
Sykes, C., 25, 28

Taylor, D., 60, 61
Taylor, G., 97

UNESCO, 43, 50, 186, 193

Van Rooyen, H., 141, 145
Vernaud, G., 76
Vygotsky, L.S., 78, 96, 168, 170

Wade, B., Minns, H. and Lutrario, C., 64, 70
Walkerdine, V., 67, 70
Walters, J., 142, 144
Whorf, B., 78
Wikelund, K., 82
Williams, R., 170
Wolf, S.A., 160, 170
Wong-Fillmore, L., 59, 61
Woodward, A., 140, 145
World Conference on Education for All, 186
Wright, R., 182
Wynne, B., 44, 50, 51

Yager, R.E., 141, 145
Yearley, S., 44, 51

Ziman, J., 44, 51

Subject Index

abstract, abstraction, 103–4, 111–12, 124, 129–30
academic practices, 4, 101, 106
  writing, 122, 166
argument, 95, 104, 106, 115, 120, 122–3, 128–31, 133
art, Arts, 11, 13–18, 20, 171
assessment, 31
Attainment Targets (AT), 185
authority, 41, 103, 105–6, 111–12, 115, 122, 126, 128, 130, 132–3, 135, 151
autonomous, 3, 80, 118, 130

boundaries, 71, 72, 123, 133

calculation, computation, 72, 76, 77, 194–5, 198–200
  calculator, 32
citizenship, 190, 191, 193
classrooms, 148, 154–5
code-switching, 91, 140
comic, comic books, 146–55, 158
comprehensibility, 140
context, 33, 37, 82, 86–7, 106, 113, 115, 122, 126, 132–5, 147, 155, 157, 163
critical, critique, 135, 152, 167, 171, 186
culture, cultural, 7, 11, 21, 31–3, 38, 63, 65–7, 80, 82, 85, 89, 101, 103, 113, 117, 119, 130, 137, 171, 184, 187, 194
  construct, 139, 163
  dominant, non-dominant, 2, 6, 65–9
  practices, 71
  reading of, 94
curriculum, 11, 22, 31, 32, 38, 188

deficit model, 41, 44, 154
developing countries, 138
dialogic, 29, 35, 128, 133–4, 150–1
didactic, 135, 139, 160–1
different registers, 164
discipline, 13, 29, 31, 33

discourse(s), 1, 13, 22, 24, 25–8, 35–6, 66–9, 95, 90, 101, 111, 122–3, 125–6, 128–9, 131–4, 155, 162, 166
  academic, 175, 183
  dominant, 102, 128, 134
dominant, 29, 41, 127, 131–2, 135, 146, 171
  practices, 71, 194

English, 41
  as second language, 93, 179
  social meanings of, 93
  teachers of, 173
  use of, 91
environmental, 8, 65, 142, 150, 168
  education, 20
epistemology, epistemological, 35, 101, 106, 116, 118, 131, 186
essay, 102, 104–5, 111, 128–9, 131
ethnographic, 13, 102, 104, 118, 158
Eurocentrism, 184, 186–7

feminist, feminism, 114–15, 131, 187
frames, 29, 41, 158
  of knowledge, 7, 41, 71, 73, 74, 78–9, 171
  of knowing, 73, 77, 78

genre, 7, 11, 102, 106, 111–12, 115, 119–20, 128–9, 131–5, 146, 151
grammar, 104, 132, 195, 197–8

humanities, 16, 20

identity, 56, 106, 116, 118, 123–6, 128, 131–2
ideology, ideological, 2, 4, 101, 132–3, 194
illiteracy, 2, 6, 43, 146, 148, 195
information, 159–64
  books, 14, 135, 161
  technology, 160
innumeracy, 3, 195
intercultural, 9, 11
intertextuality, 106, 131

knowledge, knowing, 11, 13–18, 29, 32, 33, 41, 71, 73, 90, 111, 116–17, 122, 129, 131–2, 135
  conflicts, 33, 35
  organisation of, 111–12

language, 22, 32–3, 38, 41, 71, 78, 117, 137, 155, 197–8, 200–1
  mathematics, 198, 200, 201
  multilingual, 24, 155
  skills, 154
  vernacular, 140, 142
learning, 16–18, 29, 91, 155, 157
  as social practices, 71
  in/through practice, 80, 86–7
legitimacy, legitimation, 123, 133, 187, 192
lexigraphics, 165
linguistic, 138, 140, 197–8
literacy, literacies, 2–9, 13, 20, 23, 29, 37–8, 41, 43, 52, 65–8, 71, 78–9, 104–5, 114, 116, 120, 129–30, 133, 135, 141, 147–50, 160, 163–5, 173, 180, 182, 194, 195, 197
  academic, 89, 90, 97, 101–5, 111, 113–16, 118–19, 123–4, 127–8, 130–3, 183
  activities, 2, 5, 54, 56, 58
  adult, 58, 59, 148
  as social practices, new, 52, 101, 159, 162
  computer, 9, 20, 32, 135, 159, 163
  demands, 57
  diversity, plurality, 2, 6–9, 54, 55
  dominant, 4, 62, 135, 146
  family, 41, 52, 53, 55, 57, 58, 59, 60
  functional, skills, 6, 41, 52, 148–9
  levels of, 56
  practices, 1–8, 11, 68, 79, 118, 122, 129, 132–3, 135, 146–7, 149, 159, 174, 175, 182
  programmes, 52
  scientific, functional, technological, 22, 23, 28, 43, 44, 45, 47, 48, 50, 137
  subversive, 173, 183
  types of, 6–9, 20, 26, 44, 141, 147
literate, 62, 64, 141, 162
literature, 8, 146–7, 171
  canon, 174, 181, 183

mathematics, mathematical, 11, 15, 29–39, 41, 71–4, 83–6, 101, 171, 194–7, 199
  as social practices, practices, 29, 32, 71, 72, 81, 171

culture, 32
  knowledge, 30, 71–3, 200
  Indian, 194, 195, 197–8, 201
  literature, 197
  language, oral and written, notation, 32, 75, 194, 198, 201–2
  practical, commercial, 199–201
  proof, reasoning, 33, 39, 194, 197
  relations, linearity, 73, 76–7
  representations, 73, 77
  school, 29, 37
  Western, European, 194, 198, 199–202
meaning, making, 29–30, 35–7, 95, 150
measuring, 14, 73–4, 76–7, 199
media, 147–8, 150, 155
mode-switching, 69
mother tongue, 139, 140

narrative, narrator, narration, 5, 11, 13, 15–16, 29–39, 62–5, 137, 140–1, 146, 149, 152, 159, 162
  plural, 135
  construction, 67
National Curriculum Council (NCC), 173, 183, 185, 189
non-fiction, 159, 160
non-governmental organisations (NGOs), 21
number, numerals, numerical, 14, 195–200
  anti, 194, 200
  Indo-Arabic, 199–200
  written, representation words, 196–202
numeracy, numeracies, 1–8, 41, 71, 78, 80–2, 87, 194–201
  as social practices, plurality, 2, 80–6, 101
  events, 3, 81–3, 87
  practices, 3–5, 11, 80–3, 85–7, 194, 198
  formal, informal, 41, 80–3, 85–7

objective, objectivity, 31–2, 186, 187
oral practices, vernaculars, 2, 6, 41, 62

parents, 176, 183
pedagogy, 11, 22, 29, 31, 90, 97, 131–2, 139, 143
  analysis, 164
poetry, 26
political, 4, 31, 38, 151
positivist, 189
power, power relations, 3, 33, 38, 41, 89, 97, 101–2, 106, 111–12, 115, 118, 120, 122–3, 128–33, 175, 176
practices, 53, 68

Primary Science Programme (PSP), 22, 23
process, 32, 123, 131–2, 153
  skills, 138–9

reading, 63, 140, 167
reasoning, 76, 78
represent, representation, 11, 15, 35, 71, 73, 197

science, scientific, 1, 5, 11, 13–18, 29, 31, 41, 47, 71, 101, 115, 120, 133, 154–5, 158, 171, 185, 200–1
  and technology, 20, 24
  canonical, 171
  language, 119, 197
  literacies, 146
  method, 16, 186
  practices, 4, 50, 171, 187
  texts, 135
social, socially, socio-cultural, 2–5, 29–32, 37, 38
  constructed, 66, 105
  constructivism, 142, 155
  construed, 32
story, 11, 15, 30, 32–3, 153–4, 171
  telling oral, 174, 183
study skills, 106, 118, 122
subject
  hierarchies, 192
symbolic systems, 24

systems of signs, 41, 71, 73, 75–8
  enabling, constraining, structuring, 73, 74, 76

teacher development, 15, 21
technicist, 106, 116, 122, 129, 132
technology, neutral, 62
tests, 31, 130
text, 4, 8, 11, 15, 104–6, 112, 116, 120, 123–6, 128–31, 133, 135, 147–54
  academic, 4, 111, 129
  authoritative, 154
  books, 18, 135, 147–8, 150, 157
  expository, information, 141, 143, 159, 164
  'oral', 149
text-processing strategies, 141
textual, 138, 139, 166–7
transmission, transmissible, 15, 29, 31, 147

understanding, 72, 185
universal, 5, 184, 186

value, values, 82, 85–7, 151
  conflicting, 153
  neutral, free, 1, 31, 85
  performance, social, mathematical, 84, 85–7
vernacular language, 68, 69
voices, 29, 106, 112, 125–9, 131, 133, 151–2
  conflicting, 151